# Praise for
# THE SERIAL KILLER'S APPRENTICE

"*The Serial Killer's Apprentice* is an amazing report on how Elmer Wayne Henley Jr. was groomed, participated in the 1970s killings of more than two dozen boys and young men labeled the Houston Mass Murders, and then killed his groomer. Henley cooperated from his Texas prison cell with Ramsland and Ullman to change what we knew as a case narrative for over fifty years and resets the errors made during the investigation and at trial." —**Michael Baden, M.D.**, Former Chief Medical Examiner, New York City

"Dr. Ramsland, a forensic authority who writes like a top-tier novelist, and Ullman, a documentarian with a detective-like bent, pair up to tell the tale of a far more terrible team: that of sexually perverse serial predator Dean Corll and his accomplice, Elmer Wayne Henley, Jr. An instantaneous true crime classic, it proves eye-opening for those who wish to better understand this case and the criminal mind, and, despite its nightmarish details, impossible to put down." —**Dr. Gary Brucato**, co-author of *The New Evil: Understanding the Emergence of Modern Violent Crime*

"*The Serial Killer's Apprentice* transcends traditional true crime narratives, presenting a profound exploration of a bygone era. As hidden truths emerge and old cases are redefined, this book stands as a testament to the relentless pursuit of justice. Delve into the shadows of the past and emerge with a heightened awareness of the timeless battle against predators, as we navigate the complex tapestry of justice." —**Ann Wolbert Burgess**, Professor, Boston College, and author of *A Killer by Design*

"In her distinctively insightful style, Dr. Ramsland delivers a penetrating analysis of one of the most unconscionable and notorious crimes of the 20th century. In *The Serial Killer's Apprentice*, Ramsland and Ullman skillfully unmask the shocking details of Dean Corll, a prolific serial sexual child killer who, aided by his groomed teenage accomplices, snared at least twenty-eight victims. In this sleep-stealing page turner, the authors effectively evoke consideration for an additional offender typology and sexual homicide classification by examining the motivational factors of dominant offenders and their groomed teenage accomplices." —**Gregory M. Cooper**, retired FBI Profiler and Supervisor Behavioral Profiling Unit, and Executive Director, Cold Case Foundation.

"There are few people better qualified to unravel a psychopath's psyche than Dr. Katherine Ramsland, and *The Serial Killer's Apprentice* proves that she is at the top of her game! By turns intriguing and terrifying, this book shines a spotlight onto the dark corners of a predator's mind and offers urgently needed insights for those in the law enforcement community." —**Kristin Dilley**, co-host of the Mind Over Murder podcast

"Katherine Ramsland and Tracy Ullman have ventured into the profound darkness of serial killing, sexual predation, and exploitation of vulnerable youth. They take seriously, from a psychological and social perspective, what many people simply dismiss as 'evil.' They use all their intellectual resources to illuminate the developmental and cultural forces and processes that provide a "human" explanation for what otherwise seems morally and emotionally opaque. I salute them for their intelligence, both 'emotional' and 'intellectual.' In their book they go well beyond the often superficial analysis offered by most 'true crime' writing." —**James Garbarino, PhD**, Emeritus Professor Psychology at Cornell University and Loyola University Chicago and author of *Listening to Killers: Lessons Learned from My 20 Years as a Psychological Expert Witness in Murder Cases*

"Dr. Katherine Ramsland's new book *The Serial Killer's Apprentice* reveals the incredible story of the only known accomplice to have killed the predator who lured him into a killing partnership. The urgent lessons learned from Ramsland's interviews and study are priceless to law enforcement, parents, and, most importantly, to prevent future victims from predators lurking in today's world. The story of mass murderer Dean Corll being killed by a teenager, whom he lured into his web of horror, and Corll's connection to a larger child sex ring that authorities swept under the rug, is a fascinating read. If you believe that sex trafficking is a recent phenomenon, this book is a stark reminder that this particularly organized evil has existed for decades but perhaps was more disguised. This is a must-read for the true crime fan and for every parent who worries about their child's safety."
—**Chris McDonough**, retired Homicide detective, Cold Case Foundation's Director of Investigations, host of The Interview Room podcast

"Drawing on exclusive interviews with the surviving member of one of the most horrific serial killer teams in U.S. history, Katherine Ramsland and Tracy Ullman's consistently gripping book is not only the definitive account of the infamous 'Candy Man' case—offering eye-opening information never before revealed—but a brilliant study of the minds and motivations of pedophiliac predators: both a page-turning true crime narrative and a major contribution to the field of forensic psychology." —**Harold Schechter**, author of *Murderabilia: A History of Crime in 100 Objects*

"Dr. Katherine Ramsland and journalist Tracy Ullman revisit and revise the horrifying story of Houston's 'Candy Man' Dean Corll and his teen accomplice Elmer Wayne Henley Jr.—the serial killer's apprentice. Their brilliant investigation leads to Henley disclosing the existence of the sex-trafficking organization operating at the time, and the psychological manipulation Dean Corll used to ensure Henley would remain—the serial killer's apprentice." —**Dan Zupansky**, host of the True Murder podcast

# THE
# SERIAL KILLER'S
# APPRENTICE

# THE
# SERIAL KILLER'S
# APPRENTICE

**THE TRUE STORY OF HOW HOUSTON'S DEADLIEST
MURDERER TURNED A KID INTO A KILLING MACHINE**

# KATHERINE RAMSLAND
## AND TRACY ULLMAN

NEW YORK

THE SERIAL KILLER'S APPRENTICE

Crime Ink
An Imprint of Penzler Publishers
58 Warren Street
New York, N.Y. 10007

First Crime Ink edition

Interior design by Maria Fernandez

Library of Congress Control Number: 2023918643

ISBN: 978-1-61316-495-2
eBook ISBN: 978-1-61316-496-9

10 9 8 7 6 5 4 3 2 1

Printed in the United States of America
Distributed by W. W. Norton & Company

*I dedicate this work to my alpha readers and primary emotional support system, Sally, Dana, and Sue, for whom I'm eternally grateful.*
—Katherine

*I dedicate this book to my late husband, Jeffrey Felshman, and our children—Iris, Marty, and Gabriel— some of my most profound inspirations.*
—Tracy

# Contents

# Author's Note

This book revisits and revises the story of the "Candy Man" crimes that happened in Houston, Texas, during the early 1970s. Dean Corll, an adult, recruited two teenage accomplices, David Brooks and Elmer Wayne Henley Jr., to assist him to lure more than two dozen other boys for Corll to rape, torture, and murder. Eventually, Henley killed Corll and turned himself in. At this point, he mentioned his fear of Corll's association with a sex trafficking ring in Dallas. Brooks, once in custody, also described the ring. The Houston police made a tepid effort to investigate the alleged connection before ultimately dismissing it. However, such a ring did exist. The evidence for this changes the story that's been told.

Documentary maker and investigative journalist Tracy Ullman spent over a decade looking into the traffickers' activities. She contacted Henley, the only accomplice willing to talk, and he agreed to tell what he knew. I, Katherine Ramsland, joined them to explore Henley's experience as Corll's accomplice. I'm the primary author of this book, collaborating with Ullman, who describes the bigger picture of the Corll-Brooks-Henley story from her research. This account is the first time the shocking tale has been given its full context. Henley did not ask for our present-day investigation, but he agreed to help us to better understand the way sexual predators exploit their targets' vulnerabilities.

I've communicated with and researched serial killers for more than twenty-five years. One such offender operated in the town where I grew up. He once picked up a girl on his motorcycle from a spot where I'd recently been hitchhiking. I was a kid. I'd have accepted a ride like that. This man, John Norman Collins, was arrested and convicted of one of the Michigan "Coed Murders" and suspected in the others. Later, while I was writing for Court TV's Crime Library, I corresponded with Collins. Then I contacted other serial killers. Since then, I've become a specialist on these offenders, writing books and teaching university courses with a focus on the killers' psychological development.

In my book *The Mind of a Murderer*, I examined a dozen cases from the past century that feature mental health experts who'd spent extended periods of time to learn about the lives and crimes of specific mass, spree, and serial killers. Their efforts paid off in detailed material that offered a model for my work from 2010 through 2021 with Dennis Rader, the "BTK" serial killer from Wichita, Kansas. To undertake this in-depth project, I used a format I call a guided autobiography. That is, I structured my questions to get responses about Rader's trajectory toward violence that would benefit the fields of psychology, criminology, and law enforcement.

The process allowed me to better understand the way someone like Rader experiences his world. We discussed psychological concepts like compartmentalization, or the notion that predators can pass as normal citizens while engaging in serious crimes by partitioning their lives. Rader referred to this ability as "cubing" through his various "life frames." That is, he could alternate his different facades as circumstances required. He could act as a good father and husband, the devout president of his church council, and a Boy Scout volunteer while he also stalked, stole, and killed. All roles were available to him as sides of his "cube," so he could quickly pivot among them. Thus, Rader showed me that "cubing" is a more instructive concept than that of partitioned roles for understanding how he could live a double life with such dramatic differences.

The notion of "cubing" helped me to consider Wayne Henley's experience. Although he got into some minor trouble as a teen, he might never have become criminally violent save for crossing paths with Corll. Despite assisting Corll with murder, when Henley could, he *cubed* into an ordinary kid, and this part gave him some relief from what he was doing as well as the courage, finally, to resist. He's the only known accomplice to have killed the predator who lured him into a team killer arrangement.

We don't diminish Henley's criminal responsibility (nor does he). Instead, we explored with him the psychological process in the accomplice relationship that offers lessons for counselors, criminologists, parents, and potential future victims. This book is about a predator who lured two vulnerable kids into a criminal enterprise. Both came from broken homes, difficult circumstances, and meager resources. Both were susceptible to financial enticement. David Brooks died in 2020 without fully telling his story. Henley, still alive, presents an opportunity to study the predatory process from the target's perspective.

These events happened fifty years ago. What we thought we knew about it back then has shifted with new information. Recently, we've seen other "settled" cases from earlier decades being altered—even eclipsed—by new interpretations that answer lingering questions or that better address the facts. We can't cling to the 1973 identification of a victim, for example, when a 2012 DNA analysis disproves it (as happened in this case). Staying flexible is how innocent people who were wrongfully convicted have been exonerated. It's how cover-ups have been exposed and cold cases solved. It's also how older cases like this one can give us an important perspective on current conditions.

Many of the same grooming techniques that Corll employed are still in use because they're successful. Ullman's research on the trafficking ring during the 1970s that backed up Corll's threats shows its considerable spread at that time around the country. People of influence "lost" evidence, terminated investigations, and erased associations. But sufficient traces remain to piece together much of the story.

Henley hopes to contribute something redemptive from his acts. The many hours of interviews he gave are used in this book, as direct quotes and as omniscient statements about his feelings and his perspective on the events he witnessed. His police statements from August 1973 also offer material, as do Henley's mother and a few of his childhood friends. In addition, we've used police and court records, autopsy reports, news articles, and TV news packages from the relevant time period. Sometimes we relied on items from earlier book-length accounts, but the two primary sources based on the case were published before the accomplices' trials, and both also contain factual errors. Even the district attorney's memoir, in which he discussed the trials, is inconsistent with police reports and other records. This book adds more to the story, digs deeper into accomplice dynamics, and harvests its most urgent lessons about predators for a new generation.

# CHAPTER 1

# Killing the Candy Man

A slender, curly-haired teenage boy in handcuffs and a greenish-blue prison jumpsuit guided the driver of an unmarked police car onto a rutted road. The cop led a short caravan of vehicles carrying detectives toward an L-shaped row of corrugated metal sheds at 4500 Silver Bell Street in Houston, Texas. This was Southwest Boat Storage. They stopped near unit #11. Men in suits emerged from the lead car. One helped the boy to step out. He looked dazed and could barely stand.

The detectives needed this boy. He'd just revealed that Dean Corll, a local electrician whom he'd fatally shot that morning, had killed other boys and buried them in this unit's dirt floor. The detectives had initially dismissed his claims. He was a kid, coming off a paint-sniffing high. But he'd mentioned David Hilligiest, Marty Jones, and Charles Cobble. All three had been reported missing. Two had vanished on the same day a few weeks before. Despite the stifling heat on that August afternoon in 1973, they'd come to check out the kid's disturbing claim.

Some of these cops were from Houston PD. Some were from nearby Pasadena, Texas, where Corll had been shot. They'd agreed they should work together. Around 5:30 P.M., they approached the boat stall's set of steel doors. A padlock stopped them. They located the facility owner, Mayme Meynier, who lived close, and explained why they needed access. She was distressed to hear that her tenant was dead. Dean Corll had been such a nice man, she said, always paying his monthly fee on time ever since he'd rented the stall in November 1970. The landlady had no spare key for Corll's lock, so she granted permission to the officers to break it. One used a tire iron to get the job done. When they opened the doors to the windowless, high-ceilinged 12x34-foot space, a blast of pent-up heat pushed them back.

Inside, they saw a cluttered stall. They entered to assess the contents. In the center of the space, two musty overlapping carpets covered the dirt floor. The blue one touched both walls and ran about twelve feet into the unit. Along the right side near the back, the detectives saw a tarp-covered car, two canisters of compressed gas, a small red bike, an empty furniture box, and a plastic bag full of shoes and clothing. They counted eight twenty-gallon metal containers. Two ten-pound bags of lime sat on one. Near the left wall, a crack in the lumpy dirt-and-shell floor exuded a faint odor. Two short-handled shovels and a broken rake with a white residue on its tines reinforced the ominous impression that something had been buried here beneath lime.

The boy who'd brought them here came to the threshold. He looked pale. Instead of entering the stall, he backed away, sat on the grass, and put his head in his hands. His life had changed irreparably that day. Seventeen-year-old Elmer Wayne Henley Jr. had just shot and killed Dean Corll. He'd said he'd done it to save himself and two friends whom Corll had decided to torture. Then he'd told detectives about the boat stall, with four, and possibly more, kids buried inside.

Pasadena PD Detective Dave Mullican had been with Henley since the shooting that morning. He stared at the forlorn teen. This kid knew more than he was saying, a *lot* more. He'd led them to the boat stall without difficulty, though he'd said he'd been there just once. He'd pointed out where the facility owner lived. What else did he know? What else had he *done*?

But these questions could wait. First, they had to discover if Dean Corll was the killer the boy claimed him to be.

A peek under the canvas tarp showed the stripped hulk of a Chevy Camaro, seemingly used for parts—a common way to profit from stolen cars. They'd have to check the vehicle's status, and then move it out. The kid's bike as well. The police photographer, Bill Hare, snapped photos of each item before stepping aside for the forensics unit. The crime scene processors took dirt and lime samples and lifted fingerprints from several locations. Items were packaged as potential evidence.

Around 6:30 P.M., word arrived that the Camaro appeared to be stolen, and the bike belonged to thirteen-year-old James Dreymala, a boy reported missing nearly a week earlier. *Another missing boy, and not one Henley had named.* With the other three, this made four possible graves, maybe five since Gregory Malley Winkle had gone missing with David Hilligiest in 1971. It seemed impossible. Who'd ever heard of a guy grabbing and killing several boys without anyone noticing?

Still doubtful, detectives directed two inmates they'd brought from a jail—"trusties"—to dig into the smelly dirt hump near the broken rake. The air had cleared somewhat, but it was blazing hot outside, with a dampness that stuck shirts to skin. The trusties started to dig.

Eight inches below the surface, they hit a layer of white lime. A few strokes with the shovel revealed a piece of thick, transparent plastic. As they moved the sandy earth away, they smelled it before they saw it: the swollen, nude body of a blond boy, wrapped in plastic and lying on his right side. From his size, they guessed his age to be twelve or thirteen. Maybe Dreymala? White tape bound his feet together. Nervous trusties pulled the bundle from the hole and carried it out past Henley.

Encased in muck near the hole's foot end, the diggers uncovered a deteriorated green plastic bag containing a skeleton. The victim had been in a crouched position when placed in the bag. It seemed that Henley was right: this place was a private burial ground. The detectives called for more resources. They weren't going anywhere for a while. The trusties grumbled. They disliked this job. One vomited outside. But they had to keep digging. There was a lot of ground to cover in a stall this size. The officers called for floodlights and large fans. They hauled the Camaro out.

Once the second set of remains was removed, the diggers located a spot under the grimy blue rug that showed signs of disturbance. Beneath a layer of lime, they unearthed a piece of plywood, six feet long and a foot wide. It seemed to be a marker. They pulled it out and dug deeper until they located two partially decomposed victims, wrapped in thick plastic and bound with rope. Both victims lay on their left sides, against each other head to foot, seemingly killed and buried at the same time.

Possibly, these were Marty Jones and Charles Cobble, whose disappearance cops had dismissed two weeks before as boys just running away. No effort had been made to look for them. The official excuse had been that so many teenage boys left Houston these days there seemed little reason to waste the resources. Jones and Cobble were buddies; they'd vanished on the same day. Ergo, they'd left together. Yet they were two of several boys that had gone missing since 1971 from a neighborhood known as the Houston Heights. Half a dozen had attended the same junior high school. This alone should have triggered serious questions, especially when their parents had all raised a ruckus over the lack of police response. None had believed their boys had run off. Every cop in that hot, smelly stall that night probably knew there'd be hell to pay for this oversight.

They now had four bodies—the number Henley had stated. They could call it quits, but they knew there might be more. There might also be other evidence buried here or items that could help to identify these kids. They had to keep probing.

The next hole, dug where the Camaro had sat, produced a skull and some bones. Underneath them was another plastic-wrapped set of remains so decomposed the cops couldn't determine in which direction the arms and legs were lying. That made six victims. According to crime writer Jack

Olsen, some officers felt sickened when the landlady came over to watch and told them Corll had recently asked for another stall because he was "running out of space."

Ambulances transported the remains to the Harris County morgue. Mullican watched Henley smoke a cigarette. The kid *had* stopped a killer, just like he'd said. And if he hadn't, he and his friends might have been dumped in here as well, with Corll continuing his killings for who knows how long.

Several reporters arrived. Some spotted the long-haired, acne-prone boy at the center of this unfolding horror story. He looked no more than fourteen, short and skinny, hardly a kid who could cause all this trouble. Henley alternated between weeping and assuring his guard he was okay. He complained of a headache. He wanted to call his mother. He'd been asking for hours to talk to her.

Police beat reporter Jack Cato from KPRC-TV spotted an opportunity. He offered Henley the use of his car phone. Henley accepted. It was a deal with the devil. Cato filmed the teen without his permission as he leaned against a red Mustang and broke the news to his mother, Mary Henley. The audio recording of her shock over her son's revelation was broadcast on television.

Henley's voice trembled as he said, "Mama?"

"Yes, this is Mama, baby."

A brief pause. "I killed Dean." He put his hand to his face.

"Wayne?" She sounded stunned. "Oh, Wayne, you didn't!"

"Yep. . . . Yes'm."

"Oh, God! Where are you?" She started to cry.

He told her he was at Corll's "warehouse." When she asked if she could come, he said it was okay, but then detectives directed him to tell her no. They knew he was a juvenile and a parent *should* be present, but they didn't want her silencing him. She might even bring a lawyer. Henley assured her he was all right: "I'm with the police." He'd see her later.

On his own, Henley mumbled about how he knew some of the boys and had introduced them to Corll. "It's my fault."

Cato asked for an on-camera interview, but Henley didn't want to be filmed. Cato managed to record some strained words from him while the cameraperson focused on the fans pumping the reek of decomposition out of the stall. A reporter for Channel 11 persuaded Henley to talk face-to-face for the late broadcast. The boy admitted he'd known Corll for a while, about two years. They liked to drink beer together. He said Corll had talked about an organization involved in all this, one that had paid him thousands of dollars. But the kid seemed to have some doubts, because Corll's lifestyle didn't show much for his supposed association.

The reports were now airing on televisions all over town. Henley had given his mother no idea of what she was about to see—she *and* her neighbors. Some were the parents of the boys being removed from Corll's boat stall, parents Mary Henley had previously comforted when the boys had disappeared.

"I couldn't believe it," Mary said. "That wasn't my little Wayne. He didn't do things like that. He loved everybody." At the age of five, she recalled, he'd walked down the aisle at church and declared his intention to become a minister. Until recently, he'd carried a Bible in his shirt pocket. He was a *good* kid. Mary knew he'd been upset lately. He'd said things so strange she'd made an appointment with a psychiatrist. She remembered Corll telling her just two weeks earlier that he planned to take her son traveling to where she couldn't contact him. Bristling, she'd warned Corll if he tried it, she'd send the police after him. "He must have done something terrible," Mary stated, "for Wayne to have killed him."

This case was barreling toward revelations far more shocking than the fatal shooting of Dean Corll.

Henley acted surprised as he watched body bags being removed from the boat shed. He'd known about four and had suspected one or two more, but it seemed that Corll had secrets even darker than he'd realized. And he knew there were burial sites elsewhere too. He'd initially intended to show police only this much, but the pressure to tell everything leaked out in several of Henley's comments.

"I can't help but feel guilty, like I done killed those boys myself," he lamented to one officer. "I caused them to be dead. I led them straight to Dean."

The officer told Henley he should feel lucky. He might have ended up here too. Henley hid his face in his hands. He knew he deserved no consolation. He should have killed Corll much earlier or should have gone to the police. He'd made several plans to get away, but nothing he'd tried had worked. His weakness shamed him. There had been pivotal moments when he could have done the right thing, but each time he'd surrendered to whatever Corll had wanted.

Around ten P.M., Mullican sent Henley back to the jail in Pasadena, the town where he'd fatally shot Dean Corll. Mullican believed they no longer needed Henley's help. He'd soon realize that this nightmare was only just beginning.

Hole #4, back in the right corner, produced two more bodies buried close together. It appeared that several kids had been dumped on top of one another. Under the seventh set of remains the diggers found a suede jacket with long fringes, a knotted rope, and a piece of blue terry cloth. The eighth murdered boy had been buried sitting up, seemingly bound with a piece of parachute cord. Nothing about this scene seemed real. People didn't just kill kids and bury them in a boat stall. Who *was* this Dean Corll?

After midnight, the exhausted detectives called it quits. They weren't done, but everyone needed a break. The stench and the heat overwhelmed them. Some of the trusties showed signs of trauma. No one had expected to be here this long. A routine trip to check an unlikely report had evolved into a major case with multiple bodies. So far, they'd dug holes near two walls and in the stall's center. There were many more areas to explore. The age of some of the remains suggested they'd been here a while.

A crowd of reporters shouted into cameras for TV news about the gruesome discoveries. The parents of missing boys hung on every word as they called one another. Jack Olsen depicted them as enraged over how the Houston police had declared their missing sons runaways. Mary Henley later recalled for reporters that she'd sat frozen in the home she shared with her mother, Christeen Weed, and her three younger sons. She'd known that "Elmer Wayne" had been close with Corll for a year and a half. He'd tried to tell her he was in trouble. She hadn't listened. She could only hope that what she was witnessing now would all get sorted out. It *had* to. She wanted desperately to see her eldest son, to have him explain what this was all about, but she couldn't just go running out to find him. At this late hour, she doubted she'd be allowed to see her son. For her, it was a sleepless, agonizing night.

Henley, too, had a fitful night in his bare jail cell. He hallucinated a woman entering with a dog. Then, an elderly black woman seemed to be taking pictures of him. He panicked at the intrusion. He couldn't get warm. Disoriented, he shook uncontrollably.

The following day dawned just as sweltering as the day before. More bodies were exhumed, some of them with items of clothing, such as bathing suits, shoes, and belts. The medical examiner's team began the work of giving them names. ID cards for a pair of missing brothers attested to their fates. HPD Detective Karl Siebeneicher looked in horror at the remains of Marty Jones, his murdered cousin. But other identifications would be harder. TV crews filmed the grisly business of pulling up plastic-wrapped decomposed bodies and carrying them to the waiting transport vehicles. In a couple of cases, there was evidence of genital mutilation. In one hole, the skeletal remains of two boys had commingled, making it difficult to tell which parts belonged to which kid.

Over the next few days, the "Houston Mass Murders" would become the largest case of criminal multicide thus far in the history of the United States.

## The Predator

The pressing question for public safety officials was how so many kids had gone missing from the same Houston neighborhood within the span of a few years without prompting a full-scale investigation. Also, how had a seemingly nice man like Dean Corll—called the "Candy Man" by kids who'd adored him—done the things Henley described? And how had an ordinary teen like Wayne Henley been involved? The story took shape as police and prosecutors scrambled to piece together an official narrative. They ran down multiple leads and ignored those they couldn't pursue due to vague information or lack of resources.

Ultimately, they offered a simple but incomplete story of a sexual predator and murderer operating in a limited area. This narrative has been intact for nearly fifty years. However, in the early 2010s, two separate teams of researchers, following the lead of a man named Randy White, probed a possible connection between Dean Corll and the Chicago serial killer John Wayne Gacy. This contractor was arrested in 1978, five years after Corll's death, for killing nearly three dozen boys and young men. White had worked as a "researcher" for Gacy while Gacy, imprisoned, compiled dossiers on his victims and associates. A name that repeatedly came up in reports was John David Norman. An investigation turned up records dating back to the 1950s of Norman molesting teenage boys. He'd even been committed to Washington State's McNeil Island for incorrigible sex offenders. Yet he'd never stayed incarcerated for long. During the time of Dean Corll's murders, Norman was running several "businesses" out of Texas that were related to the sexual exploitation of minors. It seems that more was at stake in August 1973 than identifying and stopping a local serial killer. In fact, signs of the broader story's substantial reach around the country had been present from the day the murders were discovered. Henley had said it: there was an organization that Corll had talked about that bought and sold boys. But as Henley began to admit complicity in the murders, he lost credibility in the eyes of police.

We have no fitting label for individuals like Henley whom predators target to convert into helpers. They're not the same as the victims they help to harm, but they're also not the same as the primary predator. They occupy a fuzzy middle ground. They're often chosen merely because they're young, vulnerable, weak, needy, or compliant and therefore easy to manipulate. Since society tends to view them as equal offenders, especially when they do heinous things, researchers haven't fully studied their unique experiences. Yet dissecting how individuals who'd never considered killing someone might do so under certain influences can reveal ways to protect future potential candidates. Corll had two known apprentices, both immature teenage boys. At Corll's behest, they learned to abduct, guard, murder, and bury other boys.

## The Predator's Approach

The concept of an apprenticeship invokes the eighteenth-century image of young people bound to master craftsmen in an arrangement aimed to cultivate competency in a skill. In exchange for this education, apprentices performed the grunt work. Each party derived benefits, but the servitude could be grueling, even abusive. Apprentices were generally teenagers, fifteen or younger, because they were easy to train. The arrangement could last for years and lead to partnerships. An apprentice might even move in with the master during the training process, becoming a lackey and handyman. Sometimes a larger organization, like a guild, supervised the arrangements.

Too late, it's become clear that there was a sex trafficking ring whose principal operators were based near Dean Corll. Two of these men lived and worked extensively in Houston and Dallas, with associations in California. Their network was documented as having tens of thousands of predators participating, with just as many boys being exploited. It's improbable that

Corll would have had no awareness of this ring, as pedophiles tend to share resources to indemnify each other.

With Corll, the focus was on murder. He'd developed a method for how to look for young prey, then bait them, reel them in, kill them, and bury them. He would likely have known that getting adolescent boys to bring other boys to his parties would reduce the risk of him being seen with a boy he later killed. Some of his Houston victims had been regulars at the pool table he used to entice young males to come to his home to hang out. One had worked in his candy business.

Often, predators offer a "mentoring" relationship, as Corll did. They quickly establish a sense of intimacy and use phrases that make them seem to care. They manipulate their accomplices with money, gifts, praise, and promises similar to the way they might groom victims. They provide a home away from home and become the adult who "understands." Corll initially handed out candy, then pills and beer, before he set up his hangout for boys. He always seemed ready to help. With his genial manner, he handily enticed two young partners (and possibly more). Once they crossed the line into crime, they were psychologically, morally, and legally implicated. Their immature personality structures made them pliable. They weren't equipped to resist a strong, dominant man like Corll. (Even many adults might be unable to do so.)

This case evolved dramatically in its first few days, forcing detectives to revise their initial notions about Dean Corll and the boy who'd killed him. At the same time, Henley was coming to terms with telling the whole truth. He wanted to unload his burden, come what may. There was more to the story. Much more.

## The Case Expands

Digging resumed inside the boat stall at 8:30 A.M. on August 9. That same morning, Detective Mullican checked Henley out of his cell to ask more questions. Henley was suffering from alcohol withdrawal and had complained that his cell was too cold. He'd slept poorly. He still hadn't been allowed to see his mother, but she'd gotten a contact from her minister for an attorney who could represent her son. The detectives knew that in Texas, at age seventeen, Henley was a minor, but he could legally make his own decisions. He'd asked several times if he needed a lawyer, but he hadn't exactly requested one. Technically, detectives could proceed. Mullican told Mary Henley that her son could remain silent if he wanted, but they'd continue to ask him questions. They wanted to keep him talking while he seemed eager to do so. Getting answers had grown urgent. A team of detectives had found more than forty files about missing Houston boys that resembled the circumstances of the murdered kids.

Henley hedged a bit under the next round of interrogation, but despite his hope to distance himself and escape the repercussions of his acts, he knew he couldn't pull it off. Once they'd exhumed more bodies (four more by noon that day), he admitted there were other burial sites farther away. Without his help, he said, the police would never find them. He didn't know what would happen to him, but he needed to come clean. Mullican encouraged him to get the load off his chest. Henley would later say he'd wanted the families to know where their boys were. He didn't realize then that his case would cause a sensation and gain Houston a reputation in the press as the "murder capital of the world."

Henley offered a revised statement, starting with how he'd met Dean Corll. He said he'd asked his friend, David Brooks, to introduce him to Corll, hoping it could result in making the kind of money Brooks always seemed to have. "David was always riding around in Dean's car and everything. . . . I thought this was great." Henley's own family lived at the poverty level, barely able to pay the bills. "David Brooks told me he could get me in on a deal where I could make some money." Eventually, Corll had mentioned sex trafficking. "Dean told me he belonged to an organization out of Dallas that bought and sold boys, ran whores and dope and stuff like that. Dean told me he would pay me $200.00 at least for every boy that I could bring him and maybe more if they were real good-looking boys. I didn't try to find any for him until about a year later, and I decided I could use the money to get better things for my people, so one day I went over to Dean's apartment . . . and told him that I would find a boy for him."

They went out in Corll's car and saw a young man hitchhiking. Henley didn't know him. "Since I had long hair and all," Henley was able to persuade the guy to accompany them to Corll's place to smoke marijuana. He described how they'd disabled the boy with a handcuff trick. "I thought Dean were going to sell him to this organization that he belonged to." Corll paid him $200. "Then a day or so later, I found out that Dean had killed the boy." Henley hadn't realized that Corll had intended to commit murder. However, Corll had told him he was now part of this criminal enterprise and would go to prison if he told, so Henley had "helped Dean get 8 or 10 other boys." He mentioned David Hilligiest, a friend of his that Corll had killed, and Malley Winkle, whom Corll and Brooks had killed. Next was one of his own victims: "Charles Cobble who I killed and we buried in the boat stall. I shot Charles in the head with Dean's pistol, over on Lamar Street in Pasadena, then we buried him in the boat stall. . . . Then Marty Jones, me and Dean choked him and buried him in the boat stall." So, not only had Henley known there were bodies in stall #11, but he'd also helped to put them there. Mullican's suspicions about Henley's involvement were confirmed.

The list continued with more names—Billy, Frank, Mark, Johnny—some choked, some shot. Some were buried at Lake Sam Rayburn, where Corll's father had a vacation house, others on a beach at High Island. Henley couldn't provide exact dates "because there has been too many of them." Some names he didn't know, but he had an overall estimate. "Dean told me that there was 24 in all, but I wasn't with him on all of them." Henley said he'd tried to tell his mother "two or three times about this stuff and she just wouldn't believe me. I even wrote a confession one time and hid it, hoping that Dean would kill me because the thing was bothering me so bad. I gave the confession to my mother and told her if I was gone for a certain length of time to turn it in." He said that he and David Brooks had discussed killing Dean to stop him. "Several times, I have come within an inch of killing him, but I just never got up enough nerve to do it until yesterday, because Dean had told me that his organization would get me if I ever did anything to him."

The confession was a relief. At one point, Henley shouted, "I don't care who knows about it. I have to get it off my chest!" When he was finally allowed to see his mother for fifteen minutes, he told her to "be happy for me," because "now I can live!" She couldn't understand what he was saying. He was ill, she could see that, suffering from withdrawal, but he seemed out of his mind. She told the detectives that he needed care. She also said she had arranged for an attorney, who would come that afternoon. One officer told her that Wayne could decide for himself how much he wanted to say before the attorney arrived. Only as more information came out did Mary realize the enormity of what her son had been involved in. News reports offered gruesome details of bodies half-wrapped, some remains reduced to teeth and bones, a few bodies buried on top of others.

By the end of that day, the diggers would have seventeen removed from the boat stall. The pit they'd dug in its dirt floor was six feet deep. At that point, they had hit a solid surface they could no longer penetrate. They'd had the dirt hauled away to examine for items not yet recovered.

News reports interrupted regular evening programming to describe the discovery of bodies. The families of missing boys in the area paid close attention. Some of them *knew*. That's what had happened to Ruben or Frank or Billy. Several called the police station. They wanted more from the cops now than those initial lame notions that these boys had just run off. During the time since Corll had rented the stall, some two dozen boys from this small neighborhood had "run off." It was preposterous.

Many questions needed answers. In 1973, nothing quite like this case had been seen before. The FBI had yet to launch its program on profiling extreme offenders and no US law enforcement agency was even using the phrase *serial killer*. It was commonly believed that sexual perverts skulked on society's fringes; they didn't live and work among decent folks. The city reeled from the unfolding revelations.

Yet not far away in Dallas, a group of sex traffickers with whom Corll had claimed financial connections had succeeded in building inroads into other places around the country. Henley's statement about them got lost in the more immediate details of a local mass murder. Although the so-called Dallas Syndicate shows up in police records as a lead to check out, they seemed to let it go without much investigative effort.

But no one had to go to Dallas to find the worst kind of deviance. It had lived in this lone predator, Dean Corll, and he'd spread his venom to others via an insidious grooming process. To understand how it works, the players' backgrounds must be explored, starting with Corll as a budding sexual sadist and David Brooks as his first handyman.

# CHAPTER 2

# Bait a Kid, Make a Killer

## The Other Graves

Just after Henley started his post–boat stall statement in Pasadena, Detective Mullican received a call that David Brooks had arrived at the Houston Police Department with his father and uncle to see Lieutenant J. D. Belcher. Brooks was offering to tell what he knew about Corll and Henley. When Mullican told Henley about this development, Henley said he was glad to hear it because now he could tell the whole truth. He expected Brooks would do the same. He didn't realize Brooks intended to throw him under the bus. When Mullican thought he needed more leverage during their session, he told Henley that Brooks was putting it all on him.

Over the course of forty minutes, Henley said that he and Brooks had both been procurers of young boys and had participated in the murders. Mullican notified Houston PD so they could coordinate a team to take Henley to the burial sites at Lake Sam Rayburn that afternoon. The detective had stopped anticipating when this case would finally conclude.

Brooks, age eighteen, had seen the news and called his brother to say he was "somewhat" involved. It was common knowledge that he'd lived with Corll for the past three years, so he apparently thought he had to say *something*. His brother told their father, Alton Brooks, who insisted they go to the police. Alton had friends at HPD: they'd know what to do. A local paving contractor with a modicum of political clout, Alton hired moonlighting cops as security for his business locations. According to author Jack Olsen, Alton worried that the stigma of his son's involvement would ruin him. It didn't help that Henley had been one of his casual employees too. Alton had to undertake damage control. He seemed to think he could leverage his connections.

Lieutenant Belcher called in Detective Jim Tucker and whomever else he wanted to bring from Homicide. In Alton's presence, David Brooks offered a "witness statement." He'd known Corll for several years and had even lived with him, Brooks said, but he'd seen no evidence of any crimes. One officer took down everything Brooks related, but the cops didn't buy it. They knew they'd need to get this young man away from his father at some point.

Brooks said he'd met Corll when he was in the sixth grade. Corll was twenty-seven. Corll had bought him a black light. This small gift had made a big impression. At this time, Brooks had allowed Corll to perform oral sex. Corll then paid him five dollars. Brooks kept going back. Corll had been nice to him. Brooks had also seen other boys who let Corll have sexual contact with them. After a while, Brooks had introduced Henley into the mix.

Over the course of several hours, Brooks told what he knew in vague terms. It's unclear whether Alton was present the entire time, but since it was just a witness statement, the officers couldn't pressure or interrogate Brooks. However, they could use strategic questions to guide him.

Brooks eventually admitted that Corll had once lived in the Yorktown townhouses and Brooks had seen two naked boys tied to a bed. Corll had been naked too. He'd said he was "just having fun." He'd offered to buy

Brooks a car if he kept quiet. Brooks said Corll had told him later that he'd killed both kids. "He gave me a car; it was a Corvette." Brooks didn't know the names of either boy, but he knew of two others, Mark Scott and Ruben Haney, who'd disappeared. He added a "Mexican boy" that had "come at" Corll when Corll was living at Bellefontaine, and Corll had shot this boy twice. "He didn't mention what he had done with the body." There was another one that Corll said he'd killed in a bathtub, breaking part of the tub. "Sometimes when we were talking, he'd say how hard it was to strangle someone . . . it took quite a while to do it."

Brooks estimated that Corll had killed twenty-five to thirty boys and young men over three years. He added that Corll had "mentioned there was a group of people in Dallas which had similar activities to his. He mentioned a man by the name of Art who he said had also killed some boys in Dallas. One day while I was at his house, I picked up a piece of paper with the name Art on it and all of a phone number but the last number, and the area code was 214 [a Dallas number]."

Brooks said that Henley and Corll had once ganged up on him. Henley hit him in the head to disable him and Corll handcuffed him. Corll then raped him all night and forced him into other depraved acts. Corll had decided to kill him, and Henley was going to help. In the end, they let him go. Inexplicably, Brooks had continued to live with Corll. He moved to other apartments with Corll several times before "Wayne had told me that Dean was talking about getting me again and so I just packed up and left." But Corll grew paranoid about what Brooks might do apart from him, so Brooks had moved back in. He didn't explain why.

Brooks ended his statement at 1:20 P.M. without implicating himself in much except hearing about some murders. The detectives marveled over how he'd stayed with his rapist. They placed him into an office to await their next step. By now, they knew that Henley had admitted to participating in eight murders and knowing about sixteen others. He'd said Brooks had been involved. They couldn't let Brooks go home, not yet.

Around 2:30 P.M., Henley was brought to the Houston PD and sent into the room with Brooks. Alton wasn't present. The plan was to see if Henley could get Brooks to confess his part. Hyped up on his own sense of relief, Henley urged Brooks to clear his conscience: Brooks should just tell the truth, because that's what *he* was doing, and he felt so much better for it. But Henley warned that if Brooks hedged, Henley would change his own story and put it all on Brooks. Although Brooks said he intended to stick to his statement, he seemed to realize he couldn't cling to his lies. He hadn't anticipated that Henley would talk so much.

Late that afternoon, Brooks was arrested due to being implicated in a felony confession and read his rights. His father broke down. As an indication of the Brooks family dysfunction, Alton once had warned Henley not to hang out with his son, believing the boy (David) would come to no good. Still, Alton had never anticipated something like this.

Brooks decided to revise his statement and "tell everything." His father hovered, urging him to say he hadn't been involved in any murder. Author Jack Olsen quotes Alton saying, "What I'm worried about is the publicity. It might could ruin my business." How he was allowed this level of interference is unclear. Olsen portrays Alton as being horrified by his son's apparent indifference to the enormity of the situation.

Meanwhile, the news media were reporting the mounting body count from the boat stall. The death toll was about to get worse.

In one of the cars in a growing caravan that now comprised this multijurisdictional investigation, Henley rode with two Pasadena detectives and one Houston detective—Dave Mullican, Sidney Smith, and Willie Young—to Lake Sam Rayburn in the piney woods one hundred seventy miles northeast of Houston. Three other detectives were in another car, and in Lufkin, two Texas Rangers, Dub Clark and Charles Neel, joined the convoy. Another car contained Sheriff John Hoyt and some of his deputies from San Augustine County. A few reporters' vehicles took up the rear. Henley told the officers in the car with him about Corll's promise of money for bringing boys but maintained that he'd been paid just once. Detective Young, sitting in the back seat with Henley, asked how he'd gotten caught up in this sordid affair, to which Henley made a revealing remark: "Well, if you had a daddy that shot at you, you might could do some things too."

Henley said there were four victims at this site. He wasn't entirely sure how to get to the graves, since Brooks had been the driver, but he knew they'd been near where Corll's family had property. He recalled the name of a town. Hoyt asked if it was near a long bridge. Henley said yes, and added that after the bridge they'd taken a dirt road to the left. Hoyt knew the way.

Back at the boat stall during the second day of digging, the exhumation efforts had grown more challenging. In some places, dirt had mixed with biological fluids, making a mucky mess that made it difficult to extract intact bodies. Investigators were mostly recovering chunks of hair and bits of bone. But three small plastic baggies dumped near a body contained a severed penis and two testicles. Another boy's penis had been gnawed nearly in half. The victims had been bound, some with their hands behind their backs. All had been placed into plastic wrapping, although some wrappings had broken open. One pair of pants looked to fit a boy younger than most, perhaps eight or nine. The city sent a backhoe, but it was the wrong type, so the trusties resumed digging with shovels.

Near Lake Sam Rayburn, Henley was given a pair of golf shoes to replace the flimsy jail sandals he wore. The place would be muddy, Hoyt warned, from several days of rain. Henley got lost a few times, delaying the procession. They drove to Farm Road 3185, where he got out and led the way one hundred yards through the woods, passing an area near a creek that he said contained a grave to arrive at a spot farther away where four sticks were crossed over each other. Henley said he'd put this marker on all the graves. Cops probed the dirt. Their shovels hit a four-foot plywood board. Henley said a body was underneath. He didn't recall the victim's name. He told them the board was placed here because the body had come to the surface, possibly from animal activity. Under the board was a layer of white lime. Soon, the diggers turned up the packaged, decomposing body.

The group returned to the first grave site, where Henley said, "Billy Lawrence is buried here." Lawrence had gone missing that past June. (Author Jack Olsen writes that Lawrence was found first, under the board, and that the second grave was deeper into the woods, but the autopsy reports indicate that the second body exhumed was Lawrence, and there was no board. The medical examiner also noted that all four bodies were found on August 9, but police reports contradict this.)

Darkness ended the day's efforts, but Henley insisted there were two more bodies to locate. The entire party stayed overnight nearby, locking Henley in a local jail. Sheriff Hoyt wanted to press charges and hold Henley in San Augustine County. According to author John Gurwell, Hoyt reported that Henley had talked with his mother by phone, yelling at her for not finding him a lawyer, but Henley said he wouldn't have yelled at her, and he hadn't wanted her to mortgage her mother's house to hire him a lawyer. He took a sedative. When Sheriff Hoyt woke him around 2:00 A.M. to ask him questions, Henley was groggy. Hoyt had brought a Justice of the Peace to read Henley his rights in preparation to file charges for murder and arrest him. Henley was barely aware of what Hoyt was doing. Early the next morning, the Rangers ensured that Henley got back in the car.

Brooks, too, spent the night in a cell. On Friday morning, he was ready to unload, to a point. He said that Corll had oral sex with many of the local boys, but sometimes Corll anally raped and killed them. Brooks returned to the murder of two boys at the Yorktown apartments to provide more details. "There were two boys there and I left before they were killed. But Dean told me he had killed them afterwards." He didn't know their names. (Corll had lived at this address in 1970, and only one of the identified victims had been killed then. Brooks either remembered incorrectly or these boys are undiscovered victims. At the time, Corll had used beaches for burial; he didn't have the boat stall. So perhaps the boys had been buried on a beach.) Brooks said Corll had told him the boys were going to be sent to California, which might have been a cover story that coincidentally used the same state as the sex trafficking network he talked about. However, Corll's statement to Brooks might also indicate Corll's actual past or concurrent association with the network.

Although Brooks's account had gaps and inconsistencies, possibly due to drug use or to an unprepared attempt to cover his involvement, he admitted to being present at the murder of Ruben Haney in August 1971 at 6363 San Felipe. "Dean did the killing, and I was just present when it happened." He'd also seen two brothers killed in a different place. "I was present when Dean killed them by strangling them, but again I did not participate. I believe that I was present when they were buried, but I don't remember where they were buried." He witnessed another murder before Henley joined them but did not name the victim. "Dean kept this boy around the house for about four days before he killed him." They had picked him up together and buried him together. "It really upset Dean to have to kill this boy because he really liked him."

When Brooks mentioned Henley, he said that his fellow accomplice had initially just helped in "getting the boys" but later took an active part in the killing. Henley had been "especially sadistic" at one place. Brooks was on a roll, but he remained careful. "Most of the killings that occurred after Wayne came into the picture involved all three of us. I still did not take part in the actual killing but nearly always all three of us were there." He said he was present when Mark Scott was killed, correcting his earlier lie that he'd left before it had happened.

Brooks described more incidents of sadism and murder in a confusion of details, minimizing his role to "standby" in case something went wrong. He said the plywood board with handcuffs that they'd found at Corll's home had been used to restrain the boys for sexual assault. He was also the driver when they transported bodies for burial. As if to put a shine on his image, Brooks added that he'd helped some of the boys, including a kid named Billy Ridinger. "I believe the only reason he is alive now is because I begged them not to kill him." (In his earlier statement, he said that Corll had made this decision.)

Brooks emphasized that "most of the boys weren't good boys." They'd been runaways, as if that helped his case. Most, he said, were buried in the boat stall. Of the seventeen found there, Brooks had been present for at least ten. "I regret that this happened, and I'm sorry for the kids' families."

Meanwhile, Henley had led the way through the Lake Sam Rayburn woods south of where they'd been the night before. He located a fallen tree that he'd stumbled over when they'd brought a body here. The search party arrived at the graves of two more murdered boys, buried within ten feet of each other. Henley said these victims had been killed at different times. He thought they might be Homer Garcia and Mike Baulch, the brother of a kid murdered the year before. A plywood board covered one victim and a cord fashioned as a hangman's noose was tied around his throat. Henley knew of no other graves in the area.

Back at the cars, Henley answered a few questions for reporters, although he seemed annoyed. The teenager admitted helping Corll to "git some boys" so Corll could rape them. "We were the pickers." When he didn't like a question, he curtly said, "No comment," especially when asked about his mother's reaction on August 8, caught on film. *That*, he said, was private. He admitted he'd been involved in these murders because "Dean had something over me."

The grim caravan then proceeded on a trek to a public beach three hours south, near the unincorporated community of High Island. The area in Chambers County bordered Jefferson and Galveston Counties. They arrived by lunch time. Sand dunes hid the beach, but wide cuts through the dunes allowed access. By now, there were dozens of cars in the convoy, along with three helicopters. Another line of vehicles coming from Houston followed the HPD officers, Jim Tucker and Jack Hamel, who were transporting

David Brooks. A backhoe and bulldozer were brought in. One photo taken that day shows Henley and Brooks sitting together on a dune, but Henley doesn't recall talking with Brooks, or even being near him. These two had once plotted to kill Corll together, and Henley had now done it. But Brooks apparently had no question or comment about it. Brooks didn't reveal to Henley what he'd told police.

As beachgoers stood by and gawked, Brooks led detectives in the sweltering heat to the first grave, marked by a large piece of broken cement. He named Ruben Watson Haney as the victim. Police found a body wrapped in plastic and buried just two feet down. Strands of dark hair were still on the skull. The remains were skeletal except for flesh on the feet. (Brooks was mistaken about the victim, as the medical examiner would later determine. Corll had shown him this marker, but Brooks hadn't been present for the burial. It would turn out to be a different young man.)

Henley found a second grave just over two hundred feet away. He pointed out several other possible spots, but nothing turned up. This area proved difficult for a search since there was only one obvious landmark. Brooks said there would be six bodies here in a row, all within half a mile of one another. A beach grader raked through a wide swath of sand from the target area while investigators poked holes here and there to try to release foul odors from decomposition. Brooks recalled a victim he hadn't mentioned before. "The youngest was about nine. His daddy ran a grocery store across the street from where Dean was living." (A pair of trousers that fit a boy that age was found in the boat stall.)

Another impromptu press conference was held, which Henley used to correct errors he'd seen in news accounts during his excursions with police. He willingly posed for pictures as he pretended to point out a grave site. This only added to the impression he'd given to detectives of his seeming indifference to what he'd done. They'd later report that he'd told them during the car ride about how difficult it was to choke someone (apparently echoing Corll). They'd wondered how he could be so chatty as they dug up decomposing boys—his *friends*. They didn't grasp the enormous relief he felt over knowing Corll couldn't do anything to anyone else, including him.

That afternoon, they turned up just two bodies, bringing the total by day's end to twenty-three. Henley and Brooks both insisted there were more on the beach, including a boy named Mark Scott, but officials called a halt to the digging. In a move that would be shocking today, the excuse was that they needed machinery, which required paperwork and funds. One city official claimed that the area was a bird sanctuary and should not be disturbed. Without an exact location, it would be difficult to tear up the whole beach even though they were searching for victims who were some families' loved ones. They'd try again on Monday, they said, but insisted that this day's work was over.

Back in Houston, Dean Corll's family and some acquaintances gathered to lay his body to rest in Grand View Memorial Park in Pasadena. A young man showed up early for the funeral and stood apart, weeping. Police later identified him as a former school friend. Corll was accorded military honors for his service in the US Army, including a flag draped across his coffin. The flag was folded and given to his father. Corll's mother, Mary West, claimed to anyone listening that Brooks and Henley had framed her son for these murders. Corll was one of their victims too.

Someone leaked Brooks's second statement to the press. Parents called HPD from all over the country to find out if their missing boy was among the victims. The officers who had to respond to these calls were overwhelmed.

Assistant District Attorney Don Lambright realized he needed to implicate Brooks with an identified victim. He pressured the detectives to get a direct, detailed statement. Late on August 10, a weary Jim Tucker found David Brooks conferring with his father. He got Brooks alone and asked him to revisit the murder of Billy Lawrence, whose body had been buried at Lake Sam Rayburn. Tucker showed him a photo collected from 2020 Lamar. Brooks recognized it and said, "I have seen the same picture before at Dean's house." He identified Billy Lawrence. On that day, Brooks said, he'd gone to Corll's house, seen a nude boy on the floor, tied to the bed. The boy remained alive overnight, but by the time they were ready to go to Lake Sam Rayburn, the kid was dead, "so I must have been there when he was killed." Coldly, Brooks admitted, "It didn't bother me to see it. I'd seen it done many times." They transported the body to Lake Sam Rayburn, slept, went fishing, ate, and then dug the grave.

Tucker typed up this account. According to writer Jack Olsen, Brooks read it and said he couldn't sign it. He wanted to change one line. Just after he'd said he'd seen murder many times, he replaced, "I just didn't like to do it myself" with, "I just wouldn't do it myself. And I never did do it myself." Seemingly, Alton Brooks's concern had influenced him. Lambright would later admit regret over allowing Brooks time alone with his father. Away from Alton, they might have gotten more out of him. David Brooks signed this final statement. Thereafter, he said nothing more. He had a lawyer.

So did Henley. His mother had hired Charles Melder, who brought in Ed Pegelow. Melder told the press that Henley was ill and disoriented from a nervous condition. Melder vowed to seek a court order to get him released. No charges had been filed in Harris County (although Hoyt had filed three charges in San Augustine County for the Lake Sam Rayburn discoveries). Melder said he would no longer allow police to question his client. They'd done it for hours without his mother present and had kept him from speaking to her. She had told officers she'd hired an attorney. Melder considered that Henley's confession had been taken under duress, while the boy was ill, and he would strive to get it thrown out. "If we had been there, he would have made no statement at all." He also said that David Brooks was far more implicated than his statement revealed, and he was likely a self-serving liar.

On Monday, the search at High Island resumed and three bodies were found near where the other two had been exhumed. In a grave that contained two victims, buried head to toe, were extra bones that belong to neither: some vertebrae, three ribs, a hip bone, an ulna, and a metatarsal. These were duly collected. A machine operator suggested that dragging the sand, which they'd done for about half a mile, might have pulled bones from a separate grave. Chambers County Sheriff Louis Otter ordered more digging in the common grave, but no other bones turned up. He couldn't guess where another grave might be, and he did not have the resources to dig random holes. They'd already begun to place a fresh layer of sand over the graded area.

Three miles away, on another beach, one more body was discovered, but its status as part of the Houston Mass Murders has been questioned. The victim, identified several months later as John Sellars, was fully clothed and had been shot with several heavy-caliber slugs. It didn't fit how the other victims had been handled, aside from being bound, and Henley had said nothing about this beach. Yet, since this body brought the total on High Island to the estimated six, the operation was halted. Henley insisted they were still missing Mark Scott. He had reason to remember that burial.

The police held a press conference to announce the victim identifications made thus far and to defend themselves against community accusations of incompetence. Author John Gurwell reports that Captain Robert Horton provided statistics to the press about missing boys from the area: his division had handled more than ten thousand cases of missing juveniles since 1971. (He might have meant calls, not cases.) In 1972, he reportedly said, they'd closed all but 402 of the 5,228 cases they had. Many of those "unclosed" cases, they believed, were kids who'd returned home without updating the HPD. The Heights wasn't even the worst hot spot in Houston for missing boys. Horton gave the impression they'd been on top of the problem and had successfully resolved most of their runaway cases. He provided the official police protocol, which involved extensive effort on each case for a minimum period of thirty days.

The parents of murdered boys disputed Horton's claims. The police had told *them* that their boys were runaways and had refused to run an investigation. One victim who'd vanished had even *named* Brooks, another had a known conflict with Brooks, and several witnesses had seen Henley with Cobble and Jones, yet police had conducted no follow-up investigation. It was true that the Heights was about two miles wide and three miles deep, but too many Heights kids had "run away" in a short period for cops to have ignored the implications. They weren't getting off the hook that easily.

The Harris County District Attorney's office requested that officers who'd listened to conversations with Brooks and Henley, or interviewed them since August 8, make a written record. Mullican, Smith, and Young provided a joint statement, dated August 23. This was two weeks after the initiating incident, with its numerous dramatic developments over several days. Memory is not a video recorder, so a joint statement based on notes, affidavits, office discussions, press reports, and the pressure of politics is likely to contain bias, if not outright error. In addition, some of the conversations had occurred in cars, when no one was taking notes.

"Henley says that Cobble was shot by him in the head," the statement reads, "Jones was choked by him and Corll, Garcia was shot by Henley, Baulch was choked by Henley and Brooks, and that he could not remember how they had killed the boy from Louisiana. He went on to say that Brooks was present and assisted in most of the killings and helped to bury all of them. He said that he and Brooks and Corll would pull their pubic hair out slowly, shove glass rods up their penis, and that they castrated some of them. . . . Henley further stated that most all of the victims were beaten severly [sic] by Corll, and they used the rubber artificial penis . . . to put in the rectum of most of the victims. Also, Henley remarked that it is not easy to choke a person like it is shown on TV. He said that it was hard to do and took a long time for a person to die when he was choking them and that he had to get Corll and Brooks to help him on most of the choking victims."

The detectives noted that Brooks had misidentified Ruben Watson Haney's grave. They had instead found the remains of Jeffrey Konen in that hole. The enormity of their task in reconstructing what had happened was daunting. In the early days, no one knew quite what to believe. The accomplices themselves seemed confused. Brooks knew more than Henley, but he was less willing to talk.

As the medical examiner's staff worked on making more victim identifications, the next task for detectives was to figure out Dean Corll. If he was the monster that Brooks and Henley had described, what could possibly have motivated him?

## Dynamics of Dominance

"I got things to do, places to go, and people to see."

Henley said this was Dean Corll's signature phrase whenever he got the itch to satisfy his lust for boys. He'd get agitated. He'd chain-smoke. He'd get out the handcuffs. He'd place a plastic sheet on the floor of his secret room and position the restraint board. He'd drive around. He'd resist all attempts to deter him.

"There were a couple of different Deans," Henley asserted. "Most of the time, he was almost childlike. We'd tease him about it. We called him Deannie Weenie. Then he had his *Mission Impossible* persona. We knew when he was in it because he'd have a pack of cigarettes in his car visor. He'd light one. He didn't inhale, but he'd puff on it. He moved in short, jerky movements. He'd look real serious. He was on a mission."

Corll dropped the stance of friend and big brother to become a lust-compelled predator too strong and dominant for a teenager to stop. They could have turned him in to police, but for reasons to be explored later, they didn't.

Predators come in all shapes and sizes. Whether they're bankers, teachers, preachers, coaches, or killers, they share a goal: to plunder others for their own gain. They devise tricks, deceptions, deflections, and whatever else it may take to ensure their stealth. When they seek partners, they look for certain signals in how individuals act and what they say, and then groom them to be ready for anything.

Most of the clinical and criminological research on the grooming methods of sexual predators focuses on how they approach and manipulate those they intend to harm. However, grooming also applies to recruiting associates who aren't eager to be involved. The methods overlap, but persuading someone not criminally inclined to commit a crime takes special finesse. It could be enticement with goods or money, a threat of violence or of removing something the target person needs, or simply developing a relationship that will soften the impact of illicit demands.

These "lesser" associates are called partners, accomplices, collaborators, helpers, abettors, apprentices, or handymen. Often, they're related to, or in love with, the dominant partner. Sometimes, they're sucked into a situation from which they can't easily escape. They might be targeted based on features of their personality or circumstances for which they aren't to blame, such as youth or a mental illness that might reduce their degree of criminal responsibility. Unless they'd willingly sought to be a criminal partner, their level of participation is not on par with the predators who drew them in. Brooks and Henley entered the criminal arena via different routes. Each participated in different ways. Neither had wanted to kill anyone and each had accepted his role according to the way Corll had maneuvered him.

Sexual predators will test for different types of vulnerability, specifically emotional, intellectual, and social. Many accomplices will be insecure and dependent, yielding easily to authority or to manipulation through guilt or fear. They will have emotional touchstones that the predator exploits, e.g., rage, desperation, curiosity, or longing. They might have needs that no one seems to be meeting. They will have little parental supervision, usually due to a broken or dysfunctional home, and few friends who might grow concerned about a change in them. They can be isolated. A secret pact might add excitement: the target person feels special in ways they never did before. They might lack confidence and a sense of responsibility for their own decisions, looking instead to someone older who can lead the way or offer more resources.

Researcher Rosaleen McElvaney presents a "lived experience" from the perspective of such a groomed individual. He wasn't an accomplice, but his story illustrates how predators like Corll operated. McElvaney's subject had been a child when he was drawn into a relationship with a benefactor who acted as a substitute parent, exploiting the child's poor relationship with his father. The abuser gradually violated the child's boundaries while concurrently making himself the adult the child most wanted to be around. He established emotional dependency in the child while also preparing the child's support community to facilitate the relationship. The abuser used gifts and money to create a random reinforcement schedule that alternated punishment or abuse with periods of affection. This cycle conditioned the boy to accept abuse as part of the anticipated reward. The longer this arrangement continued, the more reluctant the boy became to report it, especially when he thought no one would believe him. The boy even became protective of his abuser—the source of his benefits. Only in retrospect did this victim realize how much the man he'd trusted had harmed him. Yet the thought of disclosing it had felt like a betrayal.

This mechanism of intermittent reward is familiar to practitioners of sexual dominance and submission. Corll certainly exploited it. For his partner in crime, he sought a submissive person, or a "Sub." As the "Dom," he'd be in charge, and the Sub would obey. This would form an intimacy based on loyalty. When Corll committed criminal acts like rape and murder, his Subs would accommodate them, cover for them, and help clean up. He *conditioned* them into these protective acts.

For teens, especially, with their underdeveloped sense of identity, this form of compromise influences the narrative they're building for personal meaning. The Dom offers something they want and can't otherwise get, so they surrender. Once they're criminally compromised, they can be persuaded to yield responsibility to the Dom. In exchange, the Dom acquires greater control.

The psychological dynamics for those who participate in a secondary role on murder teams are often oversimplified. However, these accomplices are not all the same. A typology provides more clarity on how such arrangements work.

*Equal partners* involve two (or more) people but they're not quite accomplice-type teams. They operate together and both want to cause harm. They affirm and expand each other's depravity. With no incentive to hold back, each provides a mirror to the other, boosting the excitement. They might have different roles, but they're in full agreement. Often with equals, if law enforcement confronts them, each will turn on the other to get a deal. Sometimes one will claim to have been merely an accomplice (making them a *faux accomplice*).

*Dominant/submissive partners* are both equally committed, but one takes a leading role, due to the psychological needs of both.

*Compliant accomplices* are participants who accept a lesser role in murder due to an emotional bond with the primary killer. Outside this relationship, they wouldn't consider being involved. Most often, the accomplice is a female who insists she participated out of love for her partner and/or fear of losing him. Researchers describe compliant accomplices as having weak self-esteem from being isolated and subjected to verbal abuse. Each had been leveraged with promises, assurances, and/or threats. They'd participated reluctantly, but they'd stayed even when they had the chance to leave or do something that would end the relationship.

*Forced accomplices* participate due to a clear threat of harm or death. They don't want to be involved but feel they have no choice.

*Accessory helpers/handymen* assist a principal offender before or after a crime. They're aware of the act but do nothing to prevent it or to inform authorities. Some acquire weapons, provide transportation or a false alibi, or help with cleanup or cover-up.

Henley and Brooks would both fit the category of compliant accomplice. They were drawn in with the promise of money and the false impression that the crimes that Corll wanted them to commit would be minor. Neither had wanted to kill anyone, so neither would be considered equal partners.

## Sexual Sadism

Dean Arnold Corll wanted to be in control, but he lived in a world where he had little power. He was an insecure loner who'd discovered that being gay in Texas was a problem. Males touching males was considered aberrant. To shield his secret homosexual proclivities, he'd learned to be likable. This facade assisted him later as his impulses grew violent and he developed an appetite for murder. After his death, police interviews with his family, neighbors, coworkers, bosses, and even his killer yielded a portrait of a seemingly good guy. But this was a smoke screen. Yes, he would do things for others, but he also did things *to* others that were depraved and horrifying. Had he not been killed, he would have continued. At no time did his accomplices witness in him a troubled conscience. He did "his thing." They cleaned it up.

Corll told his accomplices about a sex trafficking network in Dallas with which he was associated. Henley came to think of it as "the Syndicate." Corll seemed to know how the ring operated, including the idea of using boys to lure other boys. There were secret pedophile rings that existed at the time, and Corll's covert savagery had likely found a home. These networks overlapped with the gay underworld, but gay men weren't necessarily pedophiles. Corll happened to be both. His attraction to the idea of a sex trafficking ring was related to his desire to acquire young sex partners he could control.

Based on published organizational newsletters and documentation from a 1977 senatorial hearing, stories were swapped about successful strategies.

The coded communications that circulated in such networks taught men who lusted for boys how to satisfy themselves without getting caught. For them, children were nothing more than food to sate their appetites. They might disguise it as love, but this was only to justify the traumatic victimization.

Evading arrest meant developing a double life: be inconspicuous or be the trusted scout leader, teacher, babysitter, youth minister, or neighbor. Grooming the community was every bit as important as preparing a victim, because people will make accommodations for someone they like. Even for those adults in the Houston Heights who thought it was odd that Corll liked hanging out with teenage boys, no alarm bells rang because few in the mainstream had an imagination for the paradox of a nice guy in public who was evil in private. The street drug culture was rampant in the low income, blue-collar Heights neighborhood. This area northwest of Houston had formerly been a planned community, a "streetcar suburb" for city workers who wanted to live near their work without being inside the city. Over the years, it had grown shabby. It was harder to find prosperous employment. Exhausted parents considered another set of guiding eyes from a man who seemed to care about kids to be beneficial. They didn't guess that Corll was appraising their sons for their innocence, naivete, sleek physique, and boyish charm.

Many people view predatory criminals who present one face to the public and another to their prey, like Corll did, as a Jekyll-and-Hyde personality. In Robert Louis Stevenson's novel, *The Strange Case of Dr. Jekyll and Mr. Hyde*, Hyde is a creature of utter self-indulgence: "The spirit of hell awoke in me and raged." He's the covert part of a respectable physician, Henry Jekyll, who passes in his community as a normal, prosocial participant. But Jekyll becomes addicted to the rush of acting without regard for laws and to fully indulging his savagery. "With a transport of glee, I mauled the unresisting body, tasting delight from every blow."

The character was based on a real person, Deacon William Brodie, who carried on a respectable trade in Edinburgh, Scotland, while fleecing people at night. During the mid-eighteenth century, he was a cabinetmaker and locksmith. As president of his guild, he sat on the town council. He also cared for his five children. He inherited a fortune but lost it gambling. Thus, he turned to thievery. Significant to the Corll story is that Brodie had three criminal accomplices. When they were caught, they implicated him. Convicted, he was hanged. Brodie's disturbing duality provided a psychological frame for an ordinary person who can hide his monstrous ways.

We can imagine sexually sadistic predators like Corll as a Jekyll/Hyde. The ordinary facade they cultivate serves as the "the cavern in which he conceals himself from pursuit." Even when they try to adhere to their morally better part, like Jekyll they're "found wanting in the strength to keep it." Each time they indulge, they experience "a more unbridled, a more furious propensity to ill." As Jekyll notes, "I have more than once observed that in my second character, my faculties seemed sharpened to a point and my spirits more tensely elastic. . . ." He embraces his wanton disregard of others.

To the outside world, predators of children act normally. They minimize suspicion by becoming stand-ins for missing parents, grandparents, or older siblings. Their presence in the child's life appears benign and offers relief to parents—especially single parents—who need support. In effect, they gain trust that comes with tacit permission to be alone with the target child. They know that most parents or guardians have been fed culturally created images of predators—the creeps who slink about near playgrounds. The predators exploit these expectations to present themselves differently. They don't skulk or act like they have something to hide. They're confident, competent, and seemingly truthful. They'll participate in things that parents consider good so they can defy anyone believing something bad about them. "He volunteers for the Boy Scouts." "He visits sick children." "He's a youth minister." It's difficult for most people to believe that such conning Jekyll/Hydes operate among them.

Yet, how do some individuals *become* the type of people who would harm children to satisfy their own desires? Although there's no formula, we do understand how this proclivity can develop.

Sexual sadism is a neurodevelopmental dysfunction involving the desire to dominate others, and some enjoy inflicting pain. Although opinions differ on its origin, the condition appears to form from certain associations about control, pleasure, and pain during the early psychosexual stages of adolescence. Even so, more than one-third of sexual sadists report discovering their perverted desires well past their teen years; they enjoy the feeling of power and authority that arises from controlling a submissive human being. Some find a way to enjoy this experience legally by acquiring consenting partners; others don't, or don't want to. They prefer to inflict pain on unwilling individuals. The latter are criminal sadists. Since they're engaging in acts that can send them to prison, they might then turn to murder to eliminate witnesses.

Human behavior ranges between ego-syntonic (internally harmonious) and ego-dystonic (disharmonious). Most sexual sadists commit ego-syntonic crimes. That is, they're comfortable with what they're doing. The more they indulge, the more they feel justified. This is called "orgasmic conditioning." A team of psychologists proposed this concept in 1965 as they studied the relationship between masturbation and deviant sexuality. They found that images, objects, and experiences that were present during an orgasm would influence the arousal mechanism. The more regularly this pairing occurred, the stronger the need became to use the image or object for gratification. A lack of social bonds could make such individuals more dependent on their solitary fantasies.

Researchers Lisa Shaffer and Julie Penn state that most sadists begin as masochists who enjoy pain or humiliation. Some who try out a dominant role find it preferable. The types of activities sadists enjoy include whipping, binding, piercing, electrocuting, hanging, raping, cutting, stomping, beating, or choking. They might use substances to induce altered states of consciousness or keep their victims imprisoned. They will usually include psychological torture, such as showing videos or playing tapes of what they did to other victims.

Criminologist Lee Mellor calls sexual sadism an "eroticized communication process" that involves a behavioral cycle: the infliction of a negative stimulus, observation of a victim's reaction, and experiencing an enhanced self-concept upon achieving success. He categorizes sexual sadists along three continuums:

- destructive vs. preservative
- brief vs. prolonged
- simple vs. elaborate

By Mellor's criteria, Corll would be a destructive/prolonged/elaborate sadist. That is, he mutilated or beat some victims while they were still alive, he kept some for a period, and he tried a variety of methods for inflicting pain. Feeling good about his dominance ensured that Corll would repeat it. Any of the steps can be sexualized, usually following an orgasmically conditioned fantasy. Sadists often derive more pleasure from extending their arousal via torment than from a sexual climax. When associated with the personality disorder psychopathy, the lack of remorse that characterizes this condition enables new ideas for pain infliction. According to former FBI profiler Robert Hazelwood, sexual sadists are "the great white sharks of deviant crime, marked by their wildly complex fantasy worlds, unequaled criminal cunning, paranoia, insatiable sexual hunger, and enormous capacity for destruction."

A study of thirty sexually sadistic male offenders by forensic psychiatrist Park Dietz and his colleagues revealed that they did not commit crimes impulsively; they had planned and carefully concealed their criminal acts. They usually retained incriminating evidence such as letters, photographs, and videotapes as mementoes that would help them to relive what they'd done.

Although Corll tossed many items belonging to victims in area dump-
sters, from a few he kept house keys, items of clothing, photos, and IDs.
Sometimes, he'd urge Henley to wear a victim's belt, or maybe a pair of
boots. "It was ghoulish," Henley recalled. "It embarrassed me. I was a
walking memorial." He'd quickly find a way to decline. For Corll, making
Henley wear something that had belonged to a boy Corll had killed allowed
him to relive what he'd done. He could see the item on his accomplice,
giving him a sense of power over two boys at once.

Former prison psychologist Al Carlisle, who evaluated serial killer
Ted Bundy, said that sexual sadists evolve through fantasy and compartmentalization. A fusion of anger and lust gives their fantasy life purpose
and direction. Mentally, they rehearse the scenario that excites them so
often it's easy to act when an opportunity occurs. "Because they might
have uncomfortable memories from childhood abuse, disappointment,
frustration, humiliation, or being bullied or disempowered," Carlisle
opined, "they use fantasies to escape, to feel powerful." If they see
someone on the street that attracts their attention, they might insert
that person into the next fantasy. Then they might seek to *do* what
they've envisioned.

The fantasy relieves stress, depression, and emptiness, Carlisle said.
"This leads to a dual identity, one being associated with reality . . . and the
secret identity which is able to manifest the power and control he would
like over others." If driven by anger, this alter identity "is usually an animal
of destruction." The killer repeatedly searches for the high that this power
confers. He senses that his dark side controls him. He might try to resist
but ultimately the gratification cannot be ignored. One offender that Carlisle interviewed told him, "It's a psychological impossibility to stop that
activity."

Typically, fantasies have been part of the process for years before the
first act. Serial killer and sexual sadist Edmund Kemper, who killed and
mutilated six young women, confirmed this when he described his acts of

rape and dismemberment: "It was something that had been thought out in fantasy, acted out, felt out, hundreds of times before it ever happened."

Often, there's a disturbed relationship with the mother, who might send mixed messages of need and rejection. She might be overprotective to the point of infantilizing. To please the mother, the boy might develop a "good boy" persona that shields his frustration. Later, he might shed the mother's smothering by dominating others. If this develops into murder, the act is empowering. Corll's pre-murder mood showed in agitation, a stiff gait, and driving around. Violating boys seemed to be a way to calm himself.

Jeff Nightbyrd, writing in 1973 for the rock music magazine *Crawdaddy*, surmised that Dean Corll had started with teen boys who'd sell themselves to get money for drugs (this was confirmed by Brooks). He thought perhaps one had pulled away, leading to Corll throttling him. Corll had discovered that he liked the experience. Or maybe his blood thirst had started as an accident during consensual sex. Once Corll crossed the murder boundary, he tried it again, this time planned. "What a movement of power, of triumph for a man who grasped secret fantasies about boys all his life but was frozen by fear of rejection! . . . Strangling is the ultimate intimacy of madness. . . . Strangling is flesh to flesh, face to face. Passion and emotion." Yet loving these boys could cause him to lose community status, so in his world it was rational to destroy them. Murder was preemptive. Accusing voices had to be silenced (this was confirmed by Henley).

A key skill that successful predators develop is cognitive flexibility. That is, they can quickly switch between different mental frames to achieve their goals. Nimble predators are ready to shift as a situation demands. In short, they have superior decision-making strategies. Researchers Daniella Laureiro-Martínez and Stefano Brusoni state that "set shifting" is an aspect of fluid intelligence. It allows someone to act on a plan without total commitment so they can easily move to another plan. Entrepreneurs are good at this. So are successful predators.

## The Candy Man

There are few sources for information on Dean Corll because his crimes were discovered only after his death. He never gave his side of the story, and many who knew him were reluctant to talk about him. Those who did talk offered only superficial descriptions. Some acquaintances spoke with detectives, leaving an official record. Author Jack Olsen included interviews that other reporters managed to get, and Harris County District Attorney Carol S. Vance summarized his office's investigation in his memoir (albeit with factual errors). Although Corll's biography is partial, there's sufficient information to see how this insecure man developed the need for control.

Vance wrote that he never understood Corll's homicidal motivation. In 1973, little was known about serial murder. Labor contractor Juan Corona had sexually assaulted, robbed, and killed twenty-five migrant workers in California in 1971, burying the bodies in mass graves in orchards along the Feather River. A decade before this, Albert DeSalvo had confessed to strangling thirteen women in Boston, while the unidentified "Zodiac" had attacked several couples north of San Francisco in 1968 and 1969, killing or injuring at least seven people, just as Charles Manson led his band of followers into the Tate–LaBianca murders in Los Angeles. Edmund Kemper and Herbert Mullin overlapped their murder sprees in Santa Cruz, California, between 1972 and '73, collectively killing twenty-one, and the FBI had just begun a teaching a program about the psychology of such homicidal offenders.

Although the 1970s would signal the start of the so-called Golden Age of serial murder, which ran into the 1990s, no one then had perspective on these crimes. In retrospect, during the 1970s, a striking number of homosexual predators had high victim totals (Dean Corll, Patrick Kearney, Randy Kraft, Juan Corona, John Wayne Gacy, Bill Bonin). Yet early in that decade—1973—the Corll case had seemed a horrific aberration.

Corll was thirty-three when he was fatally shot on August 8, 1973. His official victim toll of twenty-seven at that time might not account for the totality of his murders (another was added later, and more are suspected). Police prematurely stopped looking soon after the mass graves discovery, when conditions were best to find bodies, and Corll possibly killed an unknown number of boys on his own. (One officer expressed shock when the boat stall floor was quickly filled in before it was fully explored, and we know that at least one victim buried on High Island was never found.) Henley was the best source of information about Corll as a killer, yet he entered the picture after Corll had murdered at least a dozen victims. In addition, Corll killed several times without Brooks and Henley. Neither was able to give an accurate number, but Henley thought there were more bodies than police had found. Brooks said Corll had told him about a California victim. He also added the nine-year-old son of a grocer that was not among the identified victims, as well as a Mexican boy. Several extra bones in a grave belonged to no currently known victim, and a murdered hitchhiker from February 1972 remains unidentified.

So who was Dean Corll?

Born in Waynedale, Indiana, a suburb of Fort Wayne, on Christmas Eve in 1939, Dean was the first of two sons of a strict, combative father, Arnold Edwin Corll, and an overprotective mother, Mary Corll, née Robison. Harris County District Attorney Carol Vance writes, "Corll's father dished out macabre beatings to young Corll for the smallest of trespasses." Mary minimized Arnold's harsh discipline with excuses like "he just didn't relate with little kids." Young Dean had to endure unpredictable beatings for minor transgressions.

Mary gave birth to a second son, Stanley, but finally divorced Arnold in 1946, at a time when divorce carried a considerable stigma. Arnold was drafted into the Air Force and called up to training in Memphis, Tennessee. Mary followed, because she wanted her sons to maintain contact with him. She placed the boys into a government-run day care program, which soon folded. Mary found an elderly farmer and his wife who were willing to watch the boys while she worked. She moved her trailer onto their farm.

Eventually, she remarried Arnold. They moved to Houston in 1950, where Arnold had relatives. They fought again and ended things for good. Arnold married someone else. Mary looked for her own next mate.

Debra Niehoff, a neuropsychologist who researched multiple studies on violence, indicates that biological and environmental factors are both involved in the creation of a violent person. There's no simple formula, but in any given individual each influence modifies others such that processing a situation toward a violent resolution is unique to that person. Two boys raised in the same household could respond in different ways. A particular type of trigger, such as an abusive father, is not necessarily going to cause a child to become violent: it might influence one child and not the other. Each has their own set of genes and thus their own unique predispositions. It all gets processed through a "neurochemical profile," which defines whether the child feels that their world is safe. If not, they might develop fantasies of dominance that could one day become acts.

In the backgrounds of many sexual sadists we find unmotivated violence during childhood, a lack of solid role models, familial instability, and an absent father. The tendency to dominate often arises from a need for constancy. It might be reinforced by experience with an aggressive parental figure. Arnold Corll fits the bill.

To worsen the situation, Mary was a narcissistic parent, failing to see beyond her own concerns. Whatever damage Arnold's parenting might have done to young Dean, Mary likely minimized it or believed her son would get over it. Her dismissive manner, at least in published accounts, suggests that she didn't accept that her oldest son—the one to whom she looked as the man of the family—might need more nurturing from her. But Dean was insecure. He might have felt especially vulnerable. Although Mary was overprotective, she placed a burden on Dean to fit her idea of what her son should be. She had little idea who he really was, and he knew it.

Dean avoided socializing. He preferred to be alone. He became hyper-sensitive to criticism or rejection and bore grudges toward those who belittled him. From his development of sexual sadism, we can speculate that he enjoyed a secret fantasy life in which he controlled and punished people for any little transgression (consistent with his father's approach). Such aggression might become eroticized as he moved into puberty: it felt *good* to hurt others, even rewarding. A debilitating bout of rheumatic fever that gave him a heart murmur didn't help; he developed a nervous personality.

When it came time for sex education, Mary packed Dean off to her parents' farm in Yoder, Indiana. Possibly, she hoped he'd learned whatever he needed to know from watching animal behavior. She decided that since the boy never asked about sex, he simply wasn't curious. Whenever someone suggested he might be gay, Mary denied it. As a religious woman, she could not tolerate such deviance in her son. In fact, an astrologer had assured her he couldn't be gay. This gave Dean an early experience of rejection. He remained close to his mother while she provided a job and a place to live, but this would change.

Among Dean's preoccupations was to remain young. Mary was his pri-mary role model for this. She obsessed about being attractive to men and deeply feared being on her own. Dean seemed to absorb her insecurity. Being gay in an antigay world would only worsen his loneliness. Reports about him making advances at work show that he got rebuffed.

Mary sought desperately to attract another man. She seemed to care more that she had *a* mate than that this mate would be a good partner. Her second husband was a traveling salesman, Jake J. West. They married in 1955, and he moved her and the children to Vidor in East Texas. Dean soon gained a half sister, Joyce.

At Vidor High School, Dean got by as an average student but failed to graduate with the rest of his class. He flunked English during his senior year. His primary, perhaps sole, interest was playing the trombone in a brass band. He graduated in 1958.

West persuaded Mary to get involved in the candy business, and Dean became her assistant. He worked long hours, which included going out into the fields to pick pecans. Their efforts succeeded, and they moved back to Houston to continue their Pecan Prince business. Dean clashed at times with his stepfather, whom he disliked. Whenever his temper got the better of him, he'd close himself in his room to let off steam. No one knows what form this took. This might be where his fantasies of domination formed. By now, he was an adolescent, probably fuming over a second father figure who ordered him around.

When Dean was nineteen, the family moved to the Heights area of Houston. Reporter Jeff Nightbyrd, who describes Houston as a "small-time LA with big-time pretensions," provides a sense of this location as "a minor league teen outlaw culture of drug dealing, runaways, punk vandalism and petty thievery." Uppers and downers were easy to get. Yet residents also practiced a fundamentalist, devout Christianity. Some parents checked the pockets of visiting kids to make sure no one brought drugs into their house, but underage drinking was tolerated—often by parents too inebriated to notice. There wasn't much for kids to do outside school besides walk the tracks, play pool, and fish. Getting high was more fun.

After Dean's paternal grandfather died, Mary sent him back to her family's farm in Indiana to take care of his grandmother. He stayed for two years and met a girl who fell in love with him and announced her intention to marry him. To her dismay, he stopped seeing her. He returned to Houston in 1962.

After a fight with J. J. West, Mary left Pecan Prince to start the Corll Candy Company. As competition, they both thrived. This didn't improve her marriage, though. When Mary made her son a company vice president, West was annoyed. By 1963, he and Mary were divorced.

Mary noticed that her son seemed to lack the ability to nurture a long-term goal. He was moody and impulsive. "If he wanted something, he wanted it *right now*." In other words, Corll remained immature, and Mary protected him as if he were still a boy. In her eyes, he could do no wrong, which might have enabled his sense of entitlement.

In August 1964, Corll was drafted into the US Army. He lasted ten months. How he got an early release is a matter of interpretation. Supposedly, he (or his mother) persuaded officials that his family needed him, which got him a hardship discharge. Yet there might have been another reason. During his stint, Nightbyrd writes, Corll had some sexual encounters and came to terms with being gay. (It's unclear where Nightbyrd discovered this information, but in their book, authors Harbers and Jackson say a "longtime friend" confirmed it.) Vance echoed this explanation. Gay behavior, if discovered, would not have been tolerated at that time in the military. In any event, Corll returned to Houston to make and distribute candy. If he sought sexual partners, he kept this secret. Houston had a gay underground. All of Texas did. Corll visited bars and bathhouses, but an acquaintance said he disliked going to these places.

When Mary West's candy company relocated to West 22nd Street across from Helms Elementary School, this became Corll's testing ground: he offered kids free candy, especially chunks of Baker's Semi-Sweet Chocolate. When the word spread, more kids showed up. Thus, to a group of schoolchildren and some of their parents, Corll became the "Candy Man." He bought a pool table and a small Honda motorcycle and invited adolescent boys to hang out or go for a ride. He'd take them to the beach or the movies. Sometimes, he'd flirt with them or pinch them, to see who yielded. These kids got a different kind of candy—drugs, alcohol, and money for allowing Corll to perform oral sex. Corll grew older but preferred to hang with teens. Some adults thought it was odd, but no one tried to intervene, except perhaps police officer Willard Karmon Branch, who became enraged over

Corll's sexual advance on his son. In 1972, Branch went looking for Corll with a loaded gun but failed to find him before he cooled down.

Boys from the Heights became regulars at Corll's various apartments. He looked them over as potential candidates for a more intimate encounter. He also drove around to watch for kids to invite into his car. Most people had no idea what lay behind Corll's genial facade. He just blended in. To kids, Corll was the supplier, the cool older guy with the place where they could do whatever they wanted. He didn't say much, and they liked it that way. He also adopted the appearance that he had a girlfriend, Betty. For him, she was a mostly a beard, a front to make him seem entirely conventional. Boys like Johnny Delome, Mark Scott, Billy Ridinger, and the Baulch brothers often came over to drink, play pool or poker, and hang out. Whenever word got out that Corll was throwing a party, kids flocked to it, girls and boys alike. He took photos of boys swimming or cavorting on the beach. He also collected a few school photos of boys he liked. Occasionally, he'd proposition one. Sometimes it worked, sometimes it didn't.

Through a dating service, Mary West found another husband, a merchant seaman named Louis Wasilewski, who turned out to be abusive, unfaithful, and mentally unstable, so she annulled the marriage. This man told Mary her son was homosexual, but she insisted that *her* poor track record with relationships had probably put Dean off the idea of marriage. She was aware that a male employee had complained about a sexual advance her son had made, but she'd solved the problem by firing the kid.

Then in a repeat of her relationship with Arnold Corll, she married her third husband again. He was just as controlling during their second round, and Mary suspected he'd murdered his first wife (determined a suicide). He'd made veiled threats to bury her. Corll, now an adult, said he'd kill the guy. According to writer Jack Olsen, Mary had urged him to go ahead. She wanted to get away. Despite her staunch Christianity, Mary sought the guidance of palm readers and psychics. When one advised her to change her circumstances, she filed for her fifth divorce in June 1968.

That year, the Corll Candy Company failed, so in response to another psychic reading, Mary took her daughter and moved to Manitou Springs, Colorado, to make candy there. She expected her sons to join her, and Stanley eventually did, but Corll wanted to remain in Houston. The place was a bustling oil town, an easy place to find work. Promoters called Houston "the future of the United States." Corll signed on as an electrician testing relays at the Houston Lighting and Power Company on Hiram Clarke Road. His coworkers liked him. One man called him a good, commonsense type of guy, quiet but reliable, although Corll had made a remark during a discussion about war that seemed odd only in retrospect. According to one coworker, Corll had said, "Once you kill one, the rest come easy." At the time, they'd thought he was talking about his military experience.

To facilitate his parties, Corll stole cans of acrylic lacquer that produced a feeling of melting when "huffed." He knew the kids liked this experience. Corll also made money on the side by reducing stolen cars to parts he could sell. During this period, he didn't bother to go see his mother or siblings in Colorado. His biological father, Arnold, lived in nearby Pasadena, and the two of them developed a working relationship.

Now almost thirty, Corll was free to open his living space to teens. For a brief time, he had a roommate from high school, who then got married (and became a cop). Then he got another roommate, a young boy.

## Targets

Corll sought a submissive person to act as a criminal handyman, and perhaps as a willing assistant. Ideally, they wouldn't stand up to him or turn him in. They'd be easy to leverage. The best candidates would have already crossed a moral line, such as committing petty crimes. How Brooks or Henley fit in these categories depends on what we can believe about their stated motivations.

Predators have methods for feeling out a potential accomplice. Testing the water, they might tell a vulgar joke to watch the response. They might task them with shoplifting, setting a fire, or breaking into an empty house. They'll figure out the target's primary incentive: money, praise, sex, love, a place to live, a sense of being special, or an enticing activity the parents would never allow. Then they'll meet the need or desire. Gifts, affection, respect, money, and access to things (especially things the target cannot get) move the predator into an important role in the target's life. The emotional bond grows until the targets can't turn back. At this point, the predator might use threats or intimidation. The flow of positive incentives might dry up. Secrecy seals the bond. The targets are now compromised. The predator might convince them of their culpability and will likely make them believe they will now be diminished in the eyes of anyone who cares about them. They're isolated. Their closest friend—maybe their *only* friend—is the predator.

David Brooks was Corll's first known handyman, but whether he was genuinely the first has been debated. That Corll began his sadistic activities at the age of thirty is possible but unlikely. He'd mentioned to Brooks that some of his victims had posed a risk, as if they'd known things from their prior association with him that had put them on his list for elimination. One or more might have been used in the same way as Brooks. Corll had also hinted he'd done some things in California, including murder.

Although Brooks made several statements to police, he avoided media interviews, which makes the details of his story thin. Sometimes his memory was factually wrong. His father, Alton, offered a few items to reporters, as did people who knew Brooks as a friend of Henley's. One girl told a reporter he was "smart" because he didn't tell police anything, but Brooks did reveal things to police, and he wasn't all that bright. If not for the pressure from his father upon his arrest, Brooks might well have admitted more. Some people in the Heights felt sorry for him because it appeared that both his parents had rejected him. Tall and thin, he was socially awkward and possibly perceived as a kid who'd never amount to anything. The wire-rim glasses and stringy blond hair didn't help.

Brooks first encountered Corll when he was ten. He was among the kids who went over to the Corll Candy Company for handouts. Corll showed him the respect he hungered for. It wasn't long before Corll took Brooks places and treated him like he mattered, which hooked him into returning to stay with Corll later. And Corll didn't tease him about his glasses. When Brooks's parents divorced, his mother took him to Beaumont, over an hour from Houston, but during holidays and summer vacations when Brooks visited his father, he'd go see Corll. By then, Brooks had acquired a juvenile record for theft. Neither of Brooks's parents had much use for him. His father barely tolerated him and thought he'd come to no good—an opinion he expressed publicly. Corll, twice his age, offered a place to stay and pocket money. Brooks looked to Corll as a father figure and a man who claimed to have influence in organized crime. As Corll's live-in assistant, Brooks felt important in ways he'd never felt with other adults. Brooks wasn't inherently bad; he was just a kid with little going for him and no one to guide him.

Corll gave Brooks money whenever he asked. Soon, Corll persuaded him to earn it by letting him perform oral sex. Brooks complied. He said this began when he was thirteen or fourteen. It was easier for him to make money this way than to find a job. He was a poor student, so he was held back in school. He finally dropped out when he was fifteen.

Corll acquired a pair of handcuffs and devised the "handcuff game," pranking boys into putting them on, which rendered them helpless. The locks turned inward, making it impossible for the captive to open them. Corll showed it to Brooks and possibly trained him in how to do it.

According to police reports compiled after Corll's death, his behavior suggested that he might have had dealings with some level of organized crime. He changed his address frequently, sometimes four or five times in a year. Some landlords told police that he left an apartment damaged, or without paying the rent. Once, he stayed less than a week. Police records would later list twenty-five addresses for Corll within a five-year period.

Brooks often moved with him. One story describes a female building manager knocking at the door. Brooks answered and said he was Corll's brother. The woman mentioned concerns from neighbors and then discovered that Corll and Brooks had snuck out in the middle of the night. Another building manager said she saw them carry out a roll of plastic sheeting. When they vacated the apartment, they left behind a plywood board into which large holes had been drilled. Only later would the meaning of this item come clear. Neighbors of Corll's said they saw numerous boys go in and out of his places. Loud parties and other alarming noises generated complaints. In one apartment, someone shot through the door four times and Corll bolted a steel shield onto it. He most definitely harbored secrets.

## Making the Move

The 1970s counterculture was a time of experimentation with sex and drugs, so anyone who offered these things raised his status with teens. Even if the kids thought Corll was gay, few seemed to care. A small hippie culture flourished in Texas, with a live-and-let-live attitude.

It remains unknown exactly when Corll began to kill, but the earliest known murder happened in September 1970. Sensitive about aging, Corll was distressed over being thirty. He disliked gay bars, so he cruised around one day looking for company.

Jeffrey Alan Konen, eighteen, was going to school at the University of Texas at Austin. He decided to hitchhike to Houston in late September 1970 to visit his girlfriend. Konen was reportedly on the corner of South Voss and Westheimer Roads in Houston when Corll saw him, pulled over, and invited him to hop in. How Corll got Konen to his Yorktown apartment is unclear, since Konen had a destination, but Corll did have a .22-caliber revolver. At some point, Corll bound Konen with a three-strand nylon cord, gagged him with white adhesive tape, raped him, and strangled him. Corll wrapped the nude body in thick plastic sheeting that he'd stolen and buried this young man on the beach at High Island. He placed a large piece of broken cement to mark the grave.

How Corll felt about this murder is unknown. However, he'd later tell his accomplices that killing his rape victims was necessary to eliminate witnesses. He had vendettas with some that he targeted, but he also had a type—Caucasian, slender, and youthful.

With Konen, Corll had committed the perfect stranger murder. He'd picked up a kid he didn't know during a time when hitchhiking was common. No one who knew Konen had seen him enter Corll's car and no witnesses reported anything untoward. No one suspected Corll. He continued in his usual manner for the next two months until he spotted another opportunity in December. (Possibly, by Brooks's report, there was another double homicide before December.) By this time, Corll had rented the boat storage stall at 4500 Silver Bell, with a dirt floor and doors that would shield him from prying eyes as he dug holes and spread lime.

In a daring move, he lured two fourteen-year-old boys from the Heights, Jimmy Glass and his friend Danny Michael Yates. Corll saw Danny on the street with his brother, Bradley, a year older. He drove up and asked, "Do you want to drink some beer?" That's how Bradley Yates remembers it. He thought the guy was creepy, but Danny showed enough interest that Corll offered his phone number. A few days later, on December 13, Danny and James went off to a church rally on West Eleventh Street. No one saw them after that. It's unclear how Corll got them to his residence on December 13. Possibly Danny and Jimmy decided to use Corll's phone number that day. Danny's sister said a man matching Corll's description had given them a ride to a movie. Jimmy's older brother recalled that they went to the rally, and he saw them go down the aisle before they disappeared.

At his apartment at 3300 Yorktown Street, Corll restrained the boys with ropes and handcuffs to a four-poster bed. Brooks knew about this incident, and because his police statements are confusing, there are two possible scenarios: 1) He arrived when Corll was abusing them, and these are the only two boys Brooks saw during 1970, or 2) he was already there when Yates and Glass came (or he helped lure them), so he'd seen two *other* boys before the Yates/Glass abduction.

If the first scenario is true, Brooks entered the apartment. Corll was naked. Brooks saw the boys tied to the bed. Corll said he was "just having fun." He promised Brooks a car if he stayed quiet. Brooks did *not* leave because at some point, Brooks took Glass home. "I had taken him home one time, but he wouldn't get out because he wanted to go back to Dean's. I took him back and Dean ended up killing him." However, Brooks was acquainted with Glass and he said in his statement that he didn't know the first two boys he saw. He also said he left before anything happened. Thus, it's more likely that the second scenario is true: the car was offered for two boys killed before Yates and Glass. Their identities are currently unknown. They were not among the bodies exhumed in 1973, unless the extra bones found in the double grave on High Island are one day linked to them.

Corll did buy Brooks a bright green used 1969 Corvette. Brooks accepted it and said nothing, although he now knew that Corll had killed the boys. In that moment, he'd had an opportunity to do something. He'd decided not to. He never said that Corll had threatened him. Instead, he'd made it clear he could be bought. One of his friends would later tell a reporter, "He'd do anything for money and a car."

Some psychiatric reports later classified Corll as psychotic, as if he were out of touch with reality or disordered in his thinking. The mental health experts considered him organized enough to draw no attention but also out of control. Since he wasn't around to be properly evaluated, it seemed reasonable to believe that a sadistic murderer who put bodies in his boat stall might be delusional. However, no one who'd known Corll had sensed this about him. He'd seemed ordinary. Yet he had moods. His accomplices had witnessed his hyperactive behavior just prior to his stated need to "do my thing."

At the end of January in 1971, Corll made another move. He grabbed a pair of brothers. Donald Waldrop was fifteen and Jerry Waldrop was thirteen. Their father had dropped them off at a friend's house on West Twelfth Street. The boys told him they were going to the bowling lanes to join a league. They'd be home that evening. But they never returned. Since Donald had once left home, police classified the brothers as runaways. Mr. Waldrop was working next door to where Corll now lived at the Place One apartments on Magnum Road, so it's likely Corll saw them and possibly struck up a conversation. He invited or took them to his apartment. He bound them and tortured them.

Brooks admitted he was "present when Dean killed them by strangling them." This suggests that Corll had convinced Brooks to participate. The brothers' remains went into a single hole near the east wall of the boat stall. "I believe I was present when they were buried," Brooks stated to police, "but I don't remember where they were buried. The youngest of these two boys was the youngest killed, I think." (He'd revise this later at the beach when he said the youngest victim was nine, the son of a grocer.)

Brooks claimed he was just there to help if needed. However, the image of Brooks standing around while Corll killed and buried two kids is absurd. From Corll's known behavior during his other murders, he would have expected more. He had leverage for more. Brooks had been compromised by accepting the car, so he likely assisted with both acts. Whether he was afraid of Corll or just received more incentive is unknown, but one thing is clear: Corll was not afraid of Brooks knowing what he was doing. They'd developed some form of complicit partnership. Brooks was more than just an accessory.

When Everett Waldrop reported his missing sons to the police, an officer told him there would be no investigation since they'd likely gone off on their own. He was stunned. His boys were *not* runaways. Waldrop realized only later that while he was working that day, the boys were possibly still alive in the building next door.

Five weeks later, fifteen-year-old Randell Lee Harvey was killed. On March 17 (some reports say March 9), 1971, he rode his bike from his home in the Heights to the gas station where he worked three miles away. He never arrived, and never came home. His bicycle disappeared as well. Rumors floated that David Brooks had threatened to kill Harvey over a stolen stereo. A tipster passed this information to the police, but they never questioned Brooks. Harvey was shot in the eye with a .22-caliber pistol and strangled with a nylon cord. Brooks claimed to have witnessed this murder. Despite denying later that he'd killed anyone, he admitted to Henley that he had killed once. Perhaps this is the one—if there's only one. (Harvey's remains would go unidentified until 2008.) Brooks would pretend at the time of the effort to identify this victim that he didn't know the boy's name.

David Hilligiest was thirteen. He lived in the Heights. The blond kid was skinny and small for his age at five-foot-three. On May 29, 1971, he said he was going with his friend, Gregory Malley Winkle, sixteen, to a community swimming pool. Winkle, too, was blond and slender. David's mother knew that Winkle ran with a tough crowd. She'd tried to discourage David from hanging out with him, but David ignored her.

That day, they didn't arrive at the pool or return home. Police said they'd probably run off. Lots of kids were heading to California. They were two of over 5,800 kids missing that year from the Houston area, with one hundred eighty from the Heights. But this made no sense in reference to a kid in a swimsuit who'd just wanted to practice strokes before the family went on a vacation.

Winkle was another story. According to author Jack Olsen, Winkle hung around with a gang of older boys and had been arrested for stealing a bike. He'd taken pills, smoked dope, and sniffed glue. He had a probation officer. He'd called his mother that night to tell her he was in Freeport, sixty miles away, swimming with "some kids." When he didn't come home, she discovered that the boys had been seen talking to a man in a white van. They'd gotten in.

Flyers were made and neighborhood kids helped to hang them up. Elmer Wayne Henley Jr., who lived a block up the street, was one of them. He'd played with David when they were young kids, and their mothers were friends. The entire Hilligiest family devoted many hours to tracking down leads. None produced results. Fred Hilligiest borrowed money to offer a reward of $1,000. They hired an investigator, Vaughn Watts, who found evidence of young men being abducted by a local homosexual ring. Fearful of this possibility, the Hilligiests placed ads in underground newspapers and went to seedy areas of cities like New Orleans. At one point, Dorothy Hilligiest spotted a Plymouth GTX cruising around. She wrote down the license plate number, TMF 724, and gave it to the police. Had they responded, they might have checked out Dean Corll. He drove such a car.

Brooks and Corll had invited the boys to a "party." Winkle knew Corll from the candy company. He'd worked there for a while as a janitor and had played pool at Corll's apartment. So had Hilligiest. They'd always had fun at Corll's place. Not this time. Corll handcuffed and raped them. He'd devised a six-foot plywood board with holes so he could attach ropes or handcuffs to better restrain his victims, especially if he wanted to keep them for a while. The board allowed him to get some sleep without concern that they'd get free and run away. Brooks took care of their physical needs until Corll dispatched them. He (or he and Brooks) buried them in the same hole in the boat stall.

By this time, Brooks was a full-fledged apprentice. He had specific tasks. Under Corll's directive, he watched for kids who might be looking for a good time, or who he thought "wouldn't be missed." He handed out uppers and downers like candy. Kids sometimes brought these pills home to show their parents, naming Brooks as the source. Again, law enforcement paid no mind.

Seventeen-year-old Ruben Watson Haney knew Brooks. He'd had a few run-ins with authorities. This made him eligible, in Brooks's eyes: a "bad kid." He was also small, at five foot six and one hundred twenty pounds. On August 17, Haney went to the movies at a new shopping mall. Afterward, he called to tell his mother he was spending the evening with Brooks. (Another account indicates that he told his grandmother he was going with some boys to play in a band.) Once he was at Corll's apartment on San Felipe, he was raped, tortured, and strangled. Astonishingly, this was the second boy missing from the Heights area in the past six months with a known association to David Brooks, yet no mention is made in police records of interviewing Brooks. By then, Brooks had assisted with, or knew about, at least six murders.

Corll moved again, and Brooks reportedly helped with another victim. "I remember one boy who was killed on Columbia at Dean's house. This was before Wayne Henley came into the picture. Dean kept this boy around for about four days before he killed him. . . . It really upset Dean to have to kill this boy because he really liked him." Brooks did not remember a name or where the victim was buried. He said that Glass was also at the Columbia address, but Corll did not live there at the time of Glass's murder.

## Honing the Approach

Corll followed the pattern of what we know about sexual predators. They prepare in advance. They consider all the angles of how they might get caught and how they can explain themselves, so it's difficult to catch them red-handed. Corll learned to use a kid to lure other kids, possibly to prevent being seen approaching his prey—something he wasn't good at. His approach was amateurish if witness reports can be trusted. Several young men have posted on internet sites about their encounter during the early 1970s with *someone* in the Heights who resembled him. Certainly Corll was not the only predator in Houston. In fact, there was a widespread network of pedophiles from Houston to Dallas, with boys paid or forced into being photographed for pornography. Some boys were enlisted as "escorts" and sent to other cities.

However, one person described an encounter that sounds like Corll. It was 1970 or '71, and "John" was around fourteen. He was waiting to be picked up from a dentist's office. A man drove by, smiled, and waved as if he knew John. He turned around and pulled up to the curb. John didn't recognize him. The man slid over the bench seat and commented that John was a "pretty boy." John froze. The stranger kept up the prattle while he rubbed his crotch. He asked if John liked other boys. He mentioned parties they could go to where John could have booze and smoke dope. He urged John to just get in and they'd have a good time. A police car appeared, and the man slid back into the driver's seat and drove away. Only when John saw Corll's picture on the news in August 1973 did he realize what a close call he'd had.

With Brooks now leveraged, Corll had graduated from lone predator to a killer with an assistant—a team killer. Thus he felt empowered. And each time Brooks brought him someone, Brooks was implicated in murder, which bonded him more closely with Corll. In addition, Corll paid him. Brooks always had money for gas for his Corvette, and for dope, harder drugs, and cigarettes. He lived with Corll, so he had no rent to pay. For a high school dropout with no prospects, he was doing well.

Corll had a goal. He knew what he wanted and what it would take to get it. He had no mental inhibitions about causing damage or harm. He got aroused not by death but by domination and control. He liked to experiment and try things out.

Doms like Corll probe for barriers, searching for the most pliable, i.e., their "soft" limits, referring to those things about which the Sub is reluctant but could be enticed to do. Doms also learn about the "hard" limits, or those things the Sub will *not* do, or will do *only if* certain conditions are met.

Once soft limits are breached, it's easier to chisel at the hard limits, often through leveraging. Offer a beer, perhaps, to see if they'll accept it. Next might be a mildly euphoric drug. Many teens will want to see what that's like, especially if it makes them cool. If they comply, they've shown they're willing to defy parental rules or even the law. It's not a serious law. No one's getting hurt. So they'll do it. More challenging is to persuade kids to steal something. If they've already done some minor crime, as Brooks had, it's easier to incentivize the act with money or the sense that they'll be part of some daring criminal escapade. Brooks appeared to have participated in the movement of stolen goods. He'd helped Corll vacate apartments where he still owed rent. He'd kept Corll's secrets. He'd become a dope dealer.

Brooks was reticent to provide details, but Henley offered a firsthand account of how Corll operated with him. Although other accounts of this case have dismissed the influence of an underground culture that protected and supported men who exploited boys, that culture was alive and thriving in Texas. It became part of Corll's toolbox, as both a threat and a reward.

## CHAPTER 3

# Enter Henley

### The Organization

As the revelations of Dean Corll's dirty deeds threw Houston into a frenzy, on August 10, 1973, police in Dallas received a call from a twenty-one-year-old man, Charles Brisendine. He said he was a member of an organization called the Odyssey Foundation, adding that he was scared because he believed he'd been about to be sent to a man in Houston. He'd become disenchanted with the organization, according to an *Advocate* reporter, and thought "it might have some connection to the Houston murders." Brisendine had arrived in Dallas recently to work as a staff member but came to believe he'd been invited there to be a call-boy, or "fellow." From files he'd seen stamped with the words "Kill" or "Killed," he thought several of the other fellows were missing. He added that the man who ran the Odyssey Foundation, known as "Hitchcock," had "been on the phone to Houston all week and had seemed 'irritable' over the Houston Mass Murders."

Brisendine had also called the FBI. The agents said the only way they could intercede was through the Mann Act, but this federal law against transporting individuals over state lines for sexual purposes applied only to women. They posited the word "Kill" on the folders was probably just a publishing term for removing subjects from the manuscript. However, without an investigation, there was no way to know.

Despite the FBI's indifference, Dallas police followed up on Brisendine's call.

The Odyssey Foundation, set up for trafficking and pornography involving boys, was traced to a second-floor apartment at 3716–18 Cole Avenue. The forty-five-year-old man who ran it, John David Norman (aka Hitchcock), had been charged more than two dozen times previously for child sex crimes and had a long rap sheet charted by the FBI. He'd been arrested in Houston during the mid-1950s and had a conviction in California for sexual assault. Dallas PD began surveillance of apartment #208 there. On August 14, they got a warrant to raid it.

Henley had mentioned a trafficking organization that Corll implied he was part of. As noted earlier, he said, "Dean told me that he belonged to an organization out of Dallas that bought and sold boys, ran whores and dope and stuff like that." Brooks said something similar: "During one of our conversations, Dean mentioned that there was a group of people in Dallas which had similar activities to his. . . . The first few that Dean killed were supposed to have been sent off somewhere in California." Brooks also knew of a secret post office box that Corll had kept, from which he'd destroy mail he received, and Brooks had seen a phone number written on paper at Corll's house with a Dallas area code.

Corll had used the existence of this sinister organization to threaten Henley into compliance: "Dean had told me that his organization would get me if I ever did anything to him." Henley believed that this threat extended to his family. Corll eventually softened his rhetoric, giving the impression that Henley could get in on the moneymaking. During the summer of

1973, he told Henley they should go to Dallas so Henley could get "work experience." He mentioned the potential of earning thousands of dollars.

During the Odyssey Foundation raid in Dallas in August 1973, police reported that Norman "had a large number of files in his apartment which listed the names of out-of-town persons who were involved in committing acts of sodomy with friends of John Norman." The police report states that they confiscated "a pick-up truck-load of pornographic literature and pictures and many index cards."

Among the items was a newsletter, dated May 1973, that featured pictures and descriptions—including sexual services—of young males. They were offered as "fellows" to "sponsors" who paid fifteen dollars a year for a membership and all the expenses associated with flying these fellows to destinations around the world. The code language indicated that these young men would meet the sponsor for "personal growth and education." Although legal ages are placed by each fellow's name, as if to assure sponsors they weren't minors, some photos looked much younger than a posted age. The newsletter had recipients in thirty-five states. For just twenty to forty dollars, plus airfare, a sponsor could "expedite" a fellow's program and "share in the adventure."

Norman's apartment served as a crash pad and distribution point. Youths who were recruited went through up to three weeks of "training" to establish their "fitness." Norman and five other men were arrested and charged with possession of an illegal substance (ten pounds of marijuana) and conspiracy to commit sodomy, which suggests that no one in law enforcement was fooled by his euphemisms. A "pick-up truck-load of pornographic literature" was not part of a wholesome educational pursuit.

During the Dallas PD investigation, they discovered that over the past twenty years, Norman had operated child porn organizations in Los Angeles, Sacramento, San Diego, and Santa Monica in California, as well as in Houston, Texas. Officers in Dallas uncovered a network of business entities linking the Odyssey Foundation to Houston, New York, Florida, and California. News reports referred to "index cards" as having between fifty thousand and one hundred thousand names of "sponsors." The FBI was notified but the agency never received these index cards. Instead, inexplicably, Dallas PD sent the cards to the State Department. Journalist Ken Wooden from *60 Minutes* was allowed to examine the cards. He reported on the "Kiddie Porn" episode in 1976 that he'd seen the names of two State Department officials, a director of the New York Ballet, and several judges and elite businessmen. An attorney for the State Department dismissed the cards as not being "relevant to any fraud case concerning a passport," and didn't even respond to the startling fact that two members of the State Department appeared on the Odyssey Foundation's client list. The entire cache was destroyed. The Dallas police had kept no copies. No explanation was offered as to why these cards were not entrusted to the FBI, the US Postal Service, or the Internal Revenue Service, each of which was running its own investigation into the profitable Odyssey Foundation. Those who'd seen the cards believed there'd been a cover-up.

Norman paid a seven-thousand-dollar bond (by some reports) and was set free, pending further investigation. He fled Dallas and drove to Chicago. Using various pseudonyms, he found shelter in a suburb with one of his sponsors. There, he restarted his business. Like Corll, Norman had young handymen, a discovery that came out later.

Steven W. Becker, a Chicago-based attorney, provided a comprehensive overview of the Dallas organization based on his extensive research on its founder, John David Norman. Becker questioned why human trafficking is overlooked during homicide incidents and found that prosecutors prefer to keep cases simple, especially serial murder cases in which factors are already complex. They want the jury's emotional focus to remain on the defendant, which means paring down extraneous factors. Thus, important facets of the case can get shelved, lost, or even destroyed.

Houston PD officers were ambivalent about the claims that Henley and Brooks made about this organization. Their brief investigation amounted to a few records checks on Corll's known addresses. They regarded what Henley referred to as a "Syndicate" as nothing more than Corll's bogus ploy to make his apprentices obedient. It made little sense to the police that Corll was part of a network that traded boys for money, since he was killing them. This remains the official narrative today. However, there were ways for Corll to have participated and benefited and still have kept some boys on the side. Brooks said that Corll had sexual contact with a lot of boys—"He liked oral sex, and he paid boys to come over and let him do it to them"—and had killed only those he'd forcibly assaulted. "Once they went on the board," Brooks stated, "they were as good as dead." Some of the boys he paid for sex had been with him "for a long time."

Included in a police report from August 31, 1973, a twenty-seven-year-old man named Dale Ahern had revealed in a letter postmarked the week before just how large an industry male child pornography was in Houston. Ahern said he could show police some of Corll's victims as they appeared in various magazines with titles like *More Than 7 #1* and *Hot Rod #3*. He added that Corll was connected to Houston's largest pornographer, Roy Ames, who was also a music producer. Ahern claimed that Ames "knew Dean Corll and used him to exploit young boys." Ahern said he'd been invited to an S&M party at Corll's house at the behest of Ames and Corll, which suggests that Corll did have some type of link with the Houston operation. In fact, author Barbara Gibson indicates that detectives had discussed a statement made by the father of the Waldrop boys, that his sons had been messing around with "homosexuals," including a man named Roy Ames. Possibly, he'd taken their photos for magazines. Ahern estimated that Ames had taken 90 percent of the images of child pornography circulating in the local area.

However, at the end of the report about Ahern, someone added, "THIS PHASE OF THE INVESTIGATION HAS NOT LINKED CORLL TO THIS GROUP OF PEOPLE." Police had looked for residential areas that Corll had in common with the named pornographers and had found none. They'd also found very little information about Ames. Apparently, they decided that what they did find was all there was to the story, never considering that their limited efforts had simply fallen short. So just three weeks after the Houston Mass Murders made international headlines, the investigation of the "Syndicate" was over.

There would be more tips along these lines, and more disturbing discoveries.

As Henley awaited his fate, he began to believe there was no crime organization that might hurt him and his family. He felt he'd been played. And he hadn't been wrong to believe that no one would listen to his wild tales about Dean Corll. As he sobered up, Corll's threats just sounded hollow. He knew he was in real trouble.

## The Seeds for Murder

There are many accounts of Wayne Henley's involvement in the infamous Houston Mass Murders. Some give the impression that the same MO applied in all the murders when in fact there were multiple differences among them. There's also an impression that Henley participated in all the murders, that he'd brought his friends to be raped and killed, and that he was "especially sadistic." Since his attorneys put on no defense at his trial and his testimony at a hearing was limited, very little was learned about Henley from the legal records. He did participate in torture and murder, and in most of the burials in 1972 and 1973, but he knew only a little about Corll's prior murders or his favorite mass grave, the boat stall.

Henley was born in Houston, Texas, on May 9, 1956, the first of four sons to Elmer Henley Sr. and Mary Henley. They were just teens, sixteen and seventeen, with little means of support, so they moved in with Mary's parents in the Houston Heights until they could afford the larger house next door.

As a boy, young Wayne did the ordinary things of boyhood. He played Little League Baseball, got involved with Cub Scouts and Boy Scouts, went fishing, and played with neighborhood kids. "The neighborhood was open," he remembered. "It was not a lot of busy streets. There were trees. There was plenty of shade, plenty of open yard space." Wayne had a lively, active personality and was a highly social kid. As the family grew, he spent a lot of time with his maternal grandparents, Lance and Christeen Weed. Yet what appeared to be an all-American extended family showed signs of trouble. Mary quickly discovered that her husband used her pregnancies as an excuse to chase other women. "All he wanted was to get enough kids to tie me down so he could go do his thing," she said. Mary took over the childcare.

Wayne sometimes had serious asthma attacks, so his mother watched him closely. He developed a fear of dying in his sleep, perhaps from the nightly childhood prayer that mentioned this possibility—"If I should die before I wake"—or perhaps from the death of his closest friend in a house fire. He was terrified of suffocating.

The family's situation eventually improved. Lance Weed took his son-in-law under his wing and encouraged him to go to night school. Although Elmer's backwoods Arkansas family had little exposure to formal education, Elmer did well in an engineering program. He soon landed a good job as a stationary engineer maintaining machines at the cafeteria where Weed worked as a baker.

Wayne enjoyed the time he spent with his father during his earliest years. "I have memories of Dad walking me to school, [and] of Cub Scout and Boy Scout activities. I went to work with him, and he'd tell me about boilers and air conditioners. My father was a smart guy."

Mary focused on a solid spiritual upbringing. "The boys went to church every Sunday," she said. "Wayne walked down the aisle when he was five and said 'I wanna be a preacher.' They said he was too young, and he said, no, he wasn't. He carried a Bible everywhere in his shirt pocket."

When Wayne was seven, his world changed. His grandfather developed a serious case of emphysema. He smoked, but he also breathed in flour every day, and it had coated his lungs. He went to the hospital. The kids would wave at him through the hospital window, eager to have him back with the family. But he never came home.

This loss had a negative impact on Elmer Sr. Weed had been his role model. Elmer's family background was saturated in alcoholism and violence. Without Lance Weed around, those negative influences seeped back in. Elmer drank more and embarrassed his kids at family and school events. He grew surly and abusive. "He'd hit with his fist, and you never knew when it was coming," Mary said. "He'd knock me down. I always had a lot of bruises. I lied about them." But sometimes it got so bad she had to report Elmer, and he gained a police record.

Wayne, the oldest of four boys, tried to defend his mother. "Once Elmer had me backed into a corner and he'd raised his fist," Mary recalled, "and we heard this little voice say, 'Drop it, Dad.' We both looked and Wayne was standing there with a shotgun."

Christeen and Mary instilled in the boy a love of reading. Wayne dove into every book he could find, sometimes reading well beyond his age level. In the fourth grade, he zipped through the color-coded SRA Reading Laboratory program, which allowed students to work at their own pace to the highest reading level. Success meant moving on to the next color. Wayne enjoyed competing with himself to prove he was the ultimate reader. From fiction and movies, he developed hero fantasies, which supported his caretaking instinct. He became a crossing guard to protect the school kids from traffic hazards. He was also a flag boy, ensuring that the American flag was raised and lowered at school. Once when he saw from the classroom that it was about to rain, he dove out the window to save the flag from getting wet.

That's the kind of kid he was, and he enjoyed praise for his accomplishments. Yet no matter how well he did in school, he couldn't live up to his father's expectations. "I'd brought home a report card with mostly As and two Bs, and he'd yell at me that I should do better. I wanted him to be proud of me. You feel little when someone like that thinks little of you. I could never seem to please him."

Freddie Majors met Henley when they were around twelve and became a good friend. He recalls their "eternal search" for a place to just hang out, away from parental supervision. He liked Henley's sense of humor. As they grew up together in the Heights, they leaned toward the hippie ideas that pervaded the youth culture during the late 1960s. Both would grow their hair long and succumb to the lure of booze and dope, especially as Wayne grew bored with school.

In the fifth and sixth grades, school officials urged Mary to let her son skip a grade, so he could learn at a more advanced level. Wayne finished assignments faster than other kids his age and some teachers even put him to work grading other students' papers. However, Mary resisted this suggestion. She wanted him to stay with his friends.

The Henley home grew more stressful. One day, Elmer was beating Mary. Christeen stepped in and he turned on her. "He was beating on Mom," Henley recalled, "and Nonna tried to stop him. He knocked her down. I picked up the vacuum cleaner and busted him right upside the head and it knocked him over. That's how we got away."

Mary wanted a divorce, but she couldn't get a full-time job until her youngest boy was in school. She had to wait and endure the violence. When the time was right, she moved the boys into her mother's house and found work as a cashier. It didn't pay enough to cover the bills. Since the age of ten, Wayne had been working at odd jobs to help out, like delivering newspapers. Eventually, he'd been allowed to pump gas for customers at a ten-pump filling station. Paid in cash under the table, no one had checked his age. He was fourteen when the divorce came through and he felt the increased burden of family finances. Elmer warned Mary he'd pay no child support. He immediately married a woman with whom he'd had an affair.

Eventually, he sold the house and moved away, but he'd still show up drunk to further punish his ex-wife. He spent several stints in jail for drunkenness and abuse. A couple of serious episodes involved his son.

"I was scared of my dad," Henley admitted, "but I wanted him to like me. After my parents divorced, I saw my dad at times. He lived in Houston. I was at his house. Me and him and one or two neighbors he knew were out in the car in the driveway, drinking. I was sixteen. I told him I was making more now in a week than he was making when I was born. He took it that I was trying to put him down. I just meant it as, 'Look how good I'm doing.' We got in a fight, and he chased me off. He shot his shotgun at me. He ran and caught me, and we got into a fight, and he knocked me down in a ditch and jumped on my leg. I've limped ever since. I tried to stab him with a pocketknife but cut myself worse than I cut him. Someone called the police. I called Mom. She picked me up at a store and we went looking for him to keep the police from getting him."

Later, Wayne had another close call. "We were at the reception for my mother's second marriage [soon annulled] and my father was told not to come. He showed up. I tried to get him to leave. He knocked me down and ran to his car. I got up and he turned around [with a gun]. A friend pushed me down and got hit in the leg. They filed charges on my dad for attempted murder. We went to court on that one, but I would not testify. I was a juvenile and they couldn't force me to." But he wouldn't forget that his father had tried to *erase* him, his oldest son—his namesake.

Still just a boy, Wayne felt responsible to help his mother and grand-mother. He'd been raised to protect women. "You said, 'Yes, ma'am' and 'No, ma'am,' and you treated the ladies respectfully. You took care of family. Being a Southern gentleman is about your word and how you carry yourself in your dealings with others."

The pressure made Wayne anxious, reactive, and unable to sleep. In the ninth grade, his grades dropped. Mary took him to a doctor, who prescribed five milligrams of Valium three times per day. This loosened his inhibitions.

When teachers chided him, he'd snap back, sometimes cussing them out. One concerned teacher took him to the principal's office. They called his mother. Mary admitted that her divorce had badly affected him.

"I was anxious, scared, unhappy," Henley recalled. "I just wasn't doing well. Valium is like truth serum. You say things and there's no filter, none. They decided to take me out of school, so I had to redo the ninth grade. Which was probably the worst possible thing they could have done to me. If I had passed the ninth grade the first time around, I wouldn't have met David Brooks."

## Knocking

Corll had directed Brooks to bring him boys who wouldn't be missed—dropouts, druggies, or delinquents. The losers. "Most of the boys weren't good boys," Brooks told detectives after his arrest. "Most of them was no great loss. They was in trouble all the time, dope fiends, and one thing or another." He saw his job as that of culling the Heights of bad influences. They weren't hard to find in that area with its high rate of broken families and alcoholism. Kids who skipped school or ran away were good targets; for all anyone knew, a kid who disappeared had simply run away yet again.

School started, and Brooks returned to the ninth grade, albeit not for long. One day in the fall of 1971, Brooks spotted a kid walking away from a school building when he should have entered it. He was a truant. The curly-haired boy was thin and small—about five foot five. Brooks had poor social skills, but this kid seemed like an easy target. Brooks approached him and learned his name: Elmer Wayne Henley Jr.

"When I first met him," Henley recalls, "I had walked to Hamilton Junior High School. As soon as you stepped off campus, you were on the sidewalk by the filling station. That's where I'd meet my friends. They'd go to school, and I would leave. If you'd been watching me, you knew that's where I'd be. And David appeared, coming off the campus. I suspect he was making a point to meet me."

Brooks asked, "Are you skipping school too?"

Henley looked over this waifish, six-foot blond with his granny glasses and said, "I'm going to the pool hall to shoot pool."

Brooks fell right into step and said that was his destination as well. Henley hadn't seen this kid at the pool hall before, or in any classes at the school, but he didn't think much about it. It was nice to have a companion for a change. They talked about their families and their lack of interest in school. Henley took Brooks at face value as just a bored kid seeking company. They had things in common, including critical fathers and the kind of laid-back rebellion that pervaded teenage culture.

Brooks was a year older, despite being in the ninth grade. He admitted being held back. He was evasive about where he lived, but he had a steady girlfriend, Bridget Clark. Henley worked two jobs, so he had little time to hang out. Brooks persisted.

"He showed up with Dean at the filling station where I worked," Henley recalled. This was his first awareness of Dean Corll, an older man who seemed to be Brooks's friend. He didn't realize that Corll was checking him out as a potential victim. The boys continued to skip school together, smoke joints, and play pool. Henley wondered where Brooks had gotten the money for his Corvette. He knew Brooks had no job and while his father ran an asphalt paving company, his family wasn't wealthy. In fact, Brooks seemed to always have money or drugs. Henley thought maybe he was "queer-hustling" the old guy.

One day, Brooks and Corll drove to Henley's house, honking out front to get him to go out cruising. Mary Henley didn't like this. "I told Wayne, 'Sit right where you are,' and I went out and asked, 'Are you honking for any reason?' He [Corll] said, 'Yeah, I'm looking for Wayne.'" Mary didn't care for this. "Wayne doesn't come to parked cars that honk at him, and we don't have curb service. If you want to see one of my family, you'll come knock at the door. If I can't know who you are, where you live, and your phone number, you don't come back to my door. When you get that all straightened out, you may come back, but don't sit out here and honk."

She was surprised to see a man Corll's age hanging out with boys, but he seemed pleasant enough. She let him know she kept an eye on her boys. Corll apologized. He provided Mary Henley with his phone number and gave the impression he was just a big brother type.

Henley got in the car. Corll pulled out. Henley recalled Corll's approach. "The first thing Dean ever said to me, other than hello, was, 'Do you want to hear a joke?' It was a dirty joke. I was a fourteen-year-old. And here's this grown man telling me a joke about oral sex. I thought that was cool. It made me feel grown-up. It made me feel special."

When Henley laughed, Corll smiled. That had been a test. Henley had passed. Corll could take the next step. Had Henley been offended, Corll would have spotted a barrier. Grooming happens in increments, with little tests. Each time the target yields, soft limits have been breached. Corll wasn't yet sure what he'd do with this skinny, loquacious boy, but he liked Henley's easy manner. Corll already knew from Brooks that Henley drank and smoked dope. The kid was cocky but highly approachable. He played baseball but he wasn't a jock. Although he had no particular aspirations, he wasn't a slacker. But there was a negative: He had a protective mother. If he disappeared, he'd be missed.

Corll dropped Henley off at his home without incident, noting his younger brothers. The Heights neighborhood was full of kids, the kind he liked. But he played it cool to avoid giving the impression he was gay or predatory.

Between homework and his jobs, Henley didn't have much time to hang out with Brooks and Corll. He also looked after his three younger brothers. He worked more hours to keep up with family bills and finally dropped out of school. The fact that Brooks didn't work but had money started to wear on him. "I noticed David having more money than a guy our age and social status would have. I'd asked where his money came from. A bit at a time, he led me to believe he was doing some sort of illegal activity with that Dean dude he'd introduced me to. They were involved in a criminal enterprise."

This wasn't difficult to believe. *The Godfather* became a bestseller in 1969, making clandestine criminal operations seem cool and powerful, even sexy. Henley had read the novel, but he'd never done anything significantly illegal. He'd broken into empty houses with other kids, shoplifted a few times, and once was detained by police over a misunderstanding: Henley carried a gun when he guarded the filling station at night. He'd take cash home for safekeeping. One night before going home, he'd accompanied a friend to sneak a girl out of her house. Her mother called the cops, who arrested him, saw the gun, and held him overnight until his mother confirmed his job at the gas station. They let him go. He hesitated over getting caught again, but Brooks's Corvette, supply of dope, and roll of bills were enticing. Brooks used it as a hook.

"One day in the winter of 1972, David told me if I could get away without telling anyone where I was going, he and Dean would pick me up and lay it out for me. I was to meet them behind the Fulbright Methodist church down the street from my house at five P.M."

Henley ignored Brooks's warning to tell no one. He let his mother know about his plans. "I never went any place without telling my mom where I was and who I was with. I told her and decided to say I hadn't."

At 5:00 P.M., Corll and Brooks showed up. "I believe Dean was driving an American Motors Jaguar." They rode around town for a while, just talking. Corll might have been trying to thwart Henley from figuring out where his apartment was, should things go south. During the ride, he said nothing about a criminal enterprise. Near dusk, they arrived at a multistory building. Inside, they gathered around a bar in the kitchen, with Corll opposite Henley. Corll offered soft drinks. Brooks lit up a joint and shared it. Corll watched without comment as the kids engaged in illegal activity. Then Brooks went into another room, leaving Corll and Henley alone together. Henley expected that Corll would now tell him about the business. He recalled the moment.

"Dean began to tell me he was a member of a group that burgled places of business and some rich homes. All of the stolen items would be sold to the group that directed where to go and what to steal. There was good money to be made. He emphasized stealth. He made it sound like a *Mission Impossible* episode. . . . Dean made it sound like he was recruiting me for my intelligence and ability."

Henley had been selected, but not for his intelligence. The idea was to put out the bait—money—and make him feel special. Henley wasn't looking for a life of crime. He'd been a responsible kid, caring about family and friends. Yet adverse childhood circumstances like abuse and divorce make some kids vulnerable to acting out in later years. Henley was malleable, still figuring himself out. He had a low-paying part-time job with no means to do better. Corll worked him for a while that evening, seemingly testing his sense of loyalty and obedience. Then Corll opened a drawer and pulled out a large knife in a sheath.

Henley became alert. "Dean began talking about the need to silence anyone who caught us in the course of a burglary. Could I do it? *Would* I do it? Did I know how?"

Henley assured Corll he could do whatever was required. "I reacted to Dean's stealing scenario matter-of-factly. I was trying to seem cool and act like, 'Oh, sure. This is something I'm aware of and can do. I'm a man of the world.' I'm visualizing myself all in black, cool, creeping around like the Pink Panther. What happens if I'm spotted? Ain't gonna happen. I'm too slick."

It didn't sound like much of a challenge or nearly as dangerous as Corll suggested. As a naive kid, he couldn't see the game Corll was playing with him, but he did sense that something was off. He wondered where Brooks had gone. Corll moved slowly around the bar as he talked, with his hand on the knife and his cold dark eyes on Henley. "I can demonstrate the method," he said.

Henley felt trapped. He wasn't sure what to do. He couldn't show fear, but he didn't want Corll getting too close, either, not with that knife. Corll squinted. He seemed to have shifted into another person. Henley turned a little to protect his back. He tried to act cool, but he disliked being touched. "I think I can figure out what to do."

Just then, Brooks returned as if on cue. He looked at Henley and asked, "You didn't tell anyone where you were, right?"

Henley spotted an out. "I told my mother." He hadn't meant to say that. He'd meant to pretend he'd followed the instructions. But something told him to make it clear his mother knew.

Brooks looked annoyed. "I told you not to tell anyone."

"I always tell my mother where I'm going."

The room tone changed. Corll looked at Brooks and moved away. He no longer seemed interested in telling Henley about their gig.

"David seemed disappointed. Dean just stopped paying me attention. David immediately hustled me out of the apartment and took me home. Dean didn't come with us."

Henley was confused. He'd hoped to make some money, but it looked as if Corll had dismissed him as a solid prospect. He wasn't sure what he'd done wrong.

Corll now had to decide. Henley had seen where he lived. He'd heard about their illegal burglaries. Maybe he could be put to some use. He was more approachable and socially skilled than Brooks and seemed to know a lot of teenage boys. Adding another associate, Corll thought, might make Brooks up his game. He could play them off each other. Corll came up with another plan.

As he'd done with Brooks, Corll tried the sexual angle: money for pleasure. Henley resisted. He hadn't initially realized that Corll was gay. Once he did, he didn't give it much thought. The early 1970s was a time for testing tolerance. Gay men were fighting for their rights, including the right to be open about their sexuality. But Henley wasn't ready to fight off an advance. Corll had worked him to the point where he couldn't easily say no.

"The only time I had sexual contact with Dean was due to David," Henley said. "He set it up. I made it apparent that it was not something I was happy or comfortable with. It wasn't what I wanted to do, and it just never came up again. It was a terrible experience. Nothing like sex with a girl, which I really had not done that often. This big man loomed over me. I felt trapped. I tried to relax and get it over with, but there was no pleasure involved."

Henley was fifteen. He'd just been sexually assaulted. He couldn't tell anyone, he thought, because he'd *let* it happen. He'd been complicit. But he'd also been clear with Corll that he wouldn't do it again.

Disappointed with this failure, Corll devised a more devious plan. It would take patience, but he believed Henley would respond. He started with something insignificant. He paid Henley to steal small items to resell. That's what Henley was waiting for. But he wasn't the super slick criminal he'd envisioned. He soon got arrested.

"I got drunk and high, and I don't even know how it happened, but I went down the road from Dean and burglarized a place and took all their dope and some other stuff. I took it home by a cab. Then when I sobered up the next day, I took it back and admitted it and apologized. They made me clean their apartment. Then they called the police. I was declared a delinquent juvenile and put on probation."

Henley began hanging out at Corll's place because this adult had a job, didn't drink, and got along with people. Despite his quiet ways, he had a knack for making others feel at home. He seemed stable. He was easy to talk to. "That's what started it," Henley said. He missed his own father and sometimes felt the weight of being responsible for his family. Being with Corll let him be more of a kid because Corll was the adult. Unlike Henley's father, Corll seemed to have his life in control. Then Corll let

Henley, who had no license, drive his car, opening an exciting world to him. Within a few months, the shape-shifting strategy was in motion. Corll could compromise Henley while also making himself into the adult Henley most wanted to be with. It was a devious long game. By then, Henley had dropped out of school, which gave him more free time.

Corll used it to work on his recruit. They debated religion. Henley had admitted he'd once aspired to be a minister. He'd read the entire Bible and used it as his moral guide. Corll knew he'd have to shake Henley to his core if he expected to use him. He debated with Henley on the merits of the Christian belief system and a just, loving God who knows all and exacts vengeance on those who stray. Maybe it wasn't so simple. Maybe God didn't really care. Maybe God didn't even exist.

"I remember the first conversation where he was questioning my belief in God," Henley said. "At first, it was 'what kind of God allows Vietnam?' And 'what kind of God would allow the things that were happening to my mom and my family?' He was getting at my dad. 'Why would God allow your dad to beat you up? God can't have any power. If God had power, why does he allow bad things to happen?'"

Henley parried. He embraced his faith. His grandmother and mother were firm believers. They'd never forced him to go to church, but they clearly wanted him to walk the Christian path, especially in terms of compassion for others. His "Nonna" would help anyone, no matter how much risk she put herself into, because she was certain God would protect her. Henley admired that.

For a while, he clung to this foundation, but he wasn't prepared when Corll made these debates more personal. "He'd ask, 'Don't you want to be able to resist your dad? Your dad treats you like a weakling. He abuses you.'" Corll goaded Henley to prove that *he* had power and should learn to use it. "If you can show that you have power over people,' he'd say, 'you'd have power over your dad.' He didn't say this just once. This continued. He kept at me."

While Corll chiseled away at Henley's faith, he also suggested that Henley should advance from burglary to more serious crimes. He could prove himself to the Syndicate with something bolder and worth their time. That meant good money. *Real* good.

## A Market for People

Corll's next move was to plant a suggestion.

"It was done in steps," Henley said. "He didn't just all of a sudden say, 'Let's do this.' He'd normalize it in our conversations. Originally, we were going to be in the burglary thing, but he couldn't find an ideal place to burglarize. We were on the corner of Eleventh and Heights Boulevard, and he said, 'It's too bad there's not a market in people. They're everywhere.' I chuckled and agreed but thought it was a joke. Over the course of several conversations, Dean amplified on the subject, finally telling me there actually *was* a market. He said he knew of a group in Dallas that would buy young people. Then he started talking about wealthy people in California keeping them as houseboys. They were kept like pets. They had a good life."

Henley listened. Corll obviously knew more than he did. Corll seemed to have already been involved in moving boys through this process. Corll confirmed that he had connections. Then he sugared the trap: he'd pay Henley two hundred dollars to bring him boys—more if they were particularly attractive. In today's terms, that would be over $1,400, so it was quite a financial enticement to a kid working for peanuts. Corll said they should be the kind of kids that people wouldn't really miss, the troublemakers, the ones a family might think they were well to be rid of. Everybody wins.

Henley didn't like the sound of it, and he didn't really know kids like that. Months went by, but Corll was patient. He'd planted the seed. He believed it would grow. Money mattered to Henley, as did Corll's approval.

There really was such an organization in Dallas, the Odyssey Foundation, and Corll might have learned from the gay scene in Houston how it
operated, since the founder spent time in Houston. The Odyssey Foundation's literature showed boys who'd been leveraged into helpers, willing
or not.

Likewise, Corll wanted boys who would obey him. He'd had a few
already, who'd "disappeared" without much being done to find them.
Brooks had been a reluctant helper at best, but Corll thought Henley could
be trained. The boy was eager to please.

"I don't know when Dean and I started hanging out as me and Dean,"
Henley said. "I'd been hanging out with David, so I don't know when that
changed or how it changed. It must have been gradual."

Corll kept up the pressure, challenging Henley to prepare for what
the Syndicate wanted. He let Wayne use his .22 pistol and urged him
to learn how to use it to show he meant business. If he ever had to shoot
someone, Corll told him, Henley was to keep shooting till he dropped
the guy to the ground. Never let up. He had to understand the need for
deadly force in the kind of business they were in: no one should get the
drop on him. Eventually, Corll revealed that the Syndicate had picked up
David Hilligiest, Henley's missing friend, and sold him to wealthy people
in California. The name made Henley perk up. He wanted to find him.
He'd made a promise to David's mother. But Corll said to leave it alone;
the kid was better off now.

Undeterred, Henley wondered if he could bring David Hilligiest home
to his family. "I attribute that to my hero complex," he said. From science
fiction, he'd grown to love the heroes who took care of things. He also
admired John Wayne. He thought he could be a hero himself. He'd have
to play along, perhaps deliver a boy to prove himself to this Syndicate. He
could persuade them to trust him so he could acquire the information he
needed. In Henley's immature and inexperienced mind, the trafficking
seemed a bit dicey but not so bad if these boys ended up in nice homes. He

could pick up a stranger, someone who didn't matter to him. The higher goal was to bring David back home. And on a more practical level, he needed the money, so regardless of his hero complex, all signs pointed to acquiescence. Early in 1972, he agreed to go with Corll to look for a boy. He shut out the image of his mother's disapproval and focused on the task.

First, Corll trained him. He taught Henley how to pretend to get out of a pair of handcuffs, Houdini-style, so they could entice other kids to try it too. The trick was that Henley would have a key in his pocket. The other boys would not. Handcuffed, they'd be unable to resist being tied up. Corll would leave the handcuffs on a table, as an enticement for curious kids. Henley liked this idea. It was a challenge. He practiced. When Corll praised him, he felt good. This was fun.

On February 9, they went out in Corll's white Ford Econoline van. On Eleventh and Studewood, they saw a dark-haired teenage hitchhiker. Henley felt a little queasy. They pulled over. Henley persuaded the kid to come to Corll's to smoke dope for a while. (Some sources state this was seventeen-year-old Willard "Rusty" Branch, the son of a Houston police officer. However, Branch was still alive in November 1972, when he left home. Branch also knew Corll, so Corll could have just greeted him, but Henley said the boy they picked up was a stranger to them both.) In his confession, Henley said, "I talked to him since I had long hair and all and it was easier for me to talk to him." Thus, the identity of this hitchhiker remains unknown. Branch did end up killed by Corll, but this happened later.

Once they were all in Corll's apartment, Henley demonstrated the handcuff trick that Corll had taught him. When their "guest" tried to duplicate it and found himself trapped, Henley stepped back as Corll tackled the young man and used parachute cord to bind his hands and feet. Watching this made Henley uneasy. He reminded himself that a plush California home awaited their captive. Brooks took Henley home, telling him the Syndicate didn't yet know about his participation, so he couldn't be there when they arrived to pick up the captive.

Henley wasn't happy. He wanted the head traffickers to see his part. In his naivete, he was thinking, "How else can I prove myself so I can find David Hilligiest?"

Back at the apartment, Corll taped a wad of terry cloth in the boy's mouth and raped him. Since the boy's identify is unknown as of this writing, the cause of death remains a mystery. So does the burial place.

Corll gave Henley $200, as promised. "I took it so Mom could have medicine," said Henley, and "so we could get things off layaway. Mom wouldn't ask [about the source] because I could ease money into it. I'd always done that. I'd sold weed. When you have little, then a little more is a lot. I also bought a Sherman air rifle."

But Henley balked at further participation. "I wasn't helping him get anybody else because it ate at me. I thought, how would I feel if I were separated from my family? How did David [Hilligiest]'s family feel? If I'm not gonna meet these people, I don't want to do this." He didn't realize there was no turning back.

In Henley's second police statement, he said, "I thought Dean was going to sell him to this organization he belonged to. Then the next day, Dean paid me $200.00. Then a day or so later, I found out that Dean had killed the boy."

When Henley reread this statement years later, he said he'd misstated the timeline. He did not know soon afterward that Corll had raped and killed the boy. "There are factual errors in that statement, timeline errors. That was my confused brain [at the time]."

It would be more than a month before Corll sprang the trap.

Corll didn't take Henley out looking for more hitchhikers. He seemed settled, like he'd tested the kid and now things were square. Corll continued to supply beer, weed, and a place to party. Brooks, too, said nothing about the incident. Henley relaxed. Things began to feel normal, with kids in and out, until one day late in March.

Henley invited his friend, Frank Aguirre, to come over and smoke dope. Aguirre, eighteen, had just gotten off work at Long John Silver's fast-food restaurant and had plans to see his fiancée, fourteen-year-old Rhonda Williams. Henley drove up in the van and persuaded him to come to Corll's first. They drank beer and got high. The handcuffs were out on a table. Aguirre was curious about them. When he slipped them on, Corll overpowered and bound him.

"Dean jumped him," Henley said. "I did not know what to do."

Henley protested. Corll told him to back off. He admitted he'd raped and murdered the hitchhiker, and since Henley had lured that kid, he was as implicated in the boy's death as Corll. It was a plan of mutually assured destruction: *if I go down, you go down.* Corll said if anyone found out, the police would arrest Henley, convict him, and execute him. No one would listen to him say he hadn't known. In the eyes of the law, ignorance is no excuse. Also, the Syndicate knew about him. If Henley didn't cooperate, they'd kill him and his family.

Henley didn't know what to do. "I was fifteen. Who would believe me? I didn't have evidence. I didn't know where the bodies were. But had I gone to the police at that point, I would've been completely blameless of any murder. I only had the fact that Dean said he did that, and I was implicated. I couldn't prove it, and it's my word as a boy against this adult. And [I thought] the Syndicate would be on *his* side. So even if they [the police] arrest him, he's probably going to get out. But if he doesn't get out, then I have caused one of the Syndicate people to be imprisoned. So, they're going to be mad at me and come for me. That's what I believed. If I wasn't a weak person, I would have done something constructive. I managed filling stations at night by myself. I had been taught good morals. I knew right from wrong. I knew to accept responsibility. People died as a result of my being scared to go to the cops."

But fifteen-year-olds tend to think only of the most immediate consequences. Henley fretted over his own fate. When he stayed quiet, he became a full-fledged accomplice. No turning back.

In his confession, Henley said, "we choked" Frank Aguirre. In later accounts, he claims he left his friend at Corll's, distressed at being impotent, and came back to find him dead. Corll had gagged him and covered his face with adhesive tape. Henley was shocked. "I didn't realize I'd need to decide quickly. The next morning, Frank was dead. I was told what was going on and I failed to make a decision."

About his August 9 admission to police, Henley said, "If you read the statement, it sounds like I knew before Frank Aguirre that Dean was raping and killing people. I did not know. There are things in your life that are indelible, and I don't doubt my memory of that because that was the turning point. When he jumped on Frank Aguirre—and I did not know he was going to—and told me what he'd been doing and what I was hooked up in, that right then was pivotal. I remember that clearly. I know where I was standing. That doesn't come across in the statement."

The account devised by the three officers from Pasadena and Houston on August 23 seems to confirm this. They used their notes to connect Henley to the boys he'd said he'd killed, and Aguirre wasn't one of them.

Corll now had his leverage. Henley would have to do whatever he said. Stunned and depressed, Henley assisted in burying his friend's body at a beach on High Island, south of Houston. He also helped to bring Aguirre's blue-and-white 1967 Rambler over to Corll's boat stall so Corll could break it down into parts to sell. He didn't realize then that he was walking on the graves of other murdered boys in the boat stall's floor, although Corll now revealed that he'd also killed Henley's friend, David Hilligiest, so there was no use in looking for him. Corll kept an item from Aguirre's car as a souvenir.

Henley settled uneasily into his new role, anticipating with dread what would come next. He knew his life had dramatically changed.

"The money disappeared immediately," he said. "Because the next act was 'I have your friend. I raped and murdered the first person you helped me with, so you're already involved in murder.' I had not done anything about that, so in essence I bought into it. That's the bait-and-switch. 'Now

I don't need to give you money anymore because you're already involved in a murder. It's me and you.' It's fear. Now it's coercion . . . duress. 'You don't have any choice in the matter.' "

Corll soon changed his residence, moving to an apartment on Schuler Street. He could already see how he'd use Henley going forward. Yet Corll didn't give him a bed in his home, like he'd given Brooks, or funds for gas or cigarettes. Henley still had to work at the gas station for those things. "For some reason, I let myself be treated as an afterthought. I was treated like a dog. I felt lesser."

Not much improved in his life as a result of his relationship with Corll—maybe a couple hundred bucks and some party supplies. Corll used veiled threats, along with encouragement, to make Henley comply. It was the basic Dom/Sub strategy of conditioning someone with alternating cycles of cruelty and kindness, threat and safety. Despite everything, Henley still wanted to please Corll. He'd broken through his own guardrails—his hard limits—and gone off the road. He wasn't the hero he'd hoped to be. He was on the bad guy's side.

## The Tipping Point

Among the teens that hung out at Corll's residences were Mark Scott and Billy Ridinger. Henley knew them but sensed they were more inside Corll's inner circle than he was. They were older and had known Corll for several years. They did "business" with him. Yet Corll seemed to have grown tired of Mark Scott. He mentioned that the seventeen-year-old was giving him trouble, as if he had leverage Dean wanted to erase. Something had to be done about him.

"The story that Dean gave was that he [Mark Scott] had cheated him on a deal," said Henley. "They talked about it a lot. Mark would steal things and Dean bought things from him. Dean felt like Mark was going to get him into trouble with the police. Dean was adamant that he needed to be rid of Mark."

Corll wanted Henley's assistance. By now, he'd secured the fifteen-year-old's silence. He wanted more. He wanted Henley to prove himself. Committing murder might once have been his hard limit, but Corll had softened it.

"He insisted that I kill someone," Henley recalled. "I had to do that. I had to prove that I could do that. I had to step up and become powerful. He kept at me. It scared me."

This would be the most significant test yet: Corll could get rid of a troublemaker and gain a new helper. Brooks had made it clear he preferred not to do any killing.

Mark Scott, seventeen, was in and out at Corll's. No one had to lure him there. As Corll waited for an opportunity to act, he worked on Henley. He wanted to prepare him mentally. "Dean encouraged me that learning to do these things would make me capable of dealing with my father. And dealing with bullies. I was somewhat bullied by the boys at school. That started in the fifth grade. That was traumatic for me." He wanted to be able to stand up to people who might hurt him. That his father had shot at him, nearly killing him, still rankled him. He knew that Elmer Wayne Sr. still bothered his mother, even though they were divorced. Wayne wanted to be prepared should his father become more violent.

Finally, he gave in. If he wanted access to all that Corll offered, he'd have to prove himself. Maybe Corll was right, Henley thought. Maybe this would benefit him and make him stronger. Maybe he could be this bad guy Corll thought he could be. And maybe Mark Scott *did* have it coming.

That April, Corll made his move. Scott came over (maybe with Henley, as Brooks said, or maybe on his own) and Corll tackled him. Scott fought furiously, as if he knew what was in store, but Corll managed to bind and restrain him. Scott kept trying to talk Corll into letting him go, but Corll took him into a bedroom and raped him. Apparently, he also persuaded

Scott to write a postcard to his parents to tell them he was traveling. By now, Corll had developed a taste for torture, and he wanted Henley to imbibe alongside him. Brooks had said that Henley had been "especially sadistic" at this Schuler Street address.

Henley admitted it. "When we'd ride around, Dean would have these bright ideas. [For example,] I liked incense. I had these cones you could light, and they can get *hot*. Either Dean or I had picked one up and got burned, so Dean had decided to set one of these burning cones on someone. He did it to Mark Scott. Dean had a lot of animosity toward him."

As Scott lay groaning in pain, begging to be released after hours of torture, Corll went to bed. Henley was charged with watching the captive. Scott tried talking to Henley and Brooks, but Henley tuned him out. "David describes me as cold, but I just didn't want to hear him." This was a terrible moment of truth. Henley already knew Corll intended to kill Scott and would likely require his help. He was now going to see a young man be murdered. He could only hope his part would be minimal. Brooks just shrugged.

"That night, Dean was asleep on the bed," Henley said, "Mark was on the floor. I had fallen asleep on the floor, near Mark's legs. I was asleep when Dean woke up. Somehow, Mark had gotten a knife."

Corll came over and bent toward Scott, as if to see if he were still alive. Scott suddenly slashed at him, slicing him, and ripping through his shirt. Corll yelled in angry surprise. Henley woke up to see them thrashing around. Scott had one hand still tied, but his other hand was free. Henley hit him a few times to try to subdue him and ran to get Corll's .22. Brooks came in to help restrain Scott. Henley returned, pointed the gun at him, and ordered him to stop. Scott looked at the weapon and gave up. He seemed to know it was over. They weren't letting him go and he had no other means of defense. He formed his fingers into the shape of a gun and pointed it at his head as if urging Henley to get it over with. Corll ordered Henley to strangle him.

This was it. Corll wasn't going to kill Mark Scott, *he* was. He had to be the good capo, like in *The Godfather*. If he didn't comply, there was no telling what Corll would do to him. Tentatively, he placed parachute cord around Scott's throat and pulled it tight. His own childhood fear of suffocating added pressure. He didn't want to do this. Scott struggled, his eyes wide with terror. Henley looked away. He applied more pressure. He couldn't believe how difficult this was. Finally, Scott went unconscious. Still, his body fought. Then his face changed color and his lips turned blue. But Henley's hands ached. He couldn't do this. Corll had said it wasn't like he'd seen on TV, where people die quickly. Henley was exhausted. He had to get Corll to finish it.

Then it was over. Mark Scott lay unmoving on the plastic. Henley stared. He'd done this. He'd helped to kill someone. He could barely believe it.

He went into Corll's living room and sat on the couch. He stared. He felt slimy. He was just fifteen and he'd been involved in three murders. He'd have to pay for this, he knew, with his own life. That's what God would demand. That's what he'd always learned. A life for a life. He waited. He cringed. But nothing happened. There was no bolt of lightning from the heavens to strike him dead. He remained alive. It made no sense. Someone couldn't just die like that. His foundation for his beliefs began to crumble.

"I lost the biggest portion of my faith when I knew I had been involved in a murder. I remember sitting in Dean's living room and waiting on God to strike me dead. I knew it was coming. I knew it was going to happen. And then it didn't. I think at that time, that's when I really lost it. I lost my ability to actively resist Dean. I just felt like maybe this guy's got all the answers, you know, 'cause I certainly don't have any. I thought I was weak, I was evil."

Henley helped to bury Mark Scott's body on a stretch of beach at High Island, near where they'd placed Frank Aguirre. Again, there would be no pay. And now Henley knew that Corll had more on him than he'd had before. A *lot* more.

Mark Scott's family reported him missing. When they last saw him, he'd told them he was going on a trip with some friends, but he hadn't returned. A few days after they contacted police, they received an odd note. On a postcard, Mark had scribbled, "How are you doing? I am in Austin for a couple of days. I found a good job. I am making $3 an hour." The Scotts found this hard to believe, but Mark had given them no way to contact him to corroborate it. That was the last they heard from him.

Corll assured Henley he'd done a good job—the words Henley most wanted to hear. Despite his shock, this affirmation felt satisfying. In retrospect, Henley considered how he could have accepted praise for such an act. "Dean became my authority figure, a power that I acknowledged. I was doing something that would please him. It was all right to do that, because it was all right with Dean to do that."

Through the process of grooming, Henley had evolved from a kid who wanted to help people into a kid who wanted to please a sadistic killer. Over nearly a year, Corll had patiently trained a malleable apprentice. He'd seen that Henley was an all-or-nothing kind of kid. With time and a few more tests, he could be formed into a partner.

His compliance, Henley later mused, was due in part to the privilege of secrecy. "When you have a secret amongst people, David, Dean, and I were the only ones who existed in that world. We were the only ones who could understand each other and fully communicate. It becomes a microcosm."

It was also about social identity, which matters a lot to most humans but more during the teen years than at any other age. Henley was involved in organized crime. He had a gang.

## Once You've Done One

Henley turned sixteen on May 9. Less than two weeks later, on May 21, he was summoned to Corll's. There, he saw sixteen-year-old Johnny Delome (sometimes erroneously spelled Delone) and his seventeen-year-old friend, Billy Baulch. They were bound. "That [incident] was not on me," Henley said. "I walked into that situation. That was decided without me. They brought me in and said, 'This is what's gonna happen.' These two I had to do by myself." In other words, Henley had another test to pass, a more challenging one.

Delome, a high school dropout, had been in some trouble, and Baulch knew Corll. He'd once worked at the Corll Candy Company and used to hang out in his apartment. Corll seemed to have an issue with him like he'd had with Mark Scott. He had Brooks and Henley participate. According to Brooks, Corll's rule was that there would always be one person more to subdue the victims than the total number of victims. With two kids to bind and torture, he needed both accomplices. Once Delome and Baulch were under control, Corll forced them to write letters to their families. The wording for both was nearly identical. Billy's, sent from Madisonville, Texas, read like this:

"Dear Mom and Dad. I'm sorry to do this, But Johnny and I found a better job working for a trucker loading and unloading from Houston to Washington, and we'll be back in three to four Weeks. After a week, I will send money to help You and Mom out. Love, Billy."

Corll added one more task. He wanted Henley to have sex with one bound boy while he assaulted the other. Henley balked. He didn't want to witness Corll doing this, let alone do it *with* him. And he had no interest in sex with a male. He declined and Corll didn't push, not this time. But there was one thing Corll expected: Henley had to kill on his own. He had to complete a murder. On Corll's orders, Henley used a cord to strangle Baulch first, watching in amazement as the unconscious body resisted for nearly half an hour.

Brooks would describe for detectives what he'd seen that day. Baulch was dead on the bed and Brooks talked to Johnny to "keep him calm." He was "going wild when he seen the strangling. He knew he was fixing to go himself. . . . Wayne strangled Billy and he said, 'Hey Johnny,' and when Johnny looked up, Wayne shot him in the forehead with a .22 automatic." (It was actually a .25.) The bullet exited through his ear. Still alive, Johnny "raised up" and pleaded with Henley not to kill him, but Henley then strangled him, "and Dean helped." Henley said he did what Corll told him to do. He'd tell police later about electric shocks to genitals, the insertion of glass tubes into penises, pulling pubic hair, and other painful acts. "I did these things because Dean wanted me to do them. He'd direct me, 'try this,' 'try that.' I usually did [it but] didn't do it again."

The bodies were buried together at High Island.

The letters arrived at the missing boys' homes. Billy Baulch's parents recognized his handwriting, but the wording didn't sound like him. Johnny Delome's parents wondered how these boys had penned nearly duplicate letters. They knew Johnny couldn't spell, so they believed someone else had written his letter. They could only wait and see if the boys returned. Due to these letters, the Houston police removed the boys from the missing persons list. Billy's mother told them about Billy hanging out with Dean Corll, who'd once put handcuffs on him. She said that David Brooks, Corll's companion, had given Billy drugs. These reports spurred no action. The Baulches confronted Corll themselves, but he said he had no idea where the boys had gone.

To avoid another incident like the one involving Mark Scott, Corll made a restraining board. He drilled holes into an 8-by-2.5-foot piece of plywood, through which he could fasten handcuffs or ropes to secure his captives. He put holes on both sides so he could bind a victim spread-eagle or bind two boys to the board together. He wanted one captive to watch what he did to the other, because psychological torture added an edge.

"Dean said he had thought up the board as a means of ensuring a victim could not move around when he slept," Henley said. "Handcuffs and feet tied together at the ankles were enough to keep people subdued. It was more the hope of being let go that kept people in check."

Brooks had seen the board before. He knew what it was for. They'd abandoned one at a previous apartment. When Corll bound nineteen-year-old Billy Ridinger to it one day and repeatedly assaulted him, Brooks stepped in before Corll could kill the boy. Brooks insisted that Corll let him go. There was something about Ridinger that Brooks wanted to protect, although it was Corll who ultimately decided what to do. Henley thinks Ridinger might have been a former procurer. He'd seemed to know what being on the board meant. Corll warned him not to talk and released him. Ridinger left.

Brooks was another story. Corll thought the blond kid had to be brought into line. Kids who resisted him were kids who might talk when they shouldn't. One day, he enlisted Henley to knock Brooks unconscious. Corll bound Brooks to the board and raped him repeatedly. Brooks took the abuse, terrified he'd now be murdered. Corll started to strangle him, but after Brooks begged to be released, Corll relented. Brooks remained in the gang. Afraid Corll might do it again, he left, but then returned.

Oddly, there was little discussion between Henley and Brooks about what Corll was doing. Henley was aware that Brooks knew more about Corll than he was saying, but Brooks wouldn't talk about their past relationship or about the financial arrangement. Brooks certainly got a constant flow of money, as well as a room.

Brooks claimed that Henley and Corll killed one more boy at this address, but Henley didn't recall any others there, and records fail to support it. In fact, Henley hoped his "test" was over. He'd killed one by himself. He'd shown he could do it. What more did Corll expect?

Corll moved out of this apartment on June 26, taking up residence in an apartment in Westcott Towers. Former neighbors recalled that he was always on the balcony, scanning the streets with binoculars. They didn't realize he was likely looking for boys on bikes.

Shortly before midnight on July 19, Steven Sickman, seventeen, left his house to go to a party in the Heights, according to his sister. Whether he freely went to Corll's or was forced remains unknown, but he ended up bludgeoned badly in the chest, which fractured several ribs, before being strangled with a nylon cord. His body went into the boat stall. His family reported him missing the next day. The police response was lukewarm. The kid was a month shy of eighteen. They thought he'd just decided to leave town. The family never gave up looking.

That same summer, a tall, blond nineteen-year-old named Roy Eugene Bunton disappeared, possibly while hitchhiking to his job at a shoe store at the local mall. Corll gagged him with a towel and sealed it with adhesive tape. When he was done, he shot Bunton twice in the head. Corll might have lured Sickman and Bunton on his own, although Brooks recalled a tall, skinny kid, which describes Bunton. Still, Brooks placed the tall kid at Schuler, and Bunton seems to have disappeared after Corll had moved from that apartment.

Henley had forbidden his brothers to go to Corll's parties and had kept away his closest friends. They thought Henley was stingy, trying to keep Corll and his resources for himself. But Corll *had* pointed out kids from the Heights that attracted him. Gregory Hilligiest, David's younger brother, had caught his eye. This alarmed Henley. If Corll had a type, then Henley's brother Vernon was in that group. Only later would they all realize that Henley had been trying to protect them.

That summer, Mary Henley observed disturbing changes in her son. He'd sometimes disappear into his room, and she could hear him cry. He'd let his appearance go, a contrast to his former meticulous attention to grooming, and he seemed impatient with religion. He also drank . . . *a lot*. She grew worried as she watched him become someone she barely recognized. Neighbors would report that they'd seen him walking unsteadily during different times of the day. He was turning into his father, in the worst ways. Once a top student with plenty of drive, he now had nothing going for him.

Henley sometimes admitted to friends he drank more than he should. Still, it numbed the part of himself that might recognize he was lost.

"My life was kind of schizophrenic," Henley recalled. "I could get away from Dean and live normal. I could hang out with my friends. I could see my girlfriends. I could barbecue with the family. But there was always an undercurrent of fear of waiting for Dean to show up. At the same time, I was fearful of being left out. I didn't feel anchored anymore because the anchor was Dean. When I was with Dean, everything seemed to focus on him. So, everything is all right, as long as Dean is all right. When I was away from Dean, then I had misgivings and felt responsible and guilty. He was never able to make me guilt-free. It was like at one hand, the person that I was raised to be would start to assert himself, but when I was with Dean, nothing else mattered but Dean. There for a long time, I wondered if I wasn't some kind of crazy man."

Freddie Majors, Henley's childhood friend, remembers when he first met Corll. He didn't like the man and wasn't sure why Henley did. At some point Henley told Majors that he was involved in organized crime that dealt in gambling, prostitution, and drugs. Majors didn't know if Henley was just blowing smoke, so he didn't take it seriously.

In early October, two local youngsters went missing. Wally Jay Simoneaux was fourteen and Richard Hembree thirteen. Wally's mother inquired at their school, Hamilton Junior High, and was told they'd been there that day. A witness would later report that they'd been in a white van near a grocery store, and a young man had gotten out to shoo this observer away.

Neither Brooks nor Henley named either victim in his police statement, but one account reports that they'd picked up these kids near the junior high school where Brooks had first approached Henley. In addition, Brooks described an incident in which Henley accidentally shot a kid in the jaw, and Hembree had been wounded in this manner. "These were young boys from the Heights area," Brooks said, "but I don't know their names. . . . They didn't kill the boy right then. They killed the two boys later on that day."

Somehow, Simoneaux attempted to call his mother. He shouted, "Mama!" into the phone before someone hung it up. He was restrained on the plywood board with Hembree for Corll's cruel pleasure. He kept them all night. Both boys were strangled and taken to the boat stall. Corll seemingly did this burial on his own, placing them directly over the decomposed bodies of Jimmy Glass and Danny Yates in what police would later label as Hole #4.

As Halloween approached, Henley and Brooks discussed trying to stop Corll from "doing his thing." They thought he'd gotten worse. It seemed marginally acceptable to kill "bad" kids because of Corll's personal beef; it was another matter to randomly pick up boys to feed the monster. Henley said, "We both knew at some point Dean was gonna kill *us*. We knew we had to protect each other. David and I both tried to block him. We'd pretend to be willing participants but then would drag our feet."

Henley had a girlfriend, Lisa, so he sometimes double-dated with David and Bridget. On Halloween in 1972, they were at Dean's apartment getting ready to go out. "We had to wait for Dean to come because we wanted to use his car. When he came in, he had two sacks full of candy. And he was chortling and said he couldn't believe these kids were going to come up to his door and knock. And we're like, 'Oh no!' We couldn't leave him. Rather than go out with the girls, we brought them back to Dean's. He might have been teasing. But it was a hook. What if we come back and he's snatched a whole room full of them? We couldn't take that chance."

But they didn't hold him back for long. On November 11 (or 12), Richard Alan Kepner, nineteen, vanished on his way to a pay phone to call his fiancée. He was working as a carpenter's helper to learn the trade and lived with several roommates in a Heights home. Kepner had eaten dinner with his mother the night before and had plans to attend a rock concert two days away. He was strangled and buried at High Island Beach.

Willard Karmon "Rusty" Branch Jr. also disappeared that November. According to his sister, Susan, who was thirteen at the time, Rusty had fought with his father over attending Corll's parties. He'd admitted being propositioned by Corll, which had thrown his father, a cop, into a rage. Rusty was eighteen, so he'd decided to leave. An aunt in Mount Pleasant was the last person to see him that month when she dropped off Rusty and a friend at a spot where they could hitchhike back to Houston. Rusty ended up murdered and buried in Corll's boat shed. He was the only victim who was castrated, perhaps Corll's payback for sexual rejection.

Henley, unaware of Corll's independent activities, believed they'd successfully thwarted him. At times, he'd tried to talk with Corll about not killing anyone, but "conversations about that were a nonstarter. Dean only used euphemisms when he spoke of what he did with those guys. He would say he was 'going to go do my thing' or refer to 'my time alone' with one. Sex was just not a topic with Dean."

Corll moved to Wirt Road in January 1973. He'd last just two months there, but during that time, he murdered Joseph Allen Lyles, a seventeen-year-old artist. For the grave, Corll picked a beach south of Houston in Jefferson County. Neither accomplice assisted. Lyles's family reported him missing after they discovered him gone without his personal effects. They knew he wouldn't just leave, but they hit a brick wall asking for help from law enforcement.

Brooks knew about Lyles, but Henley didn't. Henley hoped to ease out from under Corll's influence. "I hated my hands," he later wrote to a correspondent. "I've always been proud of my hands. My nails were always clean. They were always manicured. I hated that I did the things I did with those hands. I hated a God I had always believed in because He wasn't paying attention. I hated the idea that life and death could ever be this way. I hated being weak and scared. I hated being cruel and cold. I didn't know how to get away from Dean. I wasn't sure if I could or if I even deserved to. But I didn't want to keep doing this."

What might have been happening with this crew was a form of *synchrony* in which the person influencing and mentoring others tries to "mind-meld" to replace their values. It was common during the seventies to believe that one could control others through one's mental prowess. Corll had several books on hypnosis. "Dean was trying to make a useful extension of himself," Henley mused. The psychopath wanted a subordinate as depraved and indifferent as he was. He'd managed this with Brooks and possibly with others. Corll might have viewed Henley as the right balance of susceptibility and temperament. With practice, the boy could get more attuned to the task.

But Henley was looking for ways to leave town.

# CHAPTER 4

---

# No Easy Out

### How to Leave a Fiend

In January 1973, Henley decided to talk to someone about his situation. He couldn't go to the police, but he thought an older male relative could advise him. His Uncle Johnny was driving an eighteen-wheeler across the country to Florida. Henley hitched a ride.

"I went with my Uncle Johnny in his truck. I told him about my predicament. I think he believed me, but when we got to Florida, he put me out there. He said he couldn't take me where he was going. I got picked up by a hippie, who took me to a bus, and I went to my Uncle Bobby's house in Atlanta. I tried to tell him about Dean, too, but he sent me home. He thought I was drunk or crazy."

Before Henley arrived back in Houston, Uncle Bobby had notified Mary that her son had serious problems. "Bobby called me to tell me I had a son who was completely drugged up, clear out of his head," Mary said. "He was putting him on a bus and sending him home." She couldn't believe that any of her kin would treat her son so badly, especially if there was something wrong with him. "I told him he was not welcome in my home."

Striking out with adult relatives he trusted, Henley thought he could just get out of Houston. A cousin lived in Mount Pleasant in East Texas, which would put him about four and a half hours from Corll. He could get a job there. Mount Pleasant was closer to Dallas and the Syndicate, but he didn't think Corll or his associates would come for him. By now, he wasn't so sure he believed in this organization. He'd seen no sign of Corll's participation.

Henley left in March. Corll noticed.

"Dean was upset," Henley recalled. "He had David call me to get me back. David said he couldn't tell what might happen with Gregg Hilligiest and my little brother. It was a threat. After two weeks, I went back [to Houston] because it was what I had to do [to protect my brother]."

During one of Henley's absences, Corll had invited Henley's brother Paul to his house. When Henley learned this, he threw a fit. "I spent a lot of effort keeping Dean away from my friends and keeping my little brothers away from Dean. They thought I was over there always having fun and they wanted to take part in it. I would tell them, look, never go to Dean's house or apartment without me or without talking to me first. I put that out real hard."

That same month, Corll leased a house from his father at 2020 Lamar in Pasadena, half an hour from the Heights. Henley found work laying asphalt for Brooks's father's paving company. For a couple months, things seemed quiet, perhaps because Corll had a painful medical condition, a hydrocele (collection of fluid) on his testicles that required surgery. Henley continued to watch over his brothers. At least Pasadena was farther away than Corll's earlier addresses. You couldn't walk or even bike over.

Henley and Brooks remained vigilant for some command from Corll. They even discussed killing him to stop him if necessary. Henley knew such conversations were risky. Brooks was closer to Corll than Henley and he was jealous of Corll's reliance on Henley. He might warn Corll to be careful of his second accomplice. Corll had once handcuffed Henley and burned him with a cigarette to show him he was not to act on his own, leave without permission, or think for himself. Henley remembered the time Corll had persuaded him to assault Brooks to teach Brooks a lesson.

"We were scared of Dean," Henley said. "And we were scared of each other, to be honest. I mean [Dean] had tied David up once. He tied me up. So, we had both been tied up and knowing his proclivities. . . . So, there was always that threat. The problem was that if you tied one of us up, the other was conflicted. On one hand, here's my friend you've got tied up and on the other hand, here's *you*, who I don't know how to say 'no' to. Do I go along with David? Do I try to save my own life? What? So, we were kept unbalanced. You didn't know whether you were in Dean's good graces or not. He would pull one of us to the side and spend some time with us and allude to the other as being jealous or acting against the one he was with. There were weird different pieces of trust [while] at the same time there was no complete trust.

"I think towards the end, David and I had finally come to the realization that we had been played against each other. Our only hope was that we could not allow Dean to catch us away from each other, or to pit one of us against the other. Dean talked more and more against [one of] us to the other. We were scared to sleep around Dean, so if we stayed there [at his place], we slept in the same bed."

Henley still hung out with a few friends, but he fell back into unhealthy habits. His friend Bruce Pittman worried about him. Henley seemed to drink a lot more than he should, and sometimes he even thought he should see a doctor or counselor. At one point, Henley asked Pittman if he'd ever considered being a professional hit man. It had seemed an odd thing to ask, almost as odd as Henley's friendship with Corll. Pittman had noticed that Corll just seemed to stare at the boys. It was unnerving. What could Henley be doing with this older gay guy? He suspected that something was deeply wrong.

Returning to Houston reminded Henley of his role in murder. He wanted to put it all behind him. In May, when he turned seventeen, he considered one more option, something that would take him so far away there was nothing Corll could do to force him back. He went to enlist in the Navy. He hoped to be trained as a boatswain's mate, the person that supervised the ship's maintenance duties. "I said goodbye to my mother and went down to enlist. I took a test. I must have done well, because they took me to the University of Houston to get a GED. A liaison walked me through all the departments. But then they gave me a color perception test. I got four of fourteen. I was color-blind. It made me ineligible for all these jobs in the Navy." They also determined that Henley had fraudulently signed a form that indicated he hadn't done drugs. "I said I'd never done drugs, but then I admitted that I had. I'd lied on the form, so I was ineligible." He withdrew the application.

Resigned to his dead-end life in Houston, Henley returned to hanging out with Corll. Unbeknownst to him, Corll had started a serious relationship with a nineteen-year-old man referred to in Jack Olsen's book as "Guy." It lasted three months, until sometime in July. Corll invited Guy to the Pasadena house, where he showed him a locked room and said he'd never take him in there. According to Guy, Corll sometimes talked about being forced to do things he didn't want to, but he didn't elaborate. Corll, Guy said, had been secretive.

Apparently, having a relationship didn't diminish Corll's darker impulses. Early in June, he insisted that Henley "bring him a boy." There was no getting out of this one. Brooks wasn't available, so Henley was on his own.

## Summer of Blood

Henley had spotted a friend of his girlfriend's, a fifteen-year-old named Billy Lawrence. The kid lived with his father and complained a lot about his life. He'd been sent to another school during the period of desegregation, and he disliked being away from his friends. His dad hated when he'd sneak around to drink or smoke dope. Author Jack Olsen describes their relationship as loving but tense. On the promise of a party or a trip to the lake where Corll's family had property, Henley lured Lawrence to Corll's house.

While Lawrence was being tortured, Brooks [who erroneously placed this incident in July] called Corll's house. No one answered, so he persisted until Henley finally picked up the phone. Brooks's third statement to police provides the details.

"Do you have anyone there?" Brooks asked.

"Yes," Henley told him.

"It's not a friend, is it?"

"Sort of."

Brooks wanted a name but claimed Henley wouldn't say. "So I went over there just to see who it was."

This seems strange for Brooks to do. If Corll hadn't called for him, he'd be free of his typical tasks of driving and digging. Yet he went over on his own. (He had a room there, but at the time, he was living with his fiancée, Bridget Clark.) This suggests that Brooks thought Henley might get something—money or approval—for this abduction and he didn't want to be left out. He provided no rationale for his behavior in his confession, but he added other details.

Brooks arrived and saw that Lawrence was nude and tied to a bed. By then, Billy had called his father to ask if he could go fishing "with some friends" at Lake Sam Rayburn. He'd promised to be back in three days. Whether this call had been coerced is unknown. On that day, according to his father's report to police, they'd exchanged words of affection. The next form of contact arrived five days later: a note from Lawrence that stated he'd found a job in Austin and would be gone until late in August. This note, most certainly, was coerced or forged. It resembled previous letters from Corll's victims to their families. The doomed boy had signed off with, "I hope you know I love you."

Lawrence wasn't ever going back home. Corll had plans for him. According to Brooks, Corll had "really liked" the boy, so he'd kept him handcuffed to the board for at least three days.

Brooks said he took Henley home at the end of that day and returned to Corll's. "I was so tired I went to bed in the opposite bedroom." Again, this is odd. He went to bed, indifferent to the boy's suffering. The next morning, Brooks brought Henley back, miffed that Corll wouldn't pay him for running back and forth. His mundane concerns contrast sharply with the shocking situation.

Apparently, the accomplices spent most of that day at Corll's because Mary Henley called that evening. Henley told her he was going to the lake for a couple days. Although Brooks said he thought Lawrence was still alive at this time, he added that when they left at 6:00 P.M., the boy was dead, strangled with a cord. "I must have been there when he was killed. . . . I do not remember how he was killed. I don't know if I saw it or not."

Brooks said they took the plastic-wrapped body in a wooden box to Lake Sam Rayburn, arriving close to 10:00 P.M. They slept, and in the morning he and Henley went fishing while Corll picked out a place for the body. This was the first time they had used this area for burial. Around 5:00 P.M., Brooks and Corll dug a grave while Henley kept a lookout. Brooks and Corll took the body from the box and buried it. Brooks scraped the extra dirt onto a rug to cart away so there would be no visible mound. Corll yelled at him for taking too much. When detectives showed Brooks a photograph collected from Corll's home of Billy Lawrence, he identified it as the boy he was talking about.

Henley recalled the sadistic treatment of this boy as well. He said it had been difficult for him, possibly because he was more than just passingly acquainted with Lawrence, and he'd brought Lawrence there. "That one was hard. I was trying to shoot myself up full of drugs while Dean had Billy tied up. I remember sitting there trying to hit myself up with a fistful of pills. I don't know what I was doing, trying to kill myself or just be obliterated. I recall thinking 'you don't even know what this [drug] will do to you,' and the answer was, 'I don't care.' I came up in a drug culture. I'd been taught how to do drugs. I didn't do drugs if I didn't know what they were or what they would do to me, but with Dean I was not able to control anything."

Henley didn't die. He just went home to sleep it off. Then he returned the next day. Lawrence was still alive. Dean had more ideas.

"All the things that people refer to as torture [in this case], that was all Dean getting me to do this stuff. 'Try this. Try that.' The glass rod was a thing. It did not produce the results Dean wanted. The pubic hair pulling happened as a coercion technique. It was more 'If you don't mind me, this will happen.' Once he got me to do any of it, he'd move on. But I didn't always do it. He wanted me to use a sword to kill someone. I voiced objections and wouldn't do it. Dean would get quiet, refuse to talk, not want to hang with me."

On June 15, a twenty-year-old married man from Baton Rouge, Louisiana, Raymond Stanley Blackburn, vanished while hitchhiking from his temporary residence in the Heights. He'd been there for work, and he wanted to go home to see his newborn child. His wife, Myrtle, reported him missing. A few days later, on June 21, she received a letter from Blackburn explaining that he needed to take care of something. He'd be home in a week or two. This was likely another person that Corll had forced into writing a fake message. Henley remembered him only by the town he was from. Blackburn was the second victim to be strangled and buried in the woods at Lake Sam Rayburn. The site was near Billy's grave. Corll kept Blackburn's driver's license in his toolbox as a trophy.

The signs that Corll was ready to kill came more often now. "He'd buy a pack of Marlboros and put them in the car's driver-side sun visor," Henley said. Corll didn't inhale. He'd take short puffs or keep an unlit cigarette in his mouth. He insisted that both of his accomplices ride around with him. "We would be told not to bring anyone over, or to call before we came."

This happened again in early July. Henley had enrolled in Coaches Driving School and met fifteen-year-old Homer Garcia. He invited the boy to come over to Corll's. Garcia phoned his mother to tell her he'd be spending the night with a friend. He didn't give a name. Garcia ended up shot in the head and chest. Henley placed him in Corll's bathtub to bleed out. They took his body to Lake Sam Rayburn.

On July 12, John Manning Sellars, a Marine, was reported missing. Although he's on most lists of victims associated with Dean Corll, it's not clear that he should be. Neither Brooks nor Henley remember him or the alleged circumstances, and the medical examiner, Joseph Jachimczyk, would exclude him due to multiple differences. Sellars was shot four times in the chest with a high-powered rifle. Although he'd been bound with rope in a manner similar to Corll's victims, his fully clothed body was not wrapped in plastic. Also, Sellars's car was found burned in Louisiana. Author Barbara Gibson states that Sellars had told his younger brother just before he vanished that someone wanted to kill him and had threatened to bury him on the beach. No one who knew him linked him to Dean Corll.

Still, he'd been buried on a beach three miles from the High Island graves (much farther away than Brooks described for the Corll victim burials). According to Jack Olsen, "Detectives theorized that the victim had been hunting and had stumbled on a burial scene and had been executed with his own rifle." This doesn't explain his car found burned in another state. Some reports claim that Henley and Brooks led police to his grave. In actuality, a truck driver took police to the spot, reporting that he'd seen suspicious activity there eight months earlier and had wondered about a mound of dirt. "Eight months earlier" put it well out of the range of when Sellars went missing, and Corll had trained his accomplices to level out the graves. They wouldn't have left a mound. Also, in Sellars's pocket was rifle ammunition, but he had no rifle (although he'd owned one). If Henley or Brooks had taken the rifle, they'd likely have taken the ammunition. Henley also said they'd buried bodies on the beach only at night. Jachimczyk decided the body discovery was coincidental.

Brooks got married on July 13 and moved in permanently with Bridget, who was pregnant. He continued to be involved with Corll, but the power differential shifted. Henley was now the number one accomplice. Yet Corll would also act on his own.

On July 19, the grieving Baulch family last saw Michael "Tony" Baulch, the brother of the missing Billy Baulch. He was fifteen and a frequent runaway, but lately he'd seemed settled. His mother had advised him to get his hair cut, and he'd asked for the money to cover this and a pack of cigarettes. He didn't return home. His parents checked his room, fearing another flight, but the items he'd have taken were still present. Reports to police produced the expected response: he's run away . . . again. The Baulches checked every place they could think of but found no sign of him. It seemed stunning that they now had two boys missing. It was beyond what they could bear.

Christeen Weed heard about their plight. She recalled that Tony had been at her house not long before. He'd been asking about his brother, still thinking they might figure out where he'd gone.

Both Baulch brothers had crossed paths with Corll. How Tony had arrived at Corll's house is unknown, but they had a prior acquaintance. Like his brother the year before, Tony was raped, strangled, and buried. Neither Brooks nor Henley mentioned being part of his murder, although Henley was aware of it and pointed out the likely location of his grave at Lake Sam Rayburn. When identifications were reexamined years later, it turned out the medical examiner had decided that Tony Baulch was buried in the boat stall, which led to confusion for the families. His body was actually among the remains at the lake.

Henley noticed Corll keeping him and Brooks apart, as if Corll suspected they were planning to gang up on him. A police report, taken later, indicates Corll told a friend of his that he was afraid of them, especially Brooks, and wanted to leave town. Brooks was now eighteen, Henley seventeen. They'd become harder to manage.

"He kept a wedge between David and me that he used," Henley recalled, "me against David, David against me." Corll's sixth sense about this was correct. "David and I had been plotting on what to do about Dean. We didn't know what to do about the Syndicate, but we knew what to do about Dean." A confrontation was brewing.

"He was escalating," Henley said. "I think he knew I was reaching saturation. I was drinking worse and worse. I did things to spite him. [He knew] I was trying to get away." Corll would identify boys he wanted, and Henley would deflect him. "I spent a lot of my life at that time fearful that Dean was going to run amok and kill my friends and family. He could no longer be blocked because he went off on his own. His episodes were becoming more vicious and hurried. . . . The feeling I had was that Dean would soon kill me or kill both of us. I believe Dean not only was losing control of his own self but [also knew he] was losing control of me. I had begun to spend time with a group of people Dean did not know. My drunkenness had become a near-constant."

Henley might have been right. Late in July, Corll said something to Mary Henley that disturbed her. "Dean stood in my front yard and said he was gonna take Wayne traveling because he hadn't seen anything or been anywhere. He was going to take him traveling around the United States. He said, 'You won't be able to call him or write to him because you won't know where we are. And on the way back, I'm gonna leave him with a friend of mine named Alex to get him a job.' I looked at him and said, 'Wayne is my son. I carried him and brought him into the world, and I've raised him. If you go anywhere in that car with Wayne, I'll call the law.' "

Corll's "travel plan" mirrors the letters he'd force his victims to write to their parents, assuring them they'd found a job in another town. Henley might have sensed that Corll hoped to make him disappear. Part of him wanted to believe that Corll could still open some doors to a better life, but another part suspected that leaving town with Corll was a death sentence. In the meantime, Corll still wanted to do his thing.

On July 25, Marty Ray Jones was seen with his friend, Charles Cobble, a high school dropout with a severe anxiety disorder. Cobble's uncle would later describe Cobble as fearful of everything. He had poor family bonds and few friends. He thought a lot about dying. With his blue eyes and fine, blond hair, he resembled Jones, except that at five foot five, Jones was nearly half a foot shorter.

Jones was from an abusive home and had had several stepfathers. At the age of six, he reported being raped. As a teen, he'd moved into the Cobble home, at no one's invitation. Cobble's mother described him as "deeply emotionally disturbed." The Cobbles kept kicking him out and he kept coming back. He had a record of multiple run-ins with police, especially for drugs. Cobble and Jones together developed a reputation for being bullies. Jones, a drug dealer, cheated people with inferior products.

In March 1973, Cobble had come home with a girl who was pregnant, so his parents had arranged a quick marriage and an apartment in a building across the street from Henley's home. On the Fourth of July, the couple had separated, and Jones had moved in. Near the time when these two disappeared, Jones had tried to pick a fight with Henley in a restaurant.

According to author John Gurwell, on that evening of July 25, witnesses saw Cobble and Jones with Henley. The three young men were walking single file, as if Henley was escorting them. Cobble had looked scared. They ended up at Corll's place. Near 10:00 P.M., Cobble's father, Vern, answered the phone. Charles said he was in trouble with "some people" who thought he'd "done something to them." He couldn't reveal what it was, but he had to have $1,000. He needed it *now*. But that was impossible for the Cobbles on short notice. Cobble said Jones was with him as well. In a broken voice, he said he'd provide instructions later. Then he hung up.

Vern phoned the police and was told there was nothing they could do. A call to the FBI produced similar results. Vern called Jones's father and learned that Jones had made a similar request. When the young men failed to return to their apartment, the Cobbles asked for help from a relative, a former CIA operative. He talked to dozens of kids in the Heights, including Henley, but learned only that Jones was a "rip-off artist" and a "sadist." Henley, he said, had been cooperative and sympathetic. The Cobbles offered a substantial reward for information. They received no response.

Corll bound Cobble and Jones to his board. He raped and tortured them both, then added a layer of sadism. He urged them to hit each other, falsely promising to release the one who survived. It's likely they did not believe him. Whether they beat each other at all is unclear from the autopsy reports, but Jones died first, strangled to death with a triple-looped rope. The obsessively nervous Cobble was so upset by witnessing his best friend's murder he went into cardiac arrest. Henley rushed to resuscitate him. "I wanted to get him to a doctor." Corll ordered him to stop. Cobble did revive, but under Corll's orders Henley shot him twice in the head. "It made no sense that I'd revive him," he said, "but I just reacted."

These bodies were destined for the boat stall. Corll took Henley there and locked him in while he went to get bags of quicklime. "I was locked in the boat shed for a period of time," Henley recalled. "I was horrified." He thought that his friend, David Hilligiest, had been buried in there. In fact, he probably stepped on Hilligiest's grave as he dug a large hole in the middle of the stall.

Henley wrote a letter for his mother in which he described the things he'd tried telling his uncles in January. He believed Corll might kill him and he wanted her to know what he'd done. It was partly a confession and partly a document to show to police in case he vanished. He gave the letter to her. "I tried to tell me [sic] mother two or three times about this stuff," his police statement reads," and she just wouldn't believe me. I even wrote a confession one time and hid it, hoping Dean would kill me because the thing was bothering me so bad. I gave the confession to my mother and told her if I was gone for a certain length of time to turn it in."

"When I got it," Mary recalled, "it said he killed David Hilligiest, and I knew he didn't. He didn't know Dean Corll then. So, it went on talkin' and he told about Malley Winkle, [a boy] which was with David Hilligiest. He said, 'we killed all of them,' and I knew Wayne didn't kill those two. So, I got rid of the letter for fear it would fall into the wrong hands and hurt him. I always did what I thought was best for the boys. I should've kept it because he was trying to get help. I knew he needed to see a psychiatrist, bad. I couldn't figure out what was wrong with him. I'd talk to him, but he wouldn't tell me."

Mary made an appointment for him with a psychiatrist who had a practice in the same building where she worked. It was a few weeks off, but she felt better knowing that a professional would take over. Her son had changed so much over the past year she knew something was desperately wrong.

A week after killing Cobble and Jones, according to Jack Olsen, Henley told Bruce Pittman he was considering going to Australia. He urged Pittman to go with him. He'd even pay his way, and Pittman could pay him back. He'd already calculated the cost—$1,700 a piece. Pittman wondered where Henley could have gotten this amount of money. His family had none, and he worked at low-paying jobs. He recalled Henley's query about becoming a hired assassin. Had his friend actually gotten himself into organized crime?

Corll was beginning to panic. He'd tried to persuade Guy to leave Houston with him and go to Mexico or Central America, because he wanted to start a new life where no one knew him. Guy said he wouldn't go, which had hurt Corll and made him cry. He'd seemed to Guy to be desperate to leave. Corll wouldn't say why it was so important.

## The Final Days

On August 3, thirteen-year-old James Stanton Dreymala took off on his bike in South Houston. Later that day, he called his parents to tell them he was at a party across town and wanted to stay. His father told him to come home. Brooks referred to him in his police statement as a "small blond boy." Brooks hadn't assisted with procuring Dreymala but had discovered the boy at Corll's house. Henley wasn't there. (He was at a three-day dope party with a group of girls.) Brooks said he brought the boy a pizza and spent forty-five minutes with him before leaving him to his terrible fate. Corll strangled the kid with a cord, wrapped the body in plastic, and buried it in the boat stall along the east wall. He placed Dreymala's red bike there, near a stolen Camaro.

Corll was running out of space. There were bodies along both walls, the front, and up the middle. He had room for possibly two or three more. He'd inquired about renting another stall. He was also unraveling.

A longtime female acquaintance named Betty Hawkins had noticed his personality change that summer. Corll had sometimes used her as a cover story by posing her as his fiancée. In her statement to the police after Corll's death, she described the nature of their fifteen-year association. She had met Corll when she worked for the candy company. In her late twenties at the time, she was married. After she divorced, Corll became romantically interested in her around 1968. She had two young sons, whom he loved to play with. There had been no sex. He was "a gentleman." Hawkins knew about David Brooks living with Corll and had thought he was just being kind to the boy. She also knew about three other boys who'd run around with Corll: Billy Baulch, another Billy (probably Ridinger), and someone named Leroy. Recently, Corll had said he wanted to get away from Brooks and Henley. He hadn't told her why. Then he'd abruptly asked if she would marry him and move with him to Colorado, where his mother lived. He had seemed upset. He was drinking heavily, which was uncharacteristic, and he admitted to doing some drugs. He seemed to be losing control of his life.

Hawkins had seen Corll on July 29 when they went together to his father's vacation home at Lake Sam Rayburn. His father and stepmother were present.

"He was acting so different," she said. "He wouldn't stay still. He wouldn't sit." He'd usually play with her kids but on this occasion, he ignored them. "He acted like a man with something on his mind. . . . From the expressions on his face, I knew something was bothering him." When he wouldn't stop to let her purchase cigarettes as he drove her home, she believed something was terribly wrong. He was usually considerate. (These were behavioral signals that he was ready to look for a victim.)

On Sunday, August 5, just after Corll had killed Dreymala, Corll told Betty over the phone he was "lonesome" but then said he wouldn't be taking her to Colorado after all. He'd have to get a job first. He agreed to assist her with moving to a new residence on August 9. He mentioned he'd get a check from his workplace and then just leave with no notice. He knew this was wrong but said he had no choice. "Whenever I do leave," he added, "don't tell David Brooks where I went."

Corll's mother, Mary West, also recalled his agitation. On July 29, Corll told her over the phone that he was in trouble. According to her report, he said, "I'm leaving here. I'm just gonna drop out of the picture. I might even take an overdose." He seemed to want a way out of something. When she told him he'd have to figure out how to live, whether in this life or the next, he responded, "Mother, it might be easier to do in another life." He refused to tell her what he meant, saying, "I can't talk about it." A little later, she chastised him for running up his phone bill. He said, "I'm not counting on paying it." When she called him all day on Sunday, August 5—the same day he'd told Betty he wouldn't take her with him to Colorado—he finally answered and told her he hadn't picked up earlier because he was dodging someone. She thought he might have owed someone money.

It's possible that Corll had heard that the police in San Augustine County were conducting a manhunt on Sunday, July 29, near the Lake

Sam Rayburn property. Some two hundred officers had been in the woods. Corll had been at the lake house with Betty Hawkins that same day. He might have heard about it and thought someone had discovered one of his grave sites.

Corll's stepmother, Mary Corll, received a call from him on Wednesday, August 1. Corll asked if her daughter might want to take over his lease at 2020 Lamar. She inquired if he planned to leave. He told her, "I have to." She knew he'd had some health issues earlier that year. She pressed him about what was bothering him, and he said, "I can't talk about it! I'll handle it." On August 3, she called him again at work to tell him she was worried about him. He seemed calmer. (He'd just killed James Dreymala.) He told her, "Everything's under control." He visited their home on August 6 to do his laundry and he seemed at ease.

To those who knew him best, Corll had seemed erratic that first week of August 1973, even suicidal. Then he'd suddenly seemed composed. Many people in this frame of mind do calm down once they've decided to end their lives. They're relieved. So, either Corll *had* taken care of the distressing situation, or he'd planned a desperate way out and was about to enact it.

## The Fateful Morning

The winding, tree-lined streets in the neighborhood around 2020 Lamar were generally quiet. Some residents were aware that Dean Corll had leased the single-story, olive and white, wood-frame house from his father. Corll parked his white Econoline van on the street out front and kept a Plymouth GTX in the driveway. Teenage boys came in and out for frequent parties, but the noise level was generally tolerable. The dark-haired, six-foot Corll seemed like a nice man. He smiled a lot and wore pricey clothes. Although he never joined groups of neighbors to chat, he was approachable, even helpful.

This impression changed dramatically on Wednesday, August 8. Patrol Officer J. B. Jamison heard "Shooting—homicide" over his police radio. He got the address and drove to the house, arriving at 8:26 A.M. He knew an ambulance was on the way.

He saw two teenage boys and a girl sitting on the curb. The taller boy stared vacantly across the street. The other two kids were crying. The shorter boy, wearing only a pair of jeans, seemed stoned. His large eyes were dull as he looked at Jamison and said, "I killed a man inside." A blue steel .22-caliber seven-shot Arms Co. revolver lay on the sidewalk near them.

Jamison identified this boy for the report as Elmer Wayne Henley Jr., seventeen, from 325 West Twenty-Seventh Street in Houston. Henley had made the call. Jamison placed all three kids into the patrol car and treated them as suspects in a homicide. The brunette girl, Rhonda Williams, was fifteen and the tall boy, Tim Kerley, was twenty. Jamison used a pencil to pick up the pistol and place it into the trunk of his car. Then he entered the house to see the victim.

A stocky adult male lay sprawled face down on the floor in a hallway. A quilted sleeping bag covered him. Jamison lifted it high enough to see blood drying around bullet holes in the left shoulder and back of the nude body. The long, curled cord from a red Princess-style phone was wrapped around one foot, as if the man had tripped on it. He didn't move. He was dead. Jamison went out to the patrol car and read the kids their rights. He noted that it was 8:37 A.M. before he called for a detective unit.

Henley gave his name and stated that he'd known Corll for about three years and had met him through a friend. Jamison took notes as Henley described what had happened. He'd brought the other two kids to the house between two and three that morning. High from pills, they'd huffed acrylic paint fumes for a while before passing out. When they'd woken up, they'd found themselves gagged and handcuffed. Corll (referred to in Jamison's report as the victim) had forced "the suspects" to remove their clothes. He'd threatened to sexually molest them ("eat them") and then shoot them. Henley, the only one not gagged, had persuaded Corll to untie him, promising to help. Corll had done so. Henley had then looked around the room and seen Corll's gun on a chest of drawers. He'd picked it up and shot Corll, then freed the other two. They'd called the police. That was their story. But it was far from the whole truth.

Detectives from Pasadena PD arrived around 8:45 A.M. Jamison released the pistol to another officer. He conferred with the lead detective, David Mullican, and transported the teens to the Police Department for their formal magistrate warnings. On the way, Jamison noted, Henley "mentioned that the victim, all during the morning, kept talking about a warehouse or small storage room where the victim had buried some bodies." It seemed an offhanded statement, but Jamison knew the detectives could follow up. The immediate need was to process the house and secure the kids for questioning.

Officers photographed the scene, the body, and items of evidence, while Mullican directed the activities that supported the investigation. The front door opened into a living area, separated from the kitchen by a long bar. The body lay in the hallway. Eddie Knowles, an investigator from the Harris County Medical Examiner's Office, photographed it. He noted that the victim appeared to be about six feet tall and solid, about two hundred pounds. Knowles had the body removed to the morgue.

Mullican entered the southeast bedroom. He noticed a large polyethylene sheet spread out under a long, narrow plywood board that had holes cut in the center and at each of the four corners, apparently for securing ropes and handcuffs. The scene looked sinister. He made a diagram of the residence for mapping evidence locations. He noted piles of clothing, crumbled paper sacks, a can of aerosol paint, a gas mask, a large hunting knife, eight sets of handcuffs, and a bayonet-like eighteen-inch blade. In another bedroom, he saw a gray toolbox, two marijuana joints, two eight-inch glass rods, a foot-long suppository, an electric motor with loose wires, and a seventeen-inch, two-headed dildo that was two inches in diameter. In other areas, scattered pipes attested to smoking dope. In a shed, Mullican also found a large box with what appeared to be air holes drilled into it. Corll's wallet contained his ID, two one-hundred-dollar bills, and five one-dollar bills. Mullican found nothing of note in the white van outside besides blackout window coverings, a soiled rug, a wooden crate with air holes, and a series of hooks fastened to the sides.

Inside the house, Mullican picked up a Polaroid photo of a boy and placed it into an evidence bag. In the attached garage were traces of powder that looked like lime. It would have to be tested.

Mullican did not collect a cigar box full of keys listed on a later inventory, although such a box was present (with over seventy-five keys). Some of the keys would later become important. Also left behind were books on hypnosis that sat in a pile in the dead man's closet, and three dozen photos of boys. These items would end up with Arnold Corll when he cleaned out his son's house; he'd turn them over to police to use as leads for witness statements.

Mullican returned to the Pasadena PD to interview Henley and his friends. They'd been placed in separate but adjacent rooms. He noted that a magistrate, Municipal Judge Russell Drake, had given them the required warning about their rights at 10:55 A.M. None of them had requested an attorney or asked to inform their parents about where they were. Arrangements were made to have the underage girl, Rhonda Williams, turned over to the Harris County Juvenile Division.

Each teen described the events of August 8 in affidavit form, which added more details to Henley's curt verbal account from that morning. They were still high from their early hours party, but the basic story was that Tim Kerley and Wayne Henley had gone to Corll's house. Henley said Corll had been trying to get him to bring Kerley there for sex. The boys had picked up Williams, who wanted to run away, to bring her back to the house. Then things had gone south.

In Henley's affidavit, he said he was seventeen, had completed the eighth grade, was unemployed, and lived with his mother and grandmother. "I have been knowing Dean Corll for about two or maybe three years. I have known him real well for about two years." He explained that a school friend named David Brooks, a year older than him, had introduced them. They'd ride around in Corll's car and drink beer. "After I knew him for a while, I began to figure he was queer, homosexual." He asked Corll if this was so, and Corll not only affirmed it but also asked if he "could do it to me and offered me ten dollars to let him do it." Henley claimed to have declined. Corll had persisted, "but I would never let him."

Henley noted the multiple addresses where Corll had lived, most recently at Lamar Street. Around this time, Henley had introduced Corll to Kerley. "He started talking about that he would like to have sex with Tim and asked me to have Tim come over to his place so that he could do unnatural sex acts with him. Also, during this time Dean told me about a warehouse that he had over on Hiram Clarke where he had killed some boys and buried them after he had sex with them. His reason for killing them was that he couldn't afford to let them know that (that is everybody else) that [sic] he was a queer and what he had done to the boys. I thought he was just kidding me about that part of it, but he took me over to the warehouse several times and the only thing that I ever saw in there was a car that he said was stolen."

Henley said they continued to hang out as friends. Around June, Corll talked about quitting his job so they could travel. "We decided to do this about the first of September." He knew that Rhonda Williams wanted to run away from her abusive home, so he thought they might take her with them.

Henley related that on August 7, when Corll got off work, "he picked me up at the corner of Fifteenth and Shepherd Drive, and we drove around for a while and drank a couple of beers, then he wanted me to get Tim to come over to his house so he could have sex with him. I told him I didn't want to, but we went by Tim's house, anyway. Dean said he was going to fill his van up with gas, and I stayed there at Tim's house. I guess I stayed there until after midnight, then me and Tim went over to Dean's house in Tim's car. We stayed there for about an hour, bagging [huffing paint fumes], then me and Tim went over and met Rhonda at a washateria down the street from her house."

Rhonda had an overnight bag prepared, but she hadn't shown up at the washateria. Henley had gone to her house and climbed up to knock on her second-floor window. The three kids returned to Dean's house. "I don't remember if he got up and let us in," Henley stated, "or if I just used my key." They continued the huffing party inside, with all of them passing out. "[I]t must have been just before daylight, I woke up and Dean was in the process of putting a pair of handcuffs on me, with my hands behind my back, and I said, 'Hey, what are you doing?' and Dean said, 'You just pissed me off by bringing Rhonda over here this early.' . . . Then I noticed that both Tim and Rhonda were both on their stomachs, with their hands cuffed and their feet tied. Also, they had tape over their mouths."

Corll turned a transistor radio on loud and set it between Kerley and Williams. He dragged Henley into the kitchen, "and told me again that he didn't appreciate me bringing Rhonda over there because it interfered with his plans." Henley was confused. He'd assumed that bringing a girl over would prevent Corll from making a move on Kerley, but he'd underestimated Corll's fixation. They argued over it while Henley downed more hard liquor, but once Henley realized that Corll meant to kill him, "I told him I'd do anything he wanted me to if he would just take the cuffs off of me." Corll considered this. Reportedly, he said, "I'm going to let you loose, but I'll keep the gun and knife."

Corll released Henley. Then he carried Kerley and Williams, one at a time, into the southeast bedroom where he secured them to his homemade restraint board. He removed the tape over their mouths. He tied Kerley on one side, forcing him flat on his stomach to bind one of his hands and one of his feet to the board. The young man whimpered and begged to be let go. Next, Corll tied Williams to the board on her back. A thick sheet of plastic was already laid out on the floor, intended for torture. Corll gave Henley a knife and told him to remove Williams's clothing while he did the same with Kerley. He expected them to rape the victims together. Corll removed his own clothes in preparation.

In his statement, Henley described Corll's next move. "At first, he wanted Tim to have sex with Rhonda, and Tim said he couldn't. Then he told me to have sex with her and he (Dean) would have sex with Tim. I got up and went to the bathroom and came back and was just sort of walking around."

Henley finally knelt near Williams. She watched him with frightened eyes. "Is this for real?" she asked.

He told her it was before he said to Dean, "I want to move her to another room."

Corll ignored him.

Henley persisted. "She doesn't need to see this."

Kerley yelled that he didn't want to see it either.

Henley, anxious, got up and paced as he huffed paint fumes from a bag. He knew he had to act. He thought it might be easier if he were high. He'd always been taught to protect females. He'd brought Williams there; he was responsible for her, like a big brother. He saw Corll's .22 unattended on a dresser. Corll was busy. Henley grabbed the gun.

In that instant, everything changed.

Henley pointed the weapon at Corll and shouted, "You've gone far enough, Dean!" He hoped Corll would just back off and allow them to leave. They'd all forget this had ever happened.

Corll looked up, puzzled.

Henley remained steady, his finger on the trigger. Corll had told him to never point a gun unless he meant to use it. There was no backing down. "I can't have you killing all my friends!"

But Corll was not going to let a kid—not *this* kid—intimidate him. He knew Henley. The kid usually did what he was told. Corll had burned him once to teach him the price of disobedience. Corll got up and moved toward Henley. "Go ahead, Wayne. Kill me! You won't do it. Shoot me!"

Henley swallowed. If Corll got to talking, he'd gain the leverage he always gained.

Then Corll rushed him. Henley pulled the trigger and hit Corll in the forehead. Corll recoiled. But he kept coming. Henley was shocked. Then he remembered. Corll had trained him, repeatedly insisting that if he ever shot someone, he should keep shooting until the person hit the ground. So Henley pulled the trigger, again and again. He put two bullets into Corll's left shoulder. Corll staggered back, turned, and headed through the door, passing close to Henley to enter the hallway. He got tangled in the long cord from a phone that sat on the floor in his way. Henley turned and shot three more times, hitting him in the back. Corll made an odd noise, hit the wall, and slid to the floor, bleeding. He went still.

Henley's first thought was that Corll would have been proud that he'd followed his direction to keep shooting. But then he knew he was in deep trouble. He could hardly believe what he'd just done. He'd killed a man. He'd killed his *friend*. He started shaking.

Williams shouted, urging him to help them. Henley released them and comforted Kerley, who wept and thanked him for saving his life. They quickly dressed in what they could wear of their ruined clothing, keeping an eye on Corll just in case he jumped up like an unvanquished monster in a horror film.

But he lay still. Blood drained in rivulets down his back. There was no sign of life. Williams couldn't look at the body.

"You two should just go!" Henley urged. But he had no plan. None of this was supposed to have happened.

Williams refused to leave. She thought Henley should flee. But no matter what was decided, she wasn't walking out past a corpse. Henley went over and covered Corll with a sleeping bag.

Kerley insisted they call the cops. Henley considered leaving town but knew he had no resources. He couldn't just run. He had to turn himself in. He'd shot Corll in self-defense. It would be all right.

"I think the reason I broke down and cried after shooting Dean," said Henley, "was because my life was ended. I had finally accepted that anything was preferable than to continue with Dean. I had reached a cusp of where I was able to act as a man should and to bear the consequences. I was also closing off a part of my life I had clung to regardless of consequences. I cried because I lost Dean, lost my life, lost my childhood, accepted death, and was just plain relieved. . . . From the minute Dean tied us up that morning, it was only going to end with Dean's or Rhonda's and Tim's deaths. I would have accepted Dean allowing us to leave. But I also know, now, that only Dean's death was going to release me.

"This was different from other deaths in that I've never felt the guilt. With Dean, it has been regret, chagrin, a wish that I could have left him alive to fade in his own heat, but [there was] no guilt. With the other deaths, there was always an emptiness to my life, as if something inside me was wrong. There was the wonder if God would now punish me. I always felt the horror of someone dying alone and away from loved ones.

"I should have killed Dean Corll long before I did. That sounds callous. But in my mind, I only had a limited set of possibilities. Dean was gonna kill me, which was really the most likely. Or I would manage to get away, but that just never seemed to work. Or I was gonna kill Dean Corll. . . . Eventually my upbringing, my conscience, my guilt—it overpowered the circumstances. It just got to where I could not accept or allow this anymore. I guess you would say I finally grew up. That I took that one other step to where I was willing and able to accept responsibility."

At 8:24 on that scorching August morning, Henley told a police dispatcher that he'd shot a man. "You need to come get me." He gave the address. Then he went outside, placed the pistol on the driveway, and sat on the curb. Williams and Kerley sat with him.

Henley felt sick. His life was over. His plan to travel with Corll and make a lot of money with the organization Corll had talked about would never happen. Yet he knew he'd had no choice. Corll had forced it.

But why would Corll have been so careless? He'd taught Henley himself to take out a threat. He knew Henley was high. Rushing Henley was a risky proposition.

It's possible that Corll had formed a plan to end his life. He'd been pressuring Henley to bring Tim Kerley to him so he could "do his thing." He wouldn't have anticipated that Henley would also bring Rhonda Williams, but once she was there, if Corll were still suicidal or even just ambivalent about it, he might have spotted an opportunity to provoke Henley into shooting him. Corll waited until Henley passed out, then bound him and made him believe he was about to be raped and killed. "I'm going to kill you all," Corll said. "But first I'm gonna have my fun."

However, Corll hadn't taped Henley's mouth like he'd done with the others, as if he'd wanted Henley to be able to talk him out of it. Then, without much resistance, he let Henley go. Corll had said he'd keep control of the knife and gun, but then left his gun untended where Henley could easily grab it. It's possible that Corll set up a scenario in which he'd goad Henley into acting. Henley said that multiple things were different about Corll that day. "He was agitated. I'd never seen Dean naked. I'd never seen him have sex with someone. Yet he stripped and tried to have sex with Tim in front of me."

Even when Henley pointed the pistol at Corll and told him to stop, the Candy Man came straight at him, shouting, "Kill me, Wayne. Kill me. You won't do it."

Corll could have rushed Henley, even after being shot, and tackled him. Instead, he passed him—close!—and went into the hallway. Whatever he'd been disturbed about during the weeks leading up to his death on August 8, it was now over. Maybe it was a setup, maybe not. But they'd been heading for a clash. If Corll wanted Henley dead, he'd had the perfect opportunity:

keep him bound, shoot him, and bury him with the others. If he'd wanted to stay alive, he could have cooperated with Henley until he got an advantage over the nervous, wasted kid with the gun. He was much larger and stronger than Henley. He'd always dominated him. Instead, Corll had challenged him and rushed him, knowing that Henley would shoot.

In his own affidavit, Kerley added some details to Henley's account. He said that he and Henley had gone to see another friend on their way to Corll's that night. Once at 2020 Lamar, Henley had fumbled with his key, waking Corll, who opened a window to inquire who was there. He let them in and went back to bed. Kerley had been at the house once before. Then Williams called them, he said, so they went to pick her up. (This account contradicts Henley's statement that he'd brought Williams there to protect Kerley. However, police reports indicate that Henley called Williams, not the other way around.) Kerley described waking up in handcuffs and being carried by Corll into a room. He was ordered to rape Williams, and when he couldn't, Corll molested him and attempted to rape him. At one point, Corll punched him hard with his fist. "I tensed myself up and started begging him not to do it." He heard Henley ask to take Williams out of the room. Then Henley picked up the gun and stood in the doorway. Corll came at him, but Henley sidestepped as he shot, and Corll veered into the hallway. Decades later, Kerley would tell reporters, "Dean stood up and I saw him change into a different person. There was somebody inside him and it wasn't him. It was a spirit from hell."

After Kerley was at the Pasadena Police Station for a while, he remembered some odd things Henley had said. On the way to pick up Williams that morning, Henley had made vague references to getting boys who might not be missed "but [he] never would say completely what he meant." Henley was "asking if I knew of any white young men that were fairly good-looking and could be missed without anyone raising too much of a fuss. Also, he said that if I wasn't his friend, he could get fifteen hundred dollars for me. . . . Then another time, he said he could get three thousand for me. At the time, I was kinda messed up and really wasn't paying much attention to what he was saying, but he said I was the only one who knew about this, and that he better not ever hear of me saying anything to anybody."

Rhonda Williams also made a statement. She was on probation in Harris County for possessing marijuana. She said that Corll had a fiancée. She claimed that Henley, Corll, and Kerley were planning a trip together. They had knocked on her bedroom window that night to help her get out. She related that they all had passed out around 4:00 A.M. She woke up at 7:00 A.M. to Corll kicking her in the ribs. She said Corll told Henley he was going to teach him a lesson for bringing Williams over. When Corll took her in the bedroom and said she was going to be raped, she recalled that Henley just sat there, huffing on a bag. Then he cut her clothes off. Williams described Corll's attempt to rape Tim Kerley, and Kerley's frantic resistance. At one point, Corll left the room and came back, whereupon Henley grabbed the gun and ordered Corll to stop. When it was over, Henley and Kerley both cried before Henley called the police. Williams would learn only later about the murdered boys, including her own missing fiancé, Frank Aguirre.

During Henley's interview at the police station, he again stated that Corll had a boat storage shed in Houston. According to a police report, Corll had "bragged to Henley that he had killed and buried several bodies of young men. Henley professed no personal knowledge of this, just that Corll had told him of it, and he did not know whether to believe it or not." He said he could show them the shed's location.

Detective Sergeant Sidney Smith thought the story was too fantastic to be true. Still, he knew it had to be checked out. That afternoon, he and Mullican took Henley to the Houston Police Department where they conferred with three other detectives and learned about the missing persons reports for boys that Henley had named. They all proceeded to the Silver Bell Street boat stall and discovered the first bodies.

## The Temporary Psychopath

In the aftermath, as Henley faced a trial, he wondered how he could have followed Dean's malevolent lead. Many might say Henley was just a bad seed, born evil, and Corll had merely set him loose. He wondered that, himself. But it's worth considering similarities between his experience and that of other teen accomplices who seemed like fledgling psychopaths.

The development of the condition known as psychopathy is a complex interaction of biology, culture, and environment. The Hare Psychopathy Checklist-Revised (PCL-R) is the most validated diagnostic instrument for assessing it. The scoring derives from the degree of manifestation of each of twenty traits and behaviors, organized around Factor 1, *interpersonal* and *affective* components (traits like grandiose, callous, manipulative, and lacking remorse) and Factor 2, *lifestyle* and *antisocial* behaviors (aggressive, impulsive, irresponsible, parasitic, and sensation-seeking). There are also two types. The "born" psychopath is the *primary type*, showing neurological deficits and emotional blunting but also an ability to hide their indifference with feigned charm and cooperation. They lack fear, guilt, and anxiety and appear to be high functioning. The *secondary type* results from environmental influences like deprivation and abuse. (Some professionals call this a sociopath.) This secondary type shows an early onset of antisocial misconduct, greater substance use, and more mental health problems. They're impulsive and reactive. Both types resist treatment.

The PCL-R was not in existence in 1973, so no one used it to assess the Candy Man or his handymen. In addition, the adult version would not apply to Wayne Henley, who wasn't yet eighteen. At worst, he might have been considered a kid at risk for becoming an adult psychopath. However, another concept applies to accomplices who engage in callous violence only under specific circumstances and for a limited period: the temporary or situational psychopath. It's a subtype of secondary psychopathy. Like Henley, some youths who've been recruited into crime wondered afterward

how they could have done the things they did. They claimed to barely recognize who they'd been. Afterward, they'd described shame and disbelief,
which are not typical of a psychopath. *Without remorse* is the hallmark of
this disorder. That's not how these kids felt.

So they weren't primary psychopaths. Their psychopathic callousness and
aggression had occurred within a limited frame, typically under someone
else's influence. From statements that Corll's accomplices gave to police
during the first two days after Corll's death, it's possible to examine his
influence on his helpers. That is, once he was gone, were they shocked,
ashamed, or disgusted over their acts? Did they try to rectify them? How
did they behave throughout their remaining lives?

David Brooks initially tried to deny that any crimes had been committed
in his presence. Then, when he changed this stance, he seemed to think
that procuring kids who "weren't good kids" wasn't so bad. They wouldn't
be missed. That's how Corll had framed it to him, and he'd accepted it.
He expressed no shock or remorse, only a weak apology, as well as plenty
of blame for his fellow accomplice. In fact, he stated that "it didn't bother
me" to watch boys get murdered because he'd seen it a lot. He'd made no
effort to stop Corll and he showed annoyance on August 9 that Henley
had messed up his life. He described Henley as the primary co-killer, yet
he'd helped Corll to commit or cover up many more murders. Brooks's
father was aghast that his son seemed not to grasp the enormity of what
he'd done. Nevertheless, Brooks had just gotten married and might have
hoped to downplay his role to protect his wife and unborn child.

According to Henley's confession, Brooks had also agreed that they
should do something to prevent Corll from continuing his killing spree.
"Me and David talked about killing Dean so that we could get away from
this whole thing several times." This suggests more humanity in Brooks
than a primary psychopath might show. However, had Henley never been
brought on to the team, there's no evidence that Brooks would have acted
differently than he'd done during the prior year. When he saw Henley

on August 9, he didn't show relief or say, "You did it!" Even married and living apart, Brooks had continued to participate in Corll's activities. He'd left a thirteen-year-old boy to be tortured and killed after sharing a pizza. Although he helped to find some graves on the beach, after Brooks's initial statements he shut down, except for a few interviews with officials. In one case, detectives said he'd been helpful in clarifying events.

In contrast, Henley tried multiple times to get away. He considered going to the police. He tried telling his uncles. He wrote a confession letter to his mother. He tried enlisting in the Navy. Upon his arrest on August 8, he immediately told police about the boat stall burials. Initially, he tried to minimize his involvement, but within a day he decided that the victims' families should know where their kids were. It's likely he thought this would gain him some consideration, but he could have spared himself altogether. He could have killed Corll, saved his friends, and said nothing about the boat stall or the other graves. He'd have been a hero. Kerley and Williams wouldn't have known any differently. He could have walked away with no one ever linking him to the missing boys from the Heights. Instead, he'd wanted to unburden himself and then to provide whatever help he could. He'd urged Brooks to do the same. When officials stopped the search on High Island before they'd recovered all the bodies, Henley had pleaded for them to keep going.

After his arrest and conviction a year later, Henley gave interviews in which he seemed unremorseful, even boastful, but later, he consistently showed contrition. His brief explanation for his initial response was, "Dean had just died. I was still under his influence." Beyond those first interviews, he boasted about his crimes only when his attorney urged him to. He resisted describing them. He even resisted the science that supports giving teen offenders more consideration. "I've been fearful that if I did give myself a pass, I would be taking away from the value of those kids' lives."

Certainly, there are people still aching from his acts today who would denounce any attempt to minimize them, but if we can credit Henley's description of Corll's grooming and Henley's fear of the alleged Syndicate, he's more likely than Brooks to qualify as a temporary psychopath. "The threat was enough," Henley said. "Dean led with open-ended statements, portentious sayings, and ominous rumblings." Henley knows that under Corll's influence he'd repeatedly acted with callous disregard, sometimes even with a sense of fun. "He'd even let it become something of a game. Dean was exciting. Dean made it exciting. It was an adventure. I'm kind of a 'if I'm going to do it, I'm gonna do everything' person." Yet nothing he'd done prior to meeting Corll had forewarned of Henley becoming a cold-blooded killer.

Henley has admitted shame over his part. He's recognized that apologizing doesn't adequately address the harm. He's like other accomplices who committed serious crimes under the direction of a primary offender but afterward were confused. "It's not like he was a role model or did things for me," Henley said. He does understand how he seemed to live two different lives. There's a concept for that that works well for explaining a temporary psychopath.

Psychiatrist Robert Jay Lifton studied Nazi doctors, curious about how they'd performed horrifying experiments on people but could still go home to their families and live normal lives. Lifton theorized that, under certain circumstances, the mutable human personality allows for shifts into different states. He proposed the notion of "doubling" to explain how a part of the self can act as the whole self under specific conditions, according to demands. Within each frame, some parts of the self can be temporarily eclipsed. "Doubling," says Lifton, "is the psychological means by which one invokes the evil potential of the self. That evil is neither inherent in the self nor foreign to it. To live out the doubling and call forth the evil is a moral choice for which one is responsible, whatever the level of consciousness involved."

Similarly, Henley described his doubled life: being with his friends and family contrasted with how he was around Corll. "With Dean, I was withdrawn. Prone to drink. Me, Dean, and David against everyone else. When I saw that I was entangled in Dean's stuff, I gave up and gave in to him. The 'me with Dean' wasn't nice; he also wasn't in control. The 'me with Dean' belonged to Dean. I was wholly owned and operated by Dean. I tried to be callous. I tried to dehumanize the kids, but I was not always able to. If something happened out of the ordinary that broke the routine, then my reaction was more normal. Like when [Cobble] had a heart attack, I wanted to help him. I tried to give him CPR. The Wayne-before-Dean was there."

In psychology, the doubling process is more typically called compartmentalization. It can be adaptive and there are different manifestations. Lifton says that "limited" doublers will kill only under certain permissible circumstances, such as financial or personal need that justifies it; "conflicted" doublers feel guilty but can still proceed; and "enthusiastic" doublers are pleased by their chameleonic skill. Henley once described Corll as a doubled person, probably in the third category: "He was reserved, quiet, enjoyed hisself. The man that did these killings was something else." Henley was mostly a conflicted doubler, although he sometimes showed enthusiasm to please Corll.

The concept of the temporary psychopath allows us to explore the doubling process of accomplices. Few researchers have focused on the nuances of a submissive partner's devolution from ordinary person to killing partner. We know about the *type* of person who's vulnerable, along with their traits, but we haven't yet identified how this moral melt can occur. Cognitive neuroscience offers ideas. Some research features the notion of a shared mentality, and other studies identify the effects of duress that suppress empathy. Combined, these notions provide a framework for understanding how a dominant person can condition a weaker person. Someone who never aspired to harm may be influenced to kill.

FBI Special Agent Robert Hazelwood and Janet Warren, a professor of clinical psychiatric medicine, interviewed twenty women who'd gotten involved with sadistic sexual predators. The four who'd participated in murder had backgrounds that included adverse circumstances, such as physical or sexual abuse. They'd responded to the promise of attention, gifts, and the assurance of being special. The researchers found that the predators first tested their recruits for leverage. Initially, they made the relationship seem normal. Eventually, they introduced a minor crime or a sex act that moved the targets just beyond their comfort zone. Gradually, they isolated their future partners from family and friends. The final touch involved threats, punishment, and the erosion of self-esteem so the women would become entirely dependent on them. The accomplices became so scared of losing the predator's love or approval they found ways to adapt to his deviance. To quell their moral concerns, some had used distancing strategies (doubling) or a belief that his bad acts wouldn't last.

These abettors became dependent on the predator for self-worth, companionship, and life direction. "Most of them had dependent personality disorders and low self-esteem," Hazelwood said. "Those I talked to indicated abhorrence but also complete intimidation and subservience to the male." To acquire something they needed, they had to agree to something they loathed.

In effect, the predators created the conditions for cognitive *synchrony*, i.e., mind melding. Professor of cognitive science Michael Spivey describes the essence of this connection: "A growing body of cognitive science research is showing that when two people cooperate on a shared task, their individual actions get coordinated in a way that is remarkably similar to how one person's limbs get coordinated when he or she performs a solitary task." That is, when an experience is part of a shared awareness between two (or more) people, their thinking patterns merge. A certain fluidity develops that gets the members in sync. They learn what's expected and perform accordingly.

Henley was trained for his role, practicing over and over, and he knew when and how to perform. He improved to avoid Corll's scorn and to invite his approval. "When Dean was happy, I was happy."

Former prison psychologist Al Carlisle described the process thus: "The relationship between a killer and his subservient follower is characterized by strong interdependence. The dominant person needs the follower's total loyalty in order to validate himself. The subservient follower needs the power and authority of the dominant person, so he or she attempts to become that person's shadow and to mirror the dominant person's beliefs and ethics."

Predators can achieve this fusion with reluctant accomplices by alternating methods of control—the Dom/Sub dynamics described in Chapter Two: you're weak and pathetic/you did a good job. "I can tell you that Dean goaded me and pushed me," Henley said. "I needed to do that to be a man. I needed to do that to be part of his group. He would push, push, push. You've got to do this. You have to prove yourself. I don't know how he did it. I wasn't paid, I wasn't rewarded, I wasn't treated special, I didn't rise in power . . . none of the things that you would consider to be recompense for a job well-done. He treated me like I was an underling and a coconspirator. He always made me think that he thought I was weak."

Yet even with synchronic bonding, accomplices can grow distressed over acting contrary to how they view themselves. In retrospect, they can't grasp how they'd been so indifferent to the suffering they'd witnessed or inflicted. In their pre-crime lives, they'd have loathed such behavior.

"Dean had wanted me to chop someone up with a sword, and I wouldn't," Henley recalled. "The torture thing—I couldn't sustain that. David wanted girls; I couldn't do that. I wasn't a very good person, not someone I had ever wished to be. I was a henchman. I thought of myself that way. I did that stuff, and I don't know how I did it. It's not in me to hurt things." To blunt his awareness, Henley drank excessively. "I do not remember my last month or so of being free. I was pretty much into the booze at that point. I drank to pass out. At sixteen, I was a blackout drunk. I could stay drunk, and things didn't affect me. The longer it went on, the drunker I stayed.

Nobody understood that as a teenager to be this drunk this often, it was a sign of something far deeper."

Psychopathy researchers find that adverse childhood experiences like parental conflict and abuse can elicit a reactive callousness that resembles secondary psychopathy. It's not the emotional blunting we see in a "born" or primary psychopath; it's an adaption to a hostile environment. It's *acquired*. It can manifest as rash, impulsive, and antisocial behavior, as well as an absence of empathy. Then, if a criminal partnership during a later stage of their lives produces this same emotional stress, the person might revert to defensive maneuvers adopted during childhood. Callousness gets them through it. When the predator *rewards* these behaviors, the accomplice might become even more insensitive. Whenever Brooks or Henley obeyed Corll, they received a reward. If they didn't obey, they were goaded, scolded, or deprived of his approval. He conditioned them toward indifference.

Brooks's family had treated him as if he were a disposable kid; it wasn't hard for him to recognize others like him to bring back to Corll. He felt inferior, so he'd padded his self-esteem by devaluing others. Henley, too, had a father who'd hurt him and even shot at him (and would later try to kill someone else). He'd had to struggle with how to feel about this man for whom he'd been named. Acting out against others as preparation for standing up to his father seems to have tapped into this unresolved conflict. As mentioned earlier, he'd even told a cop who'd questioned his involvement, "Well, if you had a daddy that shot at you, you might could do some things too."

This callousness develops as a means to operate—even to survive—within a specific set of circumstances. Through a series of minor psychological capitulations, vulnerable individuals retain enough of their former identity to minimize the changes. It's like being in a skiff slowly floating from shore; they think they can always get back . . . until they can't. Even when they recognize their compromise, they can distort or justify it. "When I got involved with Dean Corll, it was like going through the looking glass,"

Henley told an interviewer. "Nothing was real, and nothing was right. . . . It was a weird mesh of conflicting feelings. I was scared of him. I thought he was sick, but at the same time, I didn't want to displease him. I wanted him to be proud of me."

Once free of the contextual pressures, the compliant accomplice's sense of connection and moral behavior can be restored. The coldness that resembles a primary psychopath had worked for a specific purpose, but for those who return to their original moral code, the antisocial behavior stops. It was temporary. It had not defined them. Without the goading influence, they will not continue to behave in this manner.

For a while, as part of his association with Corll, Henley turned into what his father had become—an alcoholic capable of violence. He grew uncharacteristically evasive and unfriendly. By the summer of 1973, he'd become morose and aloof. He let his formerly neat appearance deteriorate. Yet he couldn't break the bonds. "When I was away from Dean, I had misgivings and felt responsible and guilty. It was like at one hand, the person that I was raised to be would start to assert himself, and [then] when I was with Dean, nothing else mattered but Dean."

Until the day Henley killed him.

However, eliminating one sexual predator barely scratched the surface. The sex trafficking organization that Corll had described to make Henley and Brooks do what he wanted was still flourishing. Some key participants were arrested, but the networks were well beyond what local police could manage. The case of John David Norman demonstrates the way a slick individual with leverage and connections can dupe or elude law enforcement. Many kids were still at risk.

# CHAPTER 5

# The Candy Men

## Networks

As previously noted, two days after Henley killed Corll and launched a press frenzy, Charles Brisendine contacted authorities about the Odyssey Foundation. He'd been concerned about being a potential trafficking victim and about a possible connection between the organization's founder, John David Norman, and the Houston Mass Murders. The police search had turned up index cards listing tens of thousands of clients and a newsletter that displayed photos of groomed victims. Norman, arrested, had posted bail and fled. No law enforcement agency pursued him. Dallas police turned over the cache of cards to the US State Department, keeping no copies. These cards were subsequently destroyed.

In December 1973, a police report noted that Mr. Schakel from the US Probation Department had called to report custody of Richard van Payne. This man, Payne, had described being in "the warehouse" in Houston and had "seen photographs of the dead boys in the mass murder." The information was given to Assistant District Attorney Don Lambright, who was preparing his cases against Brooks and Henley. He sent an investigator to speak with Payne. The investigator decided that Payne didn't have enough information to be helpful, although Payne did mention John David Norman as a central figure in Los Angeles and San Diego circles. It became clear only later that Norman was a more significant figure than anyone had realized in 1973.

The *Illinois State Police Intelligence Bulletin #39*, published in 1986, provided a "case study" of Norman. It seems there were other card collections in his possession in various locations, not just those from Dallas that the State Department destroyed. Attorney Steven Becker tried to acquire whatever cards he could find for his research. He failed. It's unclear where the cards ended up, but their existence is not disputed. They're mentioned in several police reports. The *Bulletin* offered some shocking revelations about Norman and his associates.

Following his flight from Dallas in August 1973, Norman went to Chicago to regroup his trafficking operation. He hung out where runaway boys tended to congregate. That October—just two months later—he was arrested and charged with committing five separate acts of "deviate sexual conduct with minors." Released on bail, he left Chicago and drove back to Dallas. Chicago police tracked him down and brought him back. He was finally jailed in Cook County in December. There, he obtained clerical work in the Records Office. He met Phillip Paske, a cross-dresser convicted in a botched robbery that resulted in the victim's death. Aged twenty at the time, Paske had been the lookout. Norman spotted a kindred soul and enlisted Paske's assistance. (Within the accomplice categories from Chapter 2, Paske would be considered an enthusiastic coequal.) They set up an operation from behind bars, enabled by guards who turned a blind eye.

In a letter to a friend, Norman wrote, "There were a lot of things I did that the guards noticed and allowed! Among them were the stairwell conferences. . . . I worked up front in the Records Office. . . . Next door to the

Records Office was the Attorney Room. When an inmate was called to see his lawyer . . . he had to ring a bell to summon an officer from the Records Office to admit him to the Attorney Room. Every Friday and Saturday night, I was alone in the place with just one officer, a black cop named Craig who was a nice guy but not the world's smartest. I'd once put myself at some risk to prevent Craig from making a mistake that would have cost him his job, so as far as he was concerned, I could do whatever I wanted. With his knowledge, when things got slow—there wasn't that much to do anyway on weekend nights—I might call E-2, the teenage tier, or any other where there was a guy who interested me, with the instruction, 'Drop inmate so-and-so for a conference with his attorney.' "

Despite Norman having done illegal business in Dallas and Houston for years, the Dallas County District Attorney dismissed all charges against him. The record of this dismissal exists, but no lawyers could be located for comment.

During this period, Norman and Paske worked up a client list of five thousand and replaced the Odyssey Foundation with the Delta Project. In February 1976, Paske's father bailed both out of jail. Norman remained in Chicago to await the resolution of his case.

But things had heated up in Houston on Dean Corll's potential association with trafficking networks. During a search for a stolen bicycle in 1975, a tip led Houston Police to a warehouse (probably the one they'd been tipped about in 1973) with large stores of pornography, including fifteen thousand color slides of boys in homosexual acts, more than one thousand magazines and paperback books, and thousands of reels of film. They arrested Roy Ames, a well-known blues music producer whose name had been on a card in Corll's wallet. A news article reported that eleven of Corll's victims appeared in Ames's extensive pornography collection. (No one was named, but author Barbara Gibson indicates that the Waldrop boys' father had named Ames to police as a person they knew.)

These photos showed up again in reports about a raid in 1976 on a sex ring in California. Corll had hinted to Brooks that he'd been involved in a murder in California, but Brooks didn't know the details. A Polaroid photo of Billy Lawrence had turned up in Corll's house. So Corll either had this type of camera or he had a connection with someone who'd come and take the photos. Henley said he didn't know of Corll taking such photos and Brooks mentioned no such activity. Yet soon police would find a photo in a porn magazine that resembled Billy Lawrence. His father would deny that it was his son, but the police report concludes that it is Billy Lawrence. Somehow, Corll had a photo of a captive who never left his house, and this same boy was featured in a porn magazine.

Corll had spent time alone with Billy, and Corll had also picked up and killed boys on his own. It's possible that Corll himself took and sold the photos that showed up in the pornographic literature or that he had someone like porn producer Roy Ames involved. The Houston PD investigators had spoken with a man named Dale Ahern, who'd shown them porn magazines that featured photos he'd said were some of Corll's victims and made the inference that Corll and Ames were connected. (This was probably the source for the news report.) Even though Houston PD dismissed or, worse yet, neglected this lead, these items strongly suggest that Corll had ties to a distribution network.

From April to November 1976, Norman and Paske operated the Delta Project from 707 West Wrightwood near a male hustling area of Chicago's North Side. The Delta Project established "Delta Dorms," or dormitories for boys operated by "dons" who sexually exploited the residents.

Then there was John Wayne Gacy, who was raping, torturing, and killing boys and young men during the 1970s in the Chicagoland area. Like Corll, he used a handcuff trick, possibly inspired by the news accounts about the Houston Mass Murders. He also relied on several young employees to dig holes in the crawl space beneath his house, where he'd deposit over two dozen bodies.

At some point, Paske worked for Gacy's construction firm, PDM Contractors, at the behest of Gacy's teen employees, David Cram and Michael Rossi (confirmed in Gacy's records). Paske might have been involved in some of the abuse Gacy inflicted. In his book *29 Below*, survivor Jeffrey Rignall describes a young man who resembled Paske at the Gacy home during his torture session. Gacy did know Paske. A 1992 transcript of an interview with Gacy by former FBI Supervisory Special Agent Robert Ressler has Gacy describing Paske as a dangerous person, alleging that he would "pimp girls, boys, for sex or movies." During the period when Paske and Norman were planted in Chicago, Gacy murdered fourteen of his thirty-three known victims.

Police documents report that after Gacy's arrest, he named Michael Rossi and David Cram as active accomplices. Paske showed up in handwritten notes from Gacy prosecutor Terry Sullivan as someone associated with the case, but there is no documentation of Paske providing an interview or testimony, as Rossi and Cram did. In a 2012 interview, the now deceased Chief of Des Plaines PD Joe Kozenczak acknowledged knowing about Paske but would say only that he "was on the periphery" of the case. A call from Tracy Ullman to Paske's brother, Tim, asking for further information was met by a death threat if she ever called again.

During interviews with various investigators, Gacy alluded to the fact that Norman had been filming the sexual assault and murder of boys—making snuff films—and two of Gacy's victims were last seen near Norman's home. Gacy told investigators to look through Norman's confiscated films to see if any of Gacy's victims appeared in them. (Pedophiles often had lines of communication that linked them, even if they'd never met.) Although Rossi and Cram were not fully investigated, suspicions remain even today about their involvement. Given what had happened in Houston earlier that same decade with Corll's teenage accomplices, it seems odd that the Chicago PD paid scant attention to Gacy's helpers. Rossi and

Cram admitted to spreading lime and digging many of the holes in Gacy's fetid crawl space. "Improved drainage" hardly explained this job.

Through the years-long investigative work of retired Chicago Police Detective William Dorsch, attorney Steven Becker, and journalists Alison True and Tracy Ullman, a body of documents was assembled that suggested that Gacy's "deep ties to Mayor Richard J. Daley's Democratic political machine in Chicago" helped to protect him through six felonious sexual assaults that were ultimately dismissed and from claims in at least two of his victims' missing persons reports that he was responsible for their disappearances. Overwhelming evidence of Gacy's crimes eventually skewered him. Any time he tried discussing the involvement of others, both the prosecution and defense minimized their role.

Two years before Gacy's murders were revealed, Norman faced the music from his 1973 charges for deviate sexual conduct. On November 30, 1976, he was sentenced to four years in prison. On January 19, 1977, a teenager who'd been instrumental in helping to get this conviction was murdered while walking home from work. Local police and the FBI suspected Norman's involvement in this incident but couldn't prove it. Since Norman and Gacy's cohort seemed to be intertwined, the FBI repeatedly interviewed Gacy to get information.

Then in 1977, a man with the unlikely name of Guy Strait was sentenced to a lengthy prison term in Rockford, Illinois, for using children in pornography. His partner, Bill Byars, heir to the Humble Oil fortune, fled to Italy. The two had produced vast amounts of pornographic films and magazines. To get information about them relevant to Texas crimes, the Houston police tried to make a deal with Roy Ames, but he laughed and told them his operation would run just as well while he was in prison. He wasn't willing to make a deal, so he received a ten-year sentence to a federal prison.

The *Chicago Tribune* ran a series in May 1977, naming the Delta Project and Norman and Paske as significant players in a major child exploitation ring. It linked operations in Los Angeles, Dallas, and Chicago. Despite the alarm the paper tried to raise, Norman was paroled once more on October 13, 1977. He resumed his sex trafficking operation. The following June, Norman was rearrested in Chicago, as police once again confiscated his client list. According to the Protection of Children Against Sexual Exploitation hearings before the Senate Subcommittee to Investigate Juvenile Delinquency on May 27, 1977, "20,000 pink index cards bear the names of customers in every state and some foreign countries. They list their sexual preferences in young boys."

Sergeant Ronald Kelly, head of the Chicago Police Department's Area 6 Youth Division, had been privy to information from Dallas officials about Norman's association with the Houston murders. Buried near the end of the 1977 report, on page 434, it says, "Dallas police told Sgt. Ronald Kelly, Head of the Area 6 youth division, that they have information associating Norman with the ring that helped transport to Texas the 27 boys murdered in Houston in 1973 in a widely publicized sex and sadism case. That case involved Dean Corll." This contrasts with police refutations from the short-lived 1973 investigation that Norman was involved. As of 2023, Dallas Police Department FOIA requests for anything related to Norman have gone unfilled.

As for Sergeant Ronald Kelly, his response to reporters regarding the information about Norman in the 1977 senatorial report was noncommittal: "We intend to go through the whole file and find out just who subscribes to child sex publications. Since Norman's release from Pontiac [state prison] last fall, he hasn't wasted any time. Norman has now reestablished his old 'Delta Project' operation under new names 'Creative Corps' and 'M C (Male Call) Publications.'" It seems that law enforcement failed time and time again to hold Norman responsible.

By December of 1978, Kelly was under the gun regarding the multiple young victims being removed from under Gacy's house. Like the situation in Houston, police had told the frantic parents of the missing boys and young men that they were runaways. No investigations had been launched until victim Rob Piest disappeared, despite Gacy being a central figure in two of the earlier reports. Now that he had a crawl space full of decomposing bodies, Kelly could make only hollow excuses.

Around this time, police in San Francisco reportedly seized an enormous file of index cards belonging to Norman. Thirty thousand of his clients—men who wanted boys—were based in California. (Corll had hinted about such an operation.) The FBI report on this raid lists Norman's fifteen aliases and his sexual offenses in California (e.g., indecent liberties with a child, contributing to the delinquency of a child). However, the report inexplicably makes no mention of incidents in Texas. Clearly, Norman was a prolific offender, with international contacts and a financially successful trafficking business. Yet the report shows that the FBI concluded that the case had no "investigative merit." Due to the cost of copying the high volume of records in the Norman collection, the agency had declined to do so. It was a startling concession.

Norman left Chicago in September 1980 for Denver. Across the country, he was continually arrested and rearrested, getting brief stints for sex crimes against kids, until he landed at his final destination in San Diego, California. There, he lived under supervision as an "elderly sex offender." When he brazenly violated parole for slipping a note to a teenage grocery worker, he was ordered to a state hospital, where he'd eventually die.

Despite Norman's death, there's no reason to believe that the ubiquitous and profitable trafficking ring had been terminated. As the "Apex Predator," Norman had been the ultimate Candy Man. He'd formed more than thirty organizations and developed twenty-five different publications devoted to sexually exploiting teenage boys. The Lavender Network based in San Diego is the last known organization Norman headed and that was in 1995. Thus, for forty years, Norman operated almost continuously. Even when he was in prison, his enterprises carried on and his client lists were continually confiscated, having a range of names from between five thousand and one hundred thousand men, as reported in various newspapers and in Clifford Linedecker's seminal book, *Children in Chains.*

Norman had developed what was ranked in 1977 in the *Chicago Tribune* as a "multi-million-dollar business"—and that's in 1970s dollars. Today, it would amount to billions. He was making enough money to have the IRS initiate an investigation for failure to pay taxes. The US Postal Inspector also opened up an investigation involving his illicit mail-order businesses. When Tracy Ullman filed a FOIA for documents from both investigations in 2022, the application was denied because Norman had a son: sharing the documents would be an invasion of this man's privacy.

In the 1977 *Chicago Tribune* article, Norman's ring was shown to be connected by membership to a New Orleans Boy Scout troop. As recently as 2019, a legal team called "Abused in Scouting" was representing eight hundred victims of three hundred fifty known pedophile scout leaders. In June 1977, members of Norman's ring were revealed as sponsors of a Franklin, Tennessee, nonprofit called Boys Farm, meant to help under-privileged boys experience the countryside under the tutelage of a Reverend Bud Vermilye. Instead, Vermilye was exploiting them for pedophile sex and pornography. When police raided the place, they found a list of sponsors and an eye-popping amount of pornography, as well as links to other pseudo-churches and educational foundations for boys.

Over the decades, other successful traffickers have followed a similar pattern, using procurers as go-betweens. The more powerful and wealthy the clients and sponsors are, the more buffered they are with political favors, protections, bribes, and mobility. Norman could have been successful only with such complicity. We can see examples of similar situations today. The Jeffrey Epstein/Ghislaine Maxwell trafficking case is an example.

In September 2022, *New York Times* journalist Amanda Taub reported on many institutions that had deflected or protected sexual abuse: "Over just

the past few months, multiple stories have broken about powerful or prestigious organizations that tolerated or concealed serious abuse for years. This
week [August 2022], for instance, Herlufsholm, an elite Danish boarding
school that was attended by Prince Christian of Denmark until his parents
pulled him out . . . has been engulfed in a bullying and abuse scandal. In
August, an Associated Press investigation found that the Church of Jesus
Christ of Latter-day Saints' abuse hotline diverted complaints of child
abuse away from law enforcement, leaving some children in dangerous or
abusive situations for years. [In May 2022], an independent investigation
found that the Southern Baptist Convention had covered up and enabled
sexual assaults and other abuse of parishioners." Taub adds that this is
not new and that "abuse scandals are just one example of a much broader
human resistance to self-police wrongdoing within our own groups and
communities."

Per a 2018 study of fifty thousand kids in the US, Europe, and Asia
published in *The Journal of Adolescent Health*, one in five American kids aged
nine to seventeen reported unwanted sexual solicitation on the internet.
The predators usually urged face-to-face contact. Cell phone apps have
only increased this risk. In the US, 15 percent of children aged twelve to
seventeen admitted to receiving sexually suggestive texts or pictures from
strangers.

How John David Norman and his ring carried on for so long without
law enforcement effectively shutting it down shows just how persistent it
was. A September 2019 *New York Times* article stated that "tech companies
reported over 45 million online photos and videos of children being sexually
abused—more than double what they found the previous year." Forty-five
million images aren't generated overnight.

Whether or not Dean Corll had a significant link to Norman's Dallas
operation or perhaps just knew some Houston associates like Roy Ames,
he exploited its existence for his own benefit. David Brooks and Wayne
Henley both attested to this.

## The Predator's Perspective

Corll's modus operandi mirrors other criminal enterprises that relied on adolescent complicity. What Henley describes is not unique. Here's an example from a century earlier:

A botched burglary revealed an intellectually gifted killer who'd spotted and groomed several accomplices. The incident occurred in Binghamton, New York, on July 5, 1870. Three men broke into the Halbert brothers' dry goods store and shot the night guard. There was a scuffle. Two of the burglars ran to the river to cross it and escape, but they drowned. The surviving burglar was caught and jailed. A resident recognized him as Edward Rulloff, who was suspected of killing his wife and child. In Rulloff's home was evidence that he'd planned the burglary. One of the accomplices was Albert Jarvis, the son of a jailer who'd worked where Rulloff had been incarcerated more than a decade earlier. No one was surprised that Albert had been recruited. Rulloff had a gift for persuasion and Albert had been vulnerable.

Rulloff had long sought to be famous. He'd written what he claimed was the most important book for humankind, *Method in the Formation of Language.* He claimed to have taught himself multiple languages in order to detect the origin of all thinking and communication. He'd been a teacher, a lawyer, and an inventor. He impressed people. When financial success eluded him, he became a thief, which earned him some prison time. In 1843, he married and had a child. Mysteriously, both disappeared. Rulloff was charged with murder, but the bodies were never found, so he was convicted of abduction. He received a ten-year sentence in Auburn Prison.

While serving his time, Rulloff tutored local boys. Sixteen-year-old Albert Jarvis was the son of the county undersheriff and jailer, Jacob Jarvis, rumored to be abusive. Rulloff spotted an advantage. The boy needed a father figure and Rulloff needed a helper. He taught Albert Latin and German, spending many hours with him. He saw that the kid was bright but "impulsive and rash." Perfect. Rulloff persuaded Albert to do small errands for him, lavishing him with praise. His parents noticed the growing intimacy, so to thwart potential intervention, Rulloff charmed Albert's mother. When Rulloff escaped in 1857, it was clear he'd had inside help. Albert Jarvis was indicted for assisting and granted release on bail. Jacob Jarvis was fired. Rulloff was tracked down, but they had no evidence to hold him. He left the area. Jarvis was angry at Rulloff for abandoning him. To heal the rift, Rulloff sent him money, and they reconnected. Another young accomplice, Billy Dexter, joined them. With two young accomplices who admired him, Rulloff launched the caper that ended their lives. He'd spotted young men vulnerable to his assurances and manipulations. Already book-smart, he was also street-smart about crime and partners. He knew how to manipulate their emotions.

During the 1980s, developmental psychologist Howard Gardner presented the concept of multiple intelligences. He dismissed the assumption that intelligence was a unitary, cognitively based IQ. Artists, musicians, shamans, and craftspeople demonstrated other forms of intelligence, so Gardner devised a definition: "An intelligence is the ability to solve problems, or to create products, that are valued within one or more cultural settings."

This includes predators. "Street-smart" offenders have developed ways to solve problems that are valued in their milieu. Some have been quite clever, inventing products or devising innovative methods. For example, when Corll needed to control victims while he was at work or in bed, he created the restraint board. Like Rulloff, he learned to use charm to allay suspicion or to get what he wanted. Even those predators who might do poorly on a standard IQ test can master the art of manipulation. Corll was no great genius, but he was a prolific and successful predator.

For well over a century, the joint disciplines of psychology, psychiatry, and criminology have sought ways to penetrate criminal minds like Corll's. Mental health professionals use psychological assessments to try to answer specific questions about a subject in order to diagnose and make treatment decisions. Often these tests measure strengths and weaknesses with respect to various traits. Professionals involved in forensic cases use a standard group of assessment instruments, such as an IQ test, the Psychopathy Checklist-Revised, and a personality scale like the Minnesota Multiphasic Personality Inventory-3. They might also consider what's commonly called emotional intelligence, or EQ—the ability to understand, use, and manage one's own emotions to relieve stress, empathize with others, overcome challenges, and defuse conflict.

No one has yet created an assessment for criminal intelligence, or a C-IQ. We would want to be able to measure proficiency in the ability to compartmentalize, to assess success with victims or accomplices, to create a ruse, to normalize or rationalize criminal acts, to elude detection, and to maintain secrecy. Predatory maneuvers are typically cold-blooded, calculated, and highly adaptable.

Successful offenders like John David Norman and others described here have learned effective ways to deflect people from discovering their secrets. They can speak convincingly about socially approved mores of right and wrong while actively violating them. Corll passed himself off as a big brother to the same boys he wanted to rape and kill. Although there is no record of how Corll felt, no one close to him reported any expression of remorse aside from his wan expression of sadness that he had to kill boys to eliminate them as witnesses. "He fell in love with them," Henley said. "He'd keep them for days." Yet, once murdered, they were just objects to be wrapped, transported, buried, and forgotten.

To better grasp predatory skills, one area of research we can tap involves a study of how magicians exploit perceptual processing. They know that humans are hardwired to focus on specific things, which tunes out background. Thus, the perceptual field can be hijacked to manipulate the spotlight of focus, or the place where we look. There are two basic types of attention. Voluntary attention is "top-down," initiated by us. We *decide* to notice something. Outside stimuli trigger "bottom-up" focus to draw our attention. Magicians exploit the latter. They form a context to direct us;

once they have us, they maintain control with motion, lighting, novelty, surprise, and a stream of patter. Our focus follows what they're doing. Then, within the perceptual shadows, they perform the trick, but we don't process it because our attention is elsewhere. Studies that tracked eye movement during a magician's trick indicate that the eye does see what they're doing on the periphery (outside the point of focus), but the brain is too attentive to the spotlight to process what's in the shadows.

In addition, we are subject to a base-rate bias: When we grow used to a certain scenario, we anticipate how it will work, so our brain relaxes. It lets us see what we expect to see, even if the thing we expect does not actually occur. This cognitive condition leaves us vulnerable.

Smart predators similarly use expectation, deflection, misdirection, and misinformation to provide their cover. Usually, it's a persona of charm, influence, and success that will engender trust. Like magicians, they use whatever works to fool the brain.

Some offenders also display a perplexing resilience, called narcissistic immunity. They have a talent for rebounding from setbacks because they're certain of their invulnerability—even when the evidence is against them. Some might feel protected because they hold secrets about those who decide their fate. It's a sense of immunity that grows from a belief about one's special destiny. They can't be caught. Or, if caught, they won't be held. Or, if held, it won't take long to get free. This seemed to be the case with John David Norman. Each time he got out of prison or escaped the law, his sense of immunity increased. This boldness hones the vigilance that predators need to successfully connect with accomplices.

## Mur-*dar*

According to Brooks, Dean Corll had sexual contact with multiple teenage boys, paying them cash. He might have had procurers other than Brooks and Henley, but law enforcement focused only on these two. We know from Brooks's statement that he was easy to bait. Insecure, teased, and lacking in family attachment, he hungered for the kind of attention Corll conferred. Even witnessing Corll naked, assaulting two boys that he later admitted killing failed to give Brooks second thoughts. He adjusted to the idea that Corll was picking off kids who weren't much good to anyone. He'd felt like a piece of discarded rubbish himself. Brooks and Henley both had engaged in minor theft and using illegal drugs, but neither had committed a major crime. Yet both had struck Corll as good candidates to be his apprentices. It's bold to believe one can twist a young mind toward murder, but Corll had his tricks. Most involved bait learned from keen observation. He knew what to look for and how to leverage it.

"I thought I had to do it to survive," Henley said. "I would not have done it on my own. He [Corll] wanted me to learn how to kill my dad. He also wanted me to learn that I didn't have to let people scare me. I didn't have to accept being bullied. But he partially failed with me. He did not fail with David, because David was never going to actively turn against Dean. He never did."

In *Serial Murderers and Their Victims*, criminologist Eric Hickey analyzed trends for more than five hundred serial killers from the nineteenth century through 2011. About 15 to 20 percent persuade someone to assist them. Sometimes, it's because they've found a kindred soul. For example, Roy Norris met Lawrence Bittaker in prison. They discovered a common preference for sadistic sexual torture. Once released, they bought a van in Los Angeles, California, dubbed it the "Murder Mac," and trolled for females. They grabbed a teenager and raped her before strangling her with a coat hanger. The next victim received an ice pick through the brain. This team tortured and killed three more girls before they were caught.

Most teams, Hickey found, involve just two offenders. Male participants outnumbered females by three to one, and just over one-third of teams in the study were male/female. "Without exception," Hickey stated, "every group of offenders had one person who psychologically maintained control."

The predator's goal is to inspire complete devotion and loyalty, pre-emptively shifting the accomplice's potential ambivalence in their favor. Among the accomplices Hickey interviewed was "Sunset Strip Killer" Carol Bundy, who teamed up with Douglas Clark. He'd conditioned her toward violence with several depraved acts, and eventually she'd committed murder on her own.

In 1980, Clark spotted Bundy in a bar. He was looking for a female whom he could persuade to invite him into her home. Having polished his ability to identify easy marks, Clark zeroed in on the overweight, bespectacled woman who'd recently been jilted. She was drinking and she looked depressed. He went over to her. His charming manner enthralled her. As Clark expected, Bundy soon invited him to move in. According to Bundy's recollection, Clark had fantasized about sexual murder before they met, and he sought a partner. His first step was to encourage her to reveal her darkest sexual fantasies. Once she'd crossed that line, Clark described his fantasy of grabbing young girls to torture and turn into sex slaves. To please him, Bundy lured an eleven-year-old girl from the neighborhood for his sexual enjoyment, sometimes taking pictures and sometimes joining them.

Clark also told Bundy about murders he'd committed and said he wanted Bundy to shoot a prostitute while he was having oral sex with the woman, so he could have the experience of her dying with her mouth on him. Bundy was intrigued. She later said she had wanted to be more intimate with the man she now loved. She thought this meant helping him to fulfill his fantasy. They tried this deviant maneuver with sex worker Exxie Wilson, but it went badly. They killed and beheaded Wilson, keeping the head in a freezer so Clark could take it out to use for his pleasure. Bundy applied the makeup.

Eventually, Bundy killed Jack Murray, a man with whom she'd once had an affair, supposedly to silence him after she'd confided what she was doing. She stabbed and shot him. When she worried that the bullets she'd used would hold evidence against her, she beheaded him and took the head with her. His body was quickly found. Thus began the unraveling of this team. Bundy got nervous and told police where Clark had hidden murder weapons. Both were arrested and charged with six counts of murder—five females and one male. Bundy got life in prison and Clark received six death sentences.

Although Clark insisted that Bundy was the mastermind, Hickey had found her to be "passive, a follower" who'd killed to prove her devotion to Clark. "He'd exploited her psychological trauma," Hickey concluded, "and worked on her, little by little."

This same dynamic occurs when females take the lead. In November 2013 in Pennsylvania, Miranda Barbour, nineteen, wanted to kill someone with her new husband, Elytte. She'd tested him for his tolerance by describing different murder scenarios and had found him eager to please her. Barbour placed a Craigslist ad for "companionship," to which Troy LeFerrara responded. Elytte hid under a blanket in the back seat as Miranda picked up their victim. At her signal, Elytte placed a cord around LeFerrara's throat while Miranda repeatedly stabbed him. They dumped him, cleaned the van, and went to a strip club to celebrate Elytte's twenty-second birthday. Police traced their phone call to the victim back to them and Elytte confessed that they had just wanted to murder someone together. Later, he would say, "I wish I knew what was running through my head that night. . . . I regret taking this man from his home. . . . I know I would not have done this."

Researchers have found that killing teams typically follow a common pattern: Two people so strongly resonate with each other that one feels safe enough to describe a violent fantasy. He or she then manipulates the listener to consider acting it out. Studies show that this weaker partner is likely to suffer from low intellect, youth, or a schizotypal personality disorder—they're malleable and/or unstable. The dominant person socially isolates them, getting them dependent before reshaping their moral norms.

Predators develop a sixth sense for the type of person they can successfully recruit. They're always vigilant for an opportunity to identify someone to seduce. Contextual cues assist with targeting. The more they watch, the better they get.

In sports psychology, this is called "the quiet eye." It's an enhanced visual perception that forms from a heightened focus that blocks distractions. It engages as stress levels rise to reduce mistakes. Skilled athletes can concentrate directly on a ball for longer periods than can inexperienced athletes. Their thinking processes slow down to absorb the most relevant information for an optimal response. A steady fixation just prior to the critical maneuver is the key to success. Predators, too, operate with such care.

"I'm always amazed at how these people vector in on each other," said former FBI Supervisory Special Agent Gregg McCrary about team killers. "There's radar, gaydar, and maybe *mur-dar.*"

McCrary, once a member of the Behavioral Analysis Unit, runs Behavioral Criminology International and coauthored *The Unknown Darkness: Profiling the Predators among Us.* He's seen this sinister sixth sense himself. He profiled a series of rapes and murders in Toronto, Canada, during the early 1990s. Police eventually arrested Karla Homolka and Paul Bernardo. Homolka had killed her younger sister while offering the girl, unconscious, to Bernardo for rape. Soon, they tortured and murdered two other girls. When police closed in, Homolka claimed she was a battered wife and reluctant accomplice. She had the bruises to prove it. Her love for Bernardo, she said, had made her vulnerable. Just seventeen when she met him, Homolka allowed Bernardo to do whatever he desired to her, and his sexual demands became increasingly more brutal. Nevertheless, her love notes had urged him to continue. Then her story fell apart. Incriminating videotapes revealed Homolka's involvement in the abduction of victim Kristen French. In addition, it was clear that she'd helped to murder her sister. On one videotape, Homolka told Bernardo she wanted to get more young virgins for him. She'd been more in sync with Bernardo than she'd admitted.

McCrary explained how mur-dar works: "It's like when normal people meet. You decide whether you're going to get along, but with these couples it takes a dark turn. They sense the excitement of a kindred spirit. It becomes electric."

Lone killers become teams when dominant offenders who yearn to share a twisted fantasy acquire a follower. "The process is exploratory," McCrary added. "The predator is like a shark waiting to see who will swim by and take the bait. If the other person reacts badly, it's easy to shrug off as a joke. When he finds the one who responds the way he's hoping, he thinks, 'This is someone who can do this with me.' He might say, 'What would you think if I were a rapist?' If she thinks it's cool, he can take the next step."

Corll bribed Brooks with a car, a home, and money; he tested Henley with a joke, then lured him with money for burglary. He also used his supposed association with a dangerous network of sex traffickers to ensure loyalty. The predator figures out how to switch on an "inner green light" that goads and permits people to act.

The story of the "Moors Murderers" during the 1960s in England demonstrates how a predator's mur-dar succeeded . . . and then failed. At age eighteen, Myra Hindley was a seemingly ordinary girl with a desire for a more exciting life than what she observed around her in the lower middle-class. She met Ian Brady at work. Slightly older, he seemed hip—the kind of man who could take her places. Hindley placed herself in Brady's path. She carried stacks of books to pretend to be intellectual. Finally, he noticed. They started dating. Then he began to tell her his ideas about superior people who could transcend social morality. Hindley's mind was fertile ground. She grew certain that Brady was her *only* route to an extraordinary life, so she accepted his increasingly rough sexual demands. Soon, Brady broached the idea of proving their superiority by killing someone. He pretended this was a philosophical experiment but in fact it would feed his sexual fantasies of wanting to sexually assault a child.

Hindley wasn't sure he meant this. Wanting to please him, she lured a child for Brady to rape and kill out on the Moors near Manchester, England. He assured her she'd done well. Then he insisted she do it again. He even made the acts fun by framing each incident with its own song. Then the couple would have sex, sometimes on top of the graves of their victims. Hindley had never considered doing a criminal act, let alone something this serious, yet she kept doing what Brady wanted. She would later say that her ability to detach had first developed in an abusive home growing up. Desperately in love with Brady, she'd decided that it was better to do as he wished than to lose him. She used the same method of detachment during a murder.

Then Brady wanted a third partner. Myra's sister had married David Smith, then seventeen. Brady's mur-dar sense identified Smith as an insecure person who would go along with anything. Smith had a record for assault and breaking into houses. Brady invited the newlyweds for drinks. He asked Smith about his arrest record. Smith was happy to have Brady's attention, along with the free booze. Over the course of a year, Brady worked him, getting him to consider Brady a mentor. Brady eventually asked Smith whether he thought he could kill someone (like Corll had asked Henley). Smith wasn't sure how to respond, but Brady seemed to think he was ready for the next step.

One morning, Hindley invited Smith over. She and Brady had picked up seventeen-year-old Edward Evans at a train station. Smith arrived. To his shock, Brady picked up an axe and hit Evans in the head over and over, killing him. Brady got a cord to strangle him. Then he wanted Smith to help carry and hide the body. Smith, afraid for his own life, complied. Once he got away, he called the police to describe what he'd witnessed.

Officers went to Brady's home and found the victim's body in an upstairs room. Brady had been so certain about Smith's compliance he'd been unprepared. The officers arrested him and Hindley. Evidence showed their involvement with five child murders, with victims aged ten to seventeen. Brady's mur-dar instinct had worked with Hindley because she'd been in love before he'd drawn her into murder. It had failed with Smith. He'd been young and impressionable, but he hadn't been ready for the horror show to which he'd been exposed. Brady had misjudged him.

## Matches Made in Hell

Neuropsychologist Kent Kiehl, executive science officer of the nonprofit Mind Research Network and author of *The Psychopath Whisperer: The Science of Those without Conscience*, evaluated Christopher Gribble after his involvement in a horrific crime. In 2009 in New Hampshire, Gribble, then seventeen, had followed Steven Spader and two others into the home of Kimberly Cates.

Spader was a high school dropout who'd formed a club he called "The Disciples of Destruction." He told his three recruits that the home invasion was to be a rite of initiation for club members. Inside the home, Spader hacked Cates to death with a machete while Gribble stabbed her eleven-year-old daughter, Jaimie. The other two young men, shocked and sickened, stood by. Jaimie played dead, which allowed her to survive and get help. The young men were arrested the following day.

Gribble told police he thought the experience was "cool." His only regret was that the girl had survived. "I thought I would feel bad," Gribble said. "I'm almost sorry to say I don't. I thought I would at least puke or something. I just felt nothing." He was chatty and upbeat as he led investigators to where he and Spader had buried the weapons.

Gribble's public defender asked Kiehl to examine him. Kiehl learned from Gribble that a psychologist had erroneously used the MMPI-2 personality inventory to diagnose him as a psychopath. "So Gribble had decided to *be* psychopathic," Kiehl relates, "like a self-fulfilling prophecy."

After performing his own evaluation, Kiehl found the homeschooled Gribble to have led a sheltered life in a devoutly Mormon household. He was socially awkward, with a low IQ. "It was like talking with a ten-year-old. He had limited social experiences, like he'd lived inside a cubicle. He had conflicts with his mother, and he talked about killing her but had never laid a hand on her. This is unusual restraint for a kid with psychopathic traits."

In other areas of his life, Gribble showed no psychopathic tendencies. "There was no glibness," said Kiehl, "no grandiosity, no history of lying, no fearlessness. There was no evidence of leeching off others. He was not impulsive or irresponsible."

It seemed likely to Kiehl that Spader, with his disturbed criminality, had influenced the suggestible, immature Gribble into accepting an identity based only on a psychologist's error. "My clinical sense is that this kid just got with the wrong crowd. He had a fragile mind. You can plant an idea into a fragile mind and get them to do anything. His belief that he's a psychopath is delusional."

Spader, on the other hand, referred to himself as the "most sick and twisted person you'll ever meet." He considered remorse an unnecessary weakness. He wrote detailed descriptions to cellmates about how he had "whacked the mother 36 times and could see brains and lots of blood and her eyeball hanging out of its socket." Gribble, a kid with no propensity to violence, had come under his influence.

## The Teenage Brain

When Brooks and Henley came under Corll's influence, they were kids. Research on adolescent brain development shows that the executive part of the brain, the frontal cortex, is immature. It develops more slowly than the rest. Thus, adolescents take longer to make mindful decisions that evaluate consequences. They consider fewer options for how to act and they react more emotionally. They're also vulnerable to peer pressure and the need to be socially affiliated.

The stage of life between ages twelve and twenty is a time of experimentation, exploration, exaggerated passions, feelings of invincibility, the emergence of creativity, and the onset of certain serious mental illnesses. "Adolescence," writes Stanford professor of biology and neurology Robert Sapolsky, "is the time of life when someone is most likely to join a cult, kill, be killed, invent an art form, help overthrow a dictator, ethnically cleanse a village, care for the needy, transform physics, adopt a hideous fashion style, commit to God, and be convinced that all the forces of history have converged to make this moment the most consequential ever."

Adolescents' personality and sense of identity is in flux. It can be a turbulent time for some individuals, when decisions are made in ignorance of their potential life-changing impacts. Their perspective on their own lives is limited, as is their ability to see things from another's point of view. Not quite infantile, they're still relatively self-absorbed and present-focused. It can be difficult for older people to grasp this.

In the prefrontal cortex, where sensible decisions get made and impulsive actions are inhibited, the volume of gray matter is greater in teenage brains than it is in the fully adult brain. As the person ages, connections among their neurons will be pruned according to the habits they develop. The limbic system, the seat of emotionality, motivates action faster in the teenage brain than it motivates planning, so emotions dominate decisions. The amygdala, which manages strong emotions like fear and anger, reacts with lightning speed. In addition, reward is magnified. Big rewards produce significantly larger responses. Small rewards disappoint.

When a decision involves risk, the immature frontal cortex cannot provide a full risk assessment. Researcher Sarah-Jayne Blakemore at University College in London ran an experiment in which she asked test subjects to estimate the likelihood of some event happening to them. In the next stage, they were told the actual chances and then tested for any shift in their ideas. Adolescents adjusted their estimations as well as adults, but for an event that might impact them negatively, like texting while driving, they failed to fully process the information. They understood the consequences, but they didn't think the risk related to them, personally. Thus, when kids take risks, they don't feel threatened. They think they'll be fine.

Teens are also highly vulnerable to peer pressure, especially when it's something dangerous, rebellious, harmful, or criminal. They feel an urgent need to belong and to have a social identity. They don't want to miss out. Brain scan studies reveal that peer influence heightens the dopamine rush in the limbic system while depressing frontal cortical activity: kids think less, feel more. Most importantly, they gravitate toward dramatic emotion-provoking events. Delayed gratification is not their style.

"In an adult," Sapolsky says, "the frontal cortex steadies the activity of parts of the limbic system, a brain region involved in emotion; in contrast, in the teenage brain, the limbic system is already going at full speed, while the frontal cortex is still trying to make sense of the assembly instructions." He adds that the frontal cortex's efficiency is diluted while the limbic system is "fully online and dopamine is careening all over the place. Meanwhile, the brain is being marinated in the ebb and flow of gonadal hormones."

As the legal system has absorbed this information from the fields of cognitive psychology and neuroscience, the assignment of criminal responsibility has grown more circumspect. The courts now recognize that when teens make snap judgments, especially in emotional situations, they're probably acting on a shortsighted impulse. Thus, according to several decisions by the US Supreme Court since 2005, teens should not be executed for serious crimes like murder (*Roper v. Simmons*), receive life sentences for non-homicidal crimes (*Graham v. Florida*), or have automatic life sentences without the possibility of parole (*Miller v. Alabama*) unless they're deemed permanently incorrigible. Yet the evaluation of "permanent incorrigibility" can hardly be made with any degree of accuracy given how much can change in a person across a lifetime; judges and jurors are not sufficiently educated in child psychology.

"Teens are different," writes forensic psychologist James Garbarino, author of *Miller's Children: Why Giving Teenage Killers a Second Chance Matters for All of Us*, "and traumatized teens are more different." Based on multiple interviews with teenage killers, Garbarino points out that "teenage killers are not playing with a full deck when it comes to making good decisions and managing emotions . . . but many of them are also playing with a stacked deck because of the developmental consequences of adverse life circumstances." Among those adverse circumstances listed by the CDC are poverty, domestic abuse, maltreatment, household substance abuse, divorce, depression in a family, and incarceration of a family member. Nearly 40 percent of adolescent killers have at least five of these factors versus 10 percent of kids from the general population. (Henley had five.)

*Miller v. Alabama* offers five scientific grounds for rejecting mandatory life without parole for teens.

1. Decision-making: less capacity to consider future consequences for impulsive behavior
2. Dependency: a home environment from which children cannot extricate themselves
3. Context: the youth's actual role in the criminal behavior
4. Competency: impaired ability to deal with police and lawyers
5. Future behavior change: potential in youth for rehabilitation

Adolescents tend to feel invulnerable. In addition, those who become compliant accomplices on a criminal team often have a background of abuse or familial instability, so they're used to threats and have devised strategies to deal with stress. They know how to adjust and accommodate. Sometimes they've already committed petty crimes. They may yield to moral compromise if they need or want something their partner can supply. They don't even notice their devolving moral frame.

Psychiatrist Dorothy Otnow Lewis and her research associates looked at nine males who'd been evaluated during adolescence and had later committed murder. They compared the subjects to a group of twenty-four incarcerated delinquents who had not become violent within six years of discharge. The goal was to identify factors common to the nine that might distinguish them from the nonviolent subjects and to develop treatment strategies. Family trauma was a key feature. Most showed paranoid thinking that bordered on psychotic. Exposure to parental brutality manifested later in violent acts.

More recently, social science researchers Sharline Cole and Susan Anderson performed a qualitative study with five male and three female high school students who showed antisocial aggressive tendencies. They had all experienced aggressive parents, leading the researchers to suggest that the family (the "first agent of socialization") plays a central role in how the child chooses to interact with others. A lack of father-son bonding, especially when the father was violent or absent, had a significant impact, as did rigid, assertive parenting from either parent. The antisocial children had looked to the nearest role model during their development, finding authoritarian-type aggression.

In a meta-analysis of thirty research studies that focused on associations between childhood attachment with caretakers and adult criminality, Dr. Claire Ogilvie and her colleagues identified a significant correlation between insecure attachment and adult criminality. Higher rates of insecure attachment showed up much more often in violent offenders than in nonviolent offenders. These kids lacked healthy nurturing.

A case in point is that of the Ranes brothers from Kalamazoo, Michigan, born a year and a half apart. Both became serial killers independent of each other. Their abusive, alcoholic father had forced them into fierce fights over little more than a handful of pennies. He also gave them alcohol. When Larry was nine and Danny was eleven, their father abandoned them. They began to engage in crimes, like stealing cars. At the age of nineteen, Larry was arrested for killing a man over a few dollars and some shoes. He confessed to four more murders. Danny was more of a sexual predator. He also used a fifteen-year-old accomplice, "B. K." This was the same year, 1972, in which Corll pulled fifteen-year-old Henley into *his* crimes. In other ways, B. K. and Henley had parallel experiences with an older, aggressive adult predator who sought a compliant accomplice.

Danny Ranes was twenty-eight. He'd just gotten out of prison in Michigan for assault. He raped and fatally stabbed a young mother, Patricia Howk, right next to her toddler. He left the child to wander in the streets. Not long afterward, he spotted a teen vagrant, B. K. The boy's mother had schizophrenia and his father was an alcoholic. B. K. had a record for burglary and car theft. Ranes befriended him with the hope of gaining an accomplice. He got B. K. a place to stay and a job at the service station where he worked. B. K. looked to him as an older brother. One day, Ranes took B. K. to a parking lot and described his assault on Patricia Howk. He wanted the boy to do something like that with him.

B. K. agreed to try it, so they put together a murder kit. On July 5, Ranes and B. K. were at the Sprinkle Road service station when Linda Clark and Claudia Bidstrup pulled in around 1:30 A.M. for gas. B. K. filled their Opel Kadett's tank while Ranes popped the hood. Ranes dismantled a wire to the spark plugs, which caused a disturbing noise. He directed the girls to drive the car into the bay. When they were inside, Ranes told the girls to keep quiet and they wouldn't be harmed. He pulled out a knife and instructed them to get into the backseat. He raped both and told B. K. to kill Claudia. B. K. attempted to strangle her with a rope, but he couldn't do it. Ranes held her down and together they killed her. B. K. killed Linda by himself. They put both women into the Opel, covered them with a blanket, and

B. K. drove the car to a wooded area. He poured gasoline over and inside the car and placed a lit cigarette on the car's floor. He left before he knew if the cigarette had ignited the accelerant well enough to burn the bodies. Ranes then showed B. K. money, two rings, a pair of earrings, and some photographs that he'd stolen from the victims.

Nearly two weeks later, on July 17, motorcycle riders came across the Opel Kadett with the decomposing bodies. They were identified. The full gas tank suggested they'd encountered their killer nearby. An investigation was underway as Ranes and B. K. struck again.

On August 5, they kidnapped eighteen-year-old Patricia Fearnow. B. K. tied her up in the back of the van, covered her with a sleeping bag, and lay next to her as Ranes drove. Over a period of six hours, they raped her. Then B. K. placed a plastic bag over her head to suffocate her. They dumped her body in the woods.

Ranes told B. K. to keep quiet about their crimes, but he revealed them to someone who went to the police. B. K. and Ranes were arrested for the July double homicide. B. K. was assigned an attorney, James Hills, who said he could make a deal if B. K. told what had happened. B. K. agreed and took them to Fearnow's body. He said Ranes had been the instigator. Shortly after this murder, he'd broken off with Ranes because Ranes told him to steal a car and go to Florida. B. K. had been fearful that Ranes was about to kill him too. He also told detectives about Ranes's confession of the murder of Patricia Howk. Ranes was subsequently charged with four murders. He received life sentences.

So did B. K. He could offer no reason why he'd participated in these brutal rapes and murders. He used his time in prison to get a law degree and participate in rehab programs.

Apparently, the neurological research on the adolescent brain influenced a parole board in Michigan, which voted to release B. K. after he'd served forty-eight years. They cited his youth during the crime as one of the factors. "I know what I did," he told the board. "I realize it was horribly wrong. But there are circumstances that got me involved in this. . . . I accept responsibility for that . . . [but] if I had not met Danny Ranes, I know in my heart that I would have never become involved in crimes like this."

Predators seeking partners rely on their mur-dar to hook them up with someone they can bring into their criminal plans. But these partnerships can have an Achilles' heel. The same traits that drew the predator to a vulnerable individual can later jeopardize the enterprise. When insecure or timid people think they'll be caught, they might preemptively alert the police. Carol Bundy and Karla Homolka made such calls. Elytte Barbour and B. K. turned on their partners. Ian Brady failed to leverage David Smith.

In Corll's case, his misjudgment proved fatal. He hadn't grasped the limits of his power over Henley. Once Henley found his nerve during a confrontation that only one of them could survive, Corll lost all leverage. But there would be consequences. Henley faced a trial that would determine his future. Even in death, Corll still had influence.

# CHAPTER 6

## Trials and Troubles

### First Hearing

A lthough Dean Corll was the primary killer, Henley became the official face of the case. News accounts featured him over and over as if he were the chief instigator. Multiple factual errors were printed, which frustrated him, especially about the degree of his participation.

"I thought the reason they focused on me," said Henley, "was because I was the one who broke the case, and I was the one who was talking. David was not talking. He did talk, but he wasn't honest. That first day of my arrest, I was a hero. I had saved Rhonda's and Tim's life. Then suddenly I was not a hero anymore."

A Houston psychiatrist summed up the frustration. Author John Gurwell quotes this unnamed source: "I'd wager almost everyone in the city wished that Corll had survived Henley's bullets. He was dead before they got a chance to weigh him properly in their minds. . . . Everything they read about him was secondhand. Thus, they can't put him in a proper niche. They are sure he was an ogre, but they can't satisfy themselves as to what kind."

Henley's attorney, Charles Melder, told the press three days after the case broke that he wanted a psychiatric examination for his client, because "the boy is not all there." He said when Henley learned about what Brooks said in his statement to police, he grew upset over Brooks's attempts to dodge responsibility. "Henley told me he saw Brooks kill several people."

On August 13, 1973, a Harris County grand jury convened to consider the evidence against Henley and Brooks. Since grand jury records are sealed, it remains unclear what some of those who testified revealed. The obvious witnesses to the Corll shooting were Tim Kerley and Rhonda Williams. Kerley had left town and had to be located and subpoenaed. The two near-victims described the events of August 7 and 8 leading up to the incident. Other witnesses seemed to know something more about the principal parties. Robert M. Etheridge, seventeen, had traveled from San Diego to talk about his acquaintance with the defendants during their school years. Former Corll associate Billy Ridinger, now twenty, also testified. He'd once come close to being killed. To hide his identity from the press, he entered the court with a paper grocery sack over his head in which holes were cut for his eyes.

Shortly after Corll was killed, Ridinger had arrived with his mother to the Pasadena police station to describe their long acquaintance with the decedent. They'd known him since the early 1960s as their neighbor in the Normandy Apartments. At the time, Corll had managed the Corll Candy Company and they'd called him the "Candy Man." They'd considered him part of their family. After the company closed, his visits were less frequent, although Corll had maintained a connection by phone with young Billy. When David Brooks moved in with Corll, the Ridingers had thought it was strange, but they knew Corll enjoyed young people. They were aware that he tended to change his residence every three or four months. They mentioned another teenage boy named Gerald McDaniel who might know Corll, but he seemed to have vanished. Billy had visited Corll at his Pasadena residence several times and had seen "nothing out of the unusual." He'd been invited to spend Memorial Day weekend that year at the Corll vacation home at Lake Sam Rayburn but had declined. For this report in front of his mother, Ridinger revealed nothing about what Corll had done to him on the board. Only Brooks had talked about that incident. However, Houston detectives noticed the omission and brought Ridinger in again on August 11. At this time, he gave the lengthy statement that made him so valuable to the grand jury. He made it clear that Corll had been a sexual sadist.

Before Ridinger described his mistreatment on the day Brooks had persuaded Corll to let him go, he provided context. He said he was ten years old when he first met Corll. Two years later, he got to know him better. "During the next seven years, I associated with Dean as a friend, and he would give me candy at the candy store and take me and other boys places, like to the show and to the beach. During this time, he never made any advances toward me sexually." He recalled a dozen separate places where Corll had lived.

Sometime during the spring of 1972, Corll made his move. "About eight or nine months ago," (Ridinger's timing is incorrect for where Corll lived when the events occurred) "Dean approached me about having homosexual relations with him and offered me ten dollars, and I refused. He mentioned it again about a week later, and I told him no. I associated with him on a fairly regular basis of about once a week." In fact, Ridinger had decided to spend a weekend at Corll's apartment on Schuler Street. Corll picked him up. Brooks and Henley were both present.

"Shortly after we got there," Ridinger said, "Dean got out one pair of handcuffs and started fooling around with them and was telling me that he could show me some tricks about getting out of handcuffs, and while he was showing me, he suddenly snapped the handcuffs on my wrists with my hands in front of me. Then someone put a pillowcase over my head, and they wrestled me to the floor and tied my ankles. I couldn't see anything, but I heard hammering. Someone took the pillowcase off my head and Dean took the tape off my mouth, which had been placed there during the struggle. Dean then tied my hands to some big metal hooks that were high up on the wall of the room and tied me there with some rope and tied a piece of the rope around my neck so that if I tried to get loose it would strangle me."

Corll used a knife to cut off Ridinger's clothes. "[H]e was playing with my penis and sucking on my penis, and when I tried to resist, he hit me in the stomach and told me if I didn't cooperate, he would call somebody else over who was worse than he was. During this time, Wayne and David were in the room, and Wayne had a pistol strapped to his belt. From the time he tied me up until around 11:00 P.M., Dean would play around with me and then go and watch television and come back to me and start again and he would rub himself against me and commit sodomy on me."

Corll forced Ridinger to drink beer and wine. Then he brought in the restraint board. "David and Dean untied me from the wall, and Wayne held a pistol while they handcuffed me to the rings on the board on my back with my hands spread, and then they tied my feet to the bottom of the board. Then Dean lay down next to me and started rubbing himself on me and sucking my penis and masturbating himself at the same time." He said that Henley watched this activity. Brooks left for several hours. When he came back, Henley and Brooks went to bed while Corll positioned himself alongside Ridinger for the rest of the night. The next day, Brooks told Ridinger he wanted to help him, but he was afraid of the other two. Corll said something similar, implicating Henley as the one holding the line. "I had the impression they might kill me." The three captors conferred in another room. "Then Wayne came into the room and told me that they were thinking about letting me go, and he said if I ever said anything it would be all over for me." Corll took him home. Not only did Ridinger say nothing, but he also returned to Corll's apartment. "I visited Dean's house about fifteen times after this happened to show them that I wasn't going to tell anyone what had happened." The last he'd seen Corll was at the Pasadena house. Corll's reason for letting Ridinger go when he'd killed so many others remained an open question.

The detectives who'd taken the statements from Henley and Brooks also testified at the grand jury hearing, as did those who'd conducted the investigations or supervised the digs. The hearing lasted six hours, with true bills returned. Henley was initially indicted for three murders: Billy Lawrence, Charles Cobble, and Marty Jones. Brooks was indicted for the murder of Billy Lawrence. The killing of Dean Corll was considered self-defense, so no further action would be taken.

Ten days later, Johnny Delome was added to Henley's list, while Brooks acquired indictments for James Glass, Ruben Watson Haney, and Johnny Delome. In a news article on September 7, Frank Aguirre and Homer Garcia appeared on Henley's list.

Members of the grand jury took one more step. They had called in several officers to answer questions and then issued a statement condemning the local police for their negligent handling of the numerous missing-persons reports from the Heights. They criticized Harris County District Attorney Carol Vance and Police Chief Herman Short. Both, they stated, had lacked "professional imagination, thoroughness, and coordination." In addition, the police had halted the exhumations too soon and the DA had failed to put enough men on the task. Detectives had waited too long to record their recollections of oral testimony and sometimes had not transcribed their notes until after the jurors had demanded it. "We were not successful until late in our term in interesting either the district attorney's office or the police department in tracking down many of the leads contained in the various reports," they stated.

In retrospect, they were correct. Restoring the boat shed floor and the sand at High Island had been too hasty. The beach had not been thoroughly searched, even after Henley insisted there was another body. The investigation into a possible sex trafficking ring had been anemic. At best, the jurors had a partial picture to work with and they weren't happy about it.

Vance and Short dismissed the citizens' scolding as ignorant, even "goofy." Instead of holding the parents accountable for their sons' behavior,

Vance said, the jury had misplaced blame and "held police responsible for the problem." Vance complained that the "activist" citizens on the grand jury were unaware of how difficult it had been to coordinate the "high volumes of work." For the first time in his tenure in that office, Vance had assigned a prosecutor to devote his time entirely to the case. In addition, he asserted, the problem with teens was far more complicated than members of the grand jury recognized.

Ted Musick, the attorney representing Brooks, and Charles Melder and Ed Pegelow for Henley attempted to get their clients freed on bond. They failed. Judge William M. Hatten appointed a psychiatric team headed by Dr. Ben Sher, the chief county psychiatrist, to conduct evaluations. Musick also hired psychiatrists Exter F. Bell Jr. and Blaine McLaughlin, and psychologists Jack Tractir and Victor Chen. Melder rejected the idea of Dr. Sher's team questioning his client but later changed his mind. He announced he'd mount an insanity defense and he wanted the trial to stay in Houston, where jurors were sophisticated enough to understand psychiatric testimony. "The boy [Henley] needs medical attention . . . he's not all there," Melder said. In contrast, Musick told a reporter, "If my client [Brooks] is found sane, I will file for a change of venue." He added that the district attorney's office agreed with this, since press coverage in Houston could thwart any attempt at fairness. Vance told Will Gray, Henley's third lawyer, that he would support a change of venue.

The insanity laws in Texas had shifted that year from the outdated M'Naghten standard set in Great Britain in 1843, which relied solely on a defendant's cognitive ability to distinguish right from wrong. The American Law Institute had expanded the criteria by adding the concept of the defendant's lack of a "substantial capacity" from a "mental disease or defect" to resist doing what they did. In other words, they might have known an act was wrong, but they couldn't conform their behavior to what they knew. This set of criteria covered a broader range of behavior.

For the arraignments, safety precautions were enhanced due to death threats against both defendants that streamed into the DA's office. "Ten bailiffs were stationed inside the courtroom and six in the hallway outside," reads one account. "The bulletproof windows in the courtroom doors were covered with paper."

Henley walked into court wearing a white T-shirt, jeans, and boots. He had a thin mustache, a goatee, and longish hair. Author John Gurwell said he carried a Bible (which Henley disputes) and described his stride as "jaunty." Brooks, with his blond hair still long, had donned a white T-shirt, tennis shoes, and trousers. He looked subdued and a bit lost. Both defendants listened to the charges and pleaded not guilty. Trial dates were set. There was no violence.

The parents of missing and murdered children mobilized to discuss law enforcement's lack of response that had enabled Corll's murders over the span of three years. A mass meeting was held at the West Fourteenth Street Baptist Church in the Heights to call local and state officials to account. Among the concerns was the announcement that the search for bodies was over. Rumors flew that, once the victim toll reached twenty-seven, Houston officials had called a halt so as not to incur further negative press for the "Murder Capital of the World." Some families had heard that the reason to cease digging was because Henley and Brooks could recall no more grave sites, but Henley had stated that Mark Scott's body was still on High Island. The medical examiner, Dr. Joseph Jachimczyk, disputed his account. Investigators lumped Henley into all the incidents to give the impression he had so many burials to recall he was likely confused. Neither accomplice had an exact figure for Corll's murder toll, since they'd relied on things Corll had said. Brooks thought Ruben Watson Haney was buried on the beach, but his remains turned up in the boat stall. Jachimczyk stood by his own work on the case (later shown to be wrong for several victims).

The grand jury admonitions would prove correct. Ego, poor assumptions, bias, and a lack of professionalism would lead to several misidentifications.

It took independent investigators years to set some of these records straight, causing further heartache to the victims' families.

Galveston city officials tried to block plans for a more extensive search. Several witnesses came forward to describe seeing a white van and a crew that resembled the defendants carrying or burying things. One report placed the date in February or March, the other in June. However, Corll, on his own, had used a different area in February, and by June, the murder crew was using the woods near Lake Sam Rayburn or the boat stall. The supposed witness reports were either wrong or irrelevant to this case. In response to criticism, the Galveston police and a Houston detective collected a team of trusties and volunteers to dig more holes at the beach. They lasted four hours before they gave up. Still, the sense that more bodies might be found persisted. Several extra bones had been found in a grave containing two intact victims. They belonged to *someone*. In addition, Brooks had described several victims not yet accounted for.

In Houston, police explored an area surrounding the former Corll Candy Company on West Twenty-Second Street after a woman said she'd seen Corll digging there after hours in 1965. They found nothing. Mary West publicly blasted the police and stated that her son had been burying stale candy, that's all.

By mid-October, news articles reported that twenty of the victims had been identified. Their families had buried most of them amid crowds of onlookers and reporters snapping photos.

With the primary predator dead, all eyes were on the two accomplices. There would be no plea deals. Vance knew that the public wanted a trial. The details of all these murders, especially the motive, had to come out. He later wrote that he'd preferred a single combined trial to spare the parents from enduring the ordeal twice, but he knew the defendants had the right to separate trials. "We decided to try Henley first," he stated. He assigned the "shotgun" seat to ADA Don Lambright, who'd already done most of the research and preparation.

Will Gray, for Henley, expressed his hope for a continuance to let the publicity die down. He wasn't interested in a change of venue. He merely wanted a later start date until such time as a fair jury could be seated. "I wondered to myself," Vance wrote, "how many years that would take." Vance wanted the trial to happen as soon as possible, for the families' sakes. For Houston's sake.

A hearing was scheduled to consider suppressing Henley's confession. After squeezing out Henley's first attorney, Charles Melder, from the lead position, Will Gray and Ed Pegelow planned to put Henley on the stand. Melder thought this strategy was a mistake. But Gray was now in charge. He wanted nothing to do with an insanity defense. He'd had significant success as an appellate attorney and thought he could win on appeal. He persuaded Henley to accept his idea.

"My memory about the discussion of how to defend me included all three lawyers," Henley recalled. "I was mostly in communication with Ed Pegelow. My understanding was that Melder saw no other avenue of defense save insanity. Ed was of the opinion that the legal definition of insanity in place in Texas at the time was not conducive to use in my case." Henley didn't think he had much chance of being found insane. He agreed with Pegelow that he was being scapegoated for Corll's crimes. Even Vance admitted that Henley had done a public service by killing Corll. But Gray was threatening to remove himself from the case if Melder got his way.

Melder went to the press to air his beefs. He told reporters that the Henley family lawyer, Sam Plotkin, had brought him into the case on August 11, 1973, before the other two were involved. *He'd* invited them in. He believed Gray's plan would trigger press coverage that would force a change of venue, which he resisted.

Henley's trial was scheduled for January 1974 in Judge William Hatten's 176th District Court in Houston, two months before Brooks would face a jury. The courtroom seats would be divided among news media representatives, lawyers, legal observers, and the public, with fifty of these seats reserved for families of murder victims. Among the media participants would be a famous face, Truman Capote. It wasn't unusual for writers to mingle among reporters at murder trials to find juicy yarns for novels, but officially Capote would be there as one of the press. He had ideas of his own.

## Setting the Tone

Capote is most renowned for his masterwork, *In Cold Blood*. Using the innovative literary form of a "nonfiction novel," he vividly recreated the heartless slaughter of four members of the Herb Clutter family in Holcomb, Kansas, in 1959. He included an intimate portrait of the feckless killers, Perry Smith and Dick Hickock, with special focus on Smith. When published in 1966, *In Cold Blood* became an international bestseller, making Capote a household name and a regular on the TV talk show circuit. In 1967, the book was turned into a critically acclaimed film. Behind the scenes, Capote played a prominent role. Whatever he decided to write next would have a lot to live up to. He undertook several research projects with other offenders, including an interview with Charles Manson's key associate, Bobby Beausoleil. But *In Cold Blood* proved to be a hard act to follow.

Capote expert Sally Keglovits supplies some background on the significant social standing that Capote had gained with this book. "There's probably no better example of this than his Black and White Ball in 1966," she said. "It was a grand party at the Plaza Hotel in New York City celebrating Katharine Graham, publisher of *The Washington Post* and *Newsweek*. Capote reigned supreme. The party garnered headlines across the country. An invitation was the hottest ticket in town. Even the *Houston Chronicle* weighed in with a front-page headline, 'Splendor Runs Over at Capote Ball of Decade.'"

However, such heady success can have a downside. "Trying to top his previous achievement, Capote, by his own admission, suffered writer's block and was unable to produce writing of much substance. As his time among the denizens of the jet set increased, his commitment to his literary career dwindled." He let alcohol and drugs run his life. He tried a gig for *Rolling Stone* magazine, embedding with the Rolling Stones rock group on a tour of North America, but he wrote no more than a few pages. Instead, he focused on pulling together previously published short stories for a collection.

A week after the Houston murders, on August 16, the news editor for *The Advocate*, a national gay newsletter with a circulation of forty thousand, invited Capote to pen a brief commentary on the situation. The editor expected to devote full coverage to the case in the next issue and thought Capote's experience in Kansas writing *In Cold Blood* made it "imperative that we sound you out on this." There's no record that Capote responded, and no such article was ever published.

As the Houston Mass Murders burgeoned into a sensational news story, Capote's manager, John O'Shea, arranged a deal. "O'Shea's first significant act as manager," says Keglovits, "was to negotiate a contract with *The Washington Post* for Capote to cover the Elmer Wayne Henley, Junior, murder trial. The contract was lucrative: $10,000 per week, plus expenses."

Capote accepted. He was interested in how a murder ring of this enormity could have happened. According to a December 16, 1973, memo from the *Post*, "a trial of considerable drama and sociological importance begins in Houston, Texas," on January 14, 1974, covering "the most sizable case of multiple murder in American history." The memo recounted the number of victims and anticipated Capote's contribution. "Under the overall title, 'Houston Diary,' Truman Capote, one of America's most distinguished writers and authorities on the homicidal mind . . . will be covering the Henley trial on a day-to-day basis." Capote would "incorporate a wider landscape—to deal with the climate, the city, the fantastic cast of peripheral characters, the side roads as well as the main streets, surrounding this historic case." Capote described his ambitious case coverage as being a "late

20th century version of *An American Tragedy*." In other words, he hoped for another literary masterpiece.

Theodore Dreiser's 1925 novel, *An American Tragedy*, was based on the 1906 case of Chester Gillette (renamed Clyde Griffiths for the novel). Gillette's parents' religious beliefs had inspired them to denounce their wealth and join the Salvation Army. Gillette's childhood was spent traveling. As he matured, he remained rootless. At a job in a skirt factory, he seduced and impregnated Grace Brown. She pressured Gillette to marry her, but he wasn't about to be tied down. Under the pretense of romance, he arranged a trip to upstate New York. Out in a rowboat, Gillette fatally bludgeoned Brown with a tennis racket and left her to drown. He fled the scene but was quickly arrested. His defense team claimed that Brown had killed herself over her situation. However, Gillette had changed his version of events several times and failed to explain Brown's injuries. His narrative lacked credibility. The jury convicted him and sentenced him to death. He was executed on March 30, 1908.

The novel's "tragedy" is that the main character's weakness and moral cowardice leads to his ruin. It's unclear why Capote linked this novel to his aspirations for the Corll case. It seems he set himself up by promising the *Post* a deeply moral tale. It was a grandiose idea, but he soon discovered how difficult it would be just to get information on Dean Corll, let alone recreate him as a tragic figure that signified something about American culture or character. Brooks and Henley were both too young to be featured as any kind of American symbol.

A note from November 1973 in the Capote file indicates that Henley's attorney, Charles Melder, offered to introduce Capote into Houston's legal circles—an incredible opportunity for close-up scrutiny of the case. Melder could have gotten him an exclusive interview with Henley. Yet Capote apparently ignored the gesture, even though his name had not opened other doors. In addition, Capote had no Harper Lee to pave the way as she'd so ably done in Kansas. A news article states that Capote had police connections, but he'd left no notes about talking with key detectives, and none of them told reporters of an encounter with the famous author. He'd collected very little on which to base the grand tale he'd hoped to tell. Yet he had an assignment, with pressing deadlines. He also had an opportunity that he seemed to be ignoring.

According to his (or O'Shea's) promise to the *Post*, Capote had planned to write about the "homosexual blood orgy" in a diary form. "I see the trial as a jumping off point," he stated. "To really tell about this whole extraordinary culture—in Texas and the Southwest, all the way to California—of aimless wandering, this uprooted, mobile life: the seven-mile-long trailer parks, the motorcycles, the campers, the people who have no addresses or even last names." He seemed to think that the victims' families had been blasé about their sons going off to swim or see a movie and then vanishing. One report states that Capote had met many of these relatives (again, no notes from him or reports from them), but he seemed to have no grasp of their desperation or the considerable efforts they'd made to find their lost boys. None had been blasé.

Brooks had stonewalled all interview invitations, and Henley had supposedly become more circumspect about the press. Absent now was his previously garrulous manner. However, he willingly spoke with whomever his attorneys wanted him to. Possibly, Gray didn't want Capote near Henley because he had his *own* plans for a literary sale to recoup his legal fee. Even when Henley's father claimed that a New York publisher had offered him a significant figure for the story, it was out of Henley's hands. He doesn't recall telling Gray about this offer. He didn't really believe it. "I told my father never to come back if all he wanted was to make money off me."

Henley says Capote never contacted him or anyone he knew. Despite Capote's vision, he seemed to lack the drive to bring it to fruition. Still, as he awaited the trial, he made an attempt. His notes from the file at the New York Public Library are undated, but his participation can be pieced together from various other sources.

"Perhaps it could have happened anywhere," Capote wrote for the *Post*, "but the fact that 27 youngsters, and very possibly more, could disappear without the merest ripple seems to me peculiar to this country at this particular time. How did it happen and why? It is my contention that there is no mystery about murder. That is one of the two reasons why I'm covering this case—to take the mystery out of it. As for the other: a recent national poll indicated that more than half of the American population has uneasy feelings about their country, think that it is affected by some serious and spreading undefinable malaise. Perhaps this is true; and if so, then the Houston case is possibly a strong symptom of it. Anyway it seems to me a matter worth exploring."

In Houston, Capote clipped articles from the local newspaper about the case, making red marks and underlines on some of them. Most cover the earliest reports. None was from the actual trial or even the trial preparation. In Capote's file, there are pictures of Brooks and Henley, items about their confessions, descriptions of the victims and their relatives, and police explanations for how they routinely handled investigations of runaways. One article covered Billy Ridinger's account of his near murder at Corll's Schuler Street apartment. Another stated that Melder intended to run an insanity defense. Henley's family minister from the Methodist church near his house had visited him, and he gave reporters a sense of Henley's good character (although he told Henley during his visit that he would never be back). Teachers talked about Henley being a good student with too much burden from his family's financial needs for a child to bear. He'd simply cracked from the strain. David Brooks's mother, Mary Chandler, admitted to the press that she loved her son but didn't condone what he'd done. Alton Brooks, one reporter said, had gone into seclusion. Corll's father and brother had refused to make statements, and one article that documented more refusals from Corll's work associates claimed that "insight into the man and his motivations may never be generally known."

Most statements about Corll, even to the police, were brief, superficial, and positive. The overall impression offered was that of a nice guy. His mother told anyone who'd listen that the accomplices were scapegoating him for something they alone had done. Capote had also collected some opinion pieces about the failure of police to investigate, as if preparing to explore this angle more deeply.

From the notes left behind, Capote seemed to have had an idea and a theme but no way to dig into the case the way he'd done with the Clutter family killers in Kansas. He seemed to miss the story of how a "nice" guy like Corll had been able to operate so close to home in such a sadistic manner without anyone suspecting (a question still worth asking). Or Capote's "Houston Diary" could have built off what *In Cold Blood* had accomplished, to show how easy it was during the mobile 1970s to dismiss missing kids as runaways. It could have been a precursor to the Gacy case, just a handful of years in the future. Capote might have investigated the human trafficking ring for boys that Brooks and Henley both said was operating in Dallas. If it was difficult to be gay in Texas before this came to light, it became worse, as people mistakenly conflated homosexuality with pedophilia, viewing every gay man as a child molester. Capote had hoped to rectify this misperception, but he never even placed himself in a position to observe it.

Capote's acquaintance, *Village Voice* writer Arthur Bell, had done so, and he'd offered to give Capote access to his notes. Bell had stayed in the "white lower middle-class redneck area" for three weeks after the murders were unearthed. His report is in Capote's file, detailing what he'd discovered in Houston Heights: "It's the Texas of *The Last Picture Show*." He said that the murders had incited pressure on local gay men, with victims' parents denouncing pornography, gay bars, and "men who dress like women." Yet reportedly, no pornography had been found in Corll's home, he did not cross-dress, and an acquaintance had said he disliked gay bars. Bell describes how he'd faced a man with a gun who threatened him and ordered him out of the neighborhood. "Not unusual, I'm told." Since the murders, he said, gay men had made themselves scarce. Bell's read on the murders was that the violence had come from boredom, repression, and stagnation. He, too, never spoke to Brooks or Henley, or anyone they knew.

Like others, Bell noted that reports about Corll were uniformly positive. He was a "swell guy," a "do-gooder," and "the most well-loved man in the neighborhood." The discovery that, as a favor, he'd stored items for family and friends in his boat shed on top of the decomposing bodies of boys he'd raped and killed confirmed his double life. People suspected there were more victims that Henley and Brooks didn't know about, raising "unanswered questions that can only be answered by a dead man." Bell also interviewed some of the families for an article for *Esquire* magazine.

Also in the Capote file is an undated handwritten set of pages, entitled "Houston Diary." This essay opens with Corll's address: 2020 Lamar Street. It seems that Capote at least visited the neighborhood to make some observations. He never went inside the murder house. With permission from the Truman Capote Literary Trust, here is the content:

> Pasadena, Texas, with its sulpherous [sic] and chemical-scented air, is not to be confused with Pasadena, California, bastion of crystal light and rose-strewn lawns. The Texas Pasadena, though a part of Greater Houston, is a community unto itself and, while not drastically shabby, the lower middle-class, middle-class vistas of Pasadena, the grimy garages, the gritty little plants withering along the humid, unshaded streets, the wood-frame five-room houses with blistered paint slowly flaking under the East Texas sun, are not specimens to set the soul soaring.
>
> Lamar Street is exactly typical of residential Pasadena. In search of it, I consulted a cruising police car—with some hesitancy, for the Pasadena police, like so much of the Texas

constabulary, has a reputation for being a bit ornery, over-zealous. But the young officer driving the car was a model of helpfulness—after studying a street directory, his instructions for how to find 2020 Lamar could not have been clearer. The surprising part was he didn't recognize the address. After all, it was at 2020 Lamar Street, only a mere six months earlier, that the ultimate scenes of the largest mass murder in modern American history had been enacted.

It is a flimsy, small wooden house with an attached one-car garage, painted a dark bilious green, the doors and the windows are trimmed in olive. The house next-door is almost identical; and, indeed, all the houses up and down the popu-lous street are somewhat interchangeable—the colors vary, tattletale-gray being the dominant tint; so does the choice of exterior decorative statuary—here a gnome, there a flamingo. Certainly, nothing very ominous hovers in the atmosphere, except perhaps the bayou-humidity. And yet, the ordinariness, the kids' skating, bicycling on the rough pavement, the rolled-sleeved men leaning around a car collectively listening to a baseball broadcast, the housewives bustling past in bursting slacks and with heads hair curler top-heavy. This ordinariness is in itself ominous. How was it possible that these gregarious people living in their walled, so closely assembled houses, how is it conceivable that they could have been unaware of the outcries, the gunshots, the traffic in corpses at number 2020?

Unfortunately, he didn't write anything more. It's likely that Capote attended Henley's suppression hearing. He was staying with a wealthy couple he knew in Houston, not in San Antonio, where the trial ended up (and not at the Houston hotel that Melder had offered to arrange). One report describes him sitting with other reporters on opening day. He was wearing a white shirt, bow tie, and a V-neck cardigan. He'd done little groundwork aside from going to Corll's house. When guards brought Henley into the courtroom, Capote watched the slender kid for a few minutes. Then he got up and left. Reportedly, he said, "I've seen this before." Capote biographer Gerald Clarke thinks he was referring to his experience with Hickock and Smith.

Clarke notes that Capote's approach to writing was not a good fit for the daily demand of newspapers. His was an observant, reflective style that ripened over time. In contrast, the *Post* had urgent needs. Clarke says Capote "accepted the assignment only because John [O'Shea] had pushed him. The ambitious piece he'd envisioned could not have been written in small doses; it would have required an effort on the scale of *In Cold Blood*. The project was doomed, and Truman must have known it."

Capote's Random House editor delivered the bad news to the *Post*. There would be no insightful dispatches from Houston, at least not from America's premier true crime writer. Capote was ill.

And he was. He drove to Palm Springs where he was hospitalized with a respiratory ailment. He'd left his cache of notes and articles in a box in a rented house in Santa Fe, New Mexico. The homeowner eventually found it, and it now resides at the New York Public Library.

For the record, Capote tried something similar when the John Wayne Gacy case broke in Chicago four years later, in 1978. However, it became one more research project that didn't get off the ground. Capote had hit his peak as a writer. If he'd been well and engaged with the stories, he might have tracked down the sex trafficking ring that played a role in both cases.

## Trial Preparations

Vance's memoir covered his work on the Henley case, albeit briefly. He made several factual errors, perhaps because he wasn't the primary researcher. News articles and legal documents fill in gaps, along with Henley's recollections. Brooks offered no comments on his own experiences, but the appeal document for his case provides his attorney's strategy. (By then Brooks had changed attorneys.)

First up was Henley's hearing to suppress his August 9 statement to police, based on irregularities in police procedure. It contained the incriminating claims he'd made about killing people. Without it, the prosecution team would have had nothing to convict Henley of murder. No physical evidence directly implicated him, and he could always say that Corll had shown him the grave sites. Gray also still hoped for a continuance. In December 1973, Judge Hatten began pretrial hearings.

Henley took the stand on January 24, 1974, to describe how he'd killed Dean Corll over fear for his life, just as he'd stated when arrested. He repudiated police testimony that he'd been given a magistrate's warning. If he won this point, the statements were out, due to the violation of his rights.

Henley recalls what happened. "They had a magistrate get up and say, 'I came down to the squad room and they pulled all three out of the holding cell, and right there in the hallway, in the squad room [I read them their rights].' But I was never in the same room with Rhonda again after our arrest. We weren't in a hallway. He said I understood it [the warning] and acknowledged it. But that was a lie." Although he'd been distraught and high on a combination of substances, Henley insisted he had not signed any paper about his rights. "Will Gray believed me. He asked [the magistrate], 'Since you remember this, what was he wearing?' [The magistrate] said I had on jeans and a shirt. But when I was arrested, I had on a pair of jeans, no shirt."

Rhonda Williams likewise said she recalled no magistrate alerting her to her rights and getting her to sign a paper. She'd had the experience before, she admitted, and to her recollection it had not happened that day. Thus, she corroborated Henley's account. However, Kerley said he'd signed such a document.

Still, Henley made other admissions that undermined him. He described his memory loss, blackouts, and hallucinations, which he said prevented him from fully recalling the events of August 8 and the days immediately following. That night, Henley said, he and Kerley had been drinking beer and moonshine, and had smoked marijuana. To this they'd added paint fumes. When Corll freed Henley from the handcuffs, Henley had gotten "loaded" again.

Vance pressed Henley on other details, possibly to demonstrate to the judge that prosecuting him was warranted. When asked if he'd cut off Rhonda's clothes, Henley said, "Dang right I did. He told me to." He said he couldn't recall shooting Corll, although he knew he had. He denied he'd taken Kerley to Corll's home for Corll to sexually assault him. "Having Rhonda there should have prevented that." In addition, Corll had been in bed, not partying with them. When Vance asked if he'd told Corll he'd kill Kerley and Williams, Henley responded, "I may have. I may have promised him a million dollars and half of Texas. I went to the extreme and I figured he might even kill me."

Henley admitted he had no memory of telling the detectives about the boat stall where bodies were buried, but he did recall that he was consistently denied the right to have an attorney or his mother present. He'd asked for his mother's attorney, but detectives claimed he'd said he'd wanted to spare her the expense. (Contradicting this, Gurwell quotes an officer at the police station near Lake Sam Rayburn recalling Henley's conversation with his mother by phone on August 9 reminding her to hire him an attorney.) Records show that Henley had asked Mullican to be his attorney, and Mullican had said he couldn't. Thus, Henley was aware he needed one.

Henley identified his signature on his affidavit and confession and on a document that indicated he'd been warned about his rights. He was aware that Kerley had said he'd seen a magistrate. Yet in retrospect, Henley says, "This is where Rhonda and Tim both lied. Actually, Rhonda didn't lie; she just said she didn't remember. Afterward, Tim apologized to my mother."

He assumes it was because Kerley had felt pressured to lie in order to avoid the serious drug charges the cops had threatened him with to make him testify.

Henley admitted to drinking and smoking dope daily, sometimes all day. It seemed that he was high most of the time. Mullican even testified that he thought Henley might fall apart. He'd exploited Henley's confusion and discomfort to get him to spill everything he knew, so he'd feel better. Just shy of being unconstitutionally coercive, urging Henley to talk while he was so vulnerable was permissible for law enforcement. However, Henley added that they'd threatened him with being turned over to HPD for "grilling" and a lie detector. It had scared him. His team argued that this tactic had violated his rights.

The court had difficulty in determining whether Henley's signed statement about understanding his rights was authentic or contrived. The judge apparently decided that Henley's memory was so bad for that period that he'd probably signed it but just didn't remember. The judge decided that the cops hadn't coerced him. The incriminating statement remained in evidence. This decision was a blow for his team.

Although Henley had been warned about his anger, he admitted he'd lost it during the prosecutor's questioning. Vance had used the false statement Henley gave to the Navy about his drug use to show he was a liar who'd try to work a situation to his own advantage. "Carol Vance got me angry. It irritates me when someone talks down to me. You might as well poke me in the eye with a stick as talk down to me. I get really upset. My little chest comes out. You can't talk to me like that. I didn't like his grandstanding and showmanship."

Due to concern about local publicity, Judge Hatten decided to delay the trial until July and to transfer it to Judge Preston Dial's court in San Antonio in Bexar County. Melder, frustrated, parted with Henley's legal team late in January and there was no more talk of an insanity defense. Gray was displeased about the change of venue, but he liked the extra time.

Despite losing this round on suppressing the statement, he believed they'd eventually prevail.

In May 1974, Elmer Wayne Henley Sr. was brought to the Harris County jail where his son was being held. Lest anyone wonder if he'd been as abusive as rumors had it, he'd just been arrested for the attempted murder of his father-in-law, as well as the aggravated assault and serious threat to take the life of his former, second wife, Emma. The father-in-law, A. A. Palmer, claimed that Elmer Henley Sr. had fired three shots at him, aimed to kill. Henley Sr. also slugged a cameraman at the courthouse.

Wayne Henley turned eighteen that May. He knew he faced a long prison stint. His only hope for leniency was in the hands of his legal team. Will Gray assured him no matter how the first trial turned out, the legal errors he'd spotted would ensure a new trial. Gray would put on no defense. He didn't think he'd need one. Thus, no one would talk about who Henley had been before meeting Corll. No one would affirm that he'd stopped the killings by slaying Corll. No one would say he had protected two kids from being killed. He was in prime position to bear the weight of all the anger and anguish the victims' families could muster.

Corll had been the mastermind, and Brooks had been with him for a longer period, but Brooks had offered far fewer incriminating details. He'd be tried for one provable murder, Billy Lawrence, versus the six with which Henley was charged: Frank Aguirre, Johnny Delome, Billy Lawrence, Homer Garcia, Charles Cobble, and Martin Jones. The criteria for selecting these cases had been that Henley had mentioned his involvement in killing them and a parent was available to testify about the identification. Henley's statements would be the primary evidence, along with ex parte statements he'd made to the detectives in the car and at the various burial sites. According to them, he'd been quite talkative.

Gray tried to get the trial shifted out of San Antonio, claiming that pretrial publicity was still too intense. Judge Dial said that if they had a difficult time seating a jury, he'd consider moving it.

The jury selection would start on July 1, 1974. Gray repeated his protest over the admission of Henley's confession, stating that Henley had not been read his rights or given an opportunity to see either his mother or a lawyer. Gray didn't prevail. Although Henley had been seventeen, considered in most contexts to be a minor, Texas law allowed for him to have made his own decisions in legal contexts. It was a gray area.

A deal might have been struck with Brooks to testify against Henley, but such a strategy would make Brooks and all he knew fair game for Henley's defense team. No prosecutor would take that risk. Vance believed their case was strong without him.

It took less than a week to seat a jury. After examining 124 candidates, the attorneys selected thirty-two for the jury panel. The twelve jurors who were picked were equally divided between men and women. Reporters from as far away as Sweden and Japan vied with mostly middle-aged female spectators for the available seats in the stuffy courtroom. Some eighty-five reporters were sent to an alternative area, although media artists were allowed to stay in the main courtroom. Christeen Weed sat with her three other grandsons behind Henley (who didn't think they should be there at all). Mary, excluded as a potential witness, stayed on a bench outside, giving media interviews about her son's innocence.

Henley pleaded "not guilty" before sitting down with his attorneys.

"Those two words," wrote Vance, "would be all the jury would hear from him for the duration."

That was on his attorney's advice. In retrospect, Henley would have wanted witnesses on his behalf and even the chance to speak for himself. Some reporters made him out to be indifferent. He'd been put on anti-anxiety medication, so he was subdued. "It was for the claustrophobia," he said. "It was phenobarbital and belladonna. I'm in a cell by myself. I needed it." In addition, Gray had coached him to stay silent. "I was not supposed to react. Do not stare at the jury. Don't frown. Don't laugh. Supposedly, I have killer eyes. I was told to look at the jurors [only] when they file out to deliberate. I was told I wasn't to stare at them or make eye contact." Henley wanted to write notes but couldn't. "I wasn't allowed to have a piece of paper and pencil. I just did what the lawyers told me."

Vance, trying the final case of his long career, made his opening statement to lay out his case. "We began our case with the maps, the blowups, the confession, the long search for the bodies, the body box, the torture boards, diagrams of the Pasadena house, scenes at the boat stall, the lake, and the beach at High Island. And of course, the clothing the youngsters were wearing when killed." There would also be testimony from dentists and the medical examiner. He'd characterize this case as "one of America's saddest atrocities."

Despite an investigation, no one had managed to explain what had driven Dean Corll to sexually torture and murder over two dozen boys and young men. Little was known then about sexually sadistic serial killers and their drive to dominate and terminate. Vance recognized the immaturity of the two accomplices but decided not to parse out their specific roles. He had a signed confession from Henley in which he'd admitted to being the sole or team perpetrator in ten murders (actually, nine), and that was good enough. They had the bodies, and the boy had helped with the identifications. "Without the bodies," Vance wrote, "we would have had no case and no idea of who had been murdered." Also, Brooks had described Henley's actions as sadistic, helping to associate Henley with Corll's depravity. Vance assumed that Brooks and Henley had received their payments, with money as their primary motivator. (News reports from 1974 show that Vance said Henley was paid once and then just enjoyed killing.)

To get boys over to Corll's house had been easy, Vance said: just find out what they wanted and promise to supply it. He made Henley the primary player in the handcuff trick, getting the boys to agree to put them on. He believed Henley had participated in some of the torture as well. Certainly he was the handyman who finished them off and carted the bodies in a homemade body box to their destination. Hair recovered from

Charles Cobble's clothing was consistent with that of Henley and Corll. Hair recovered from the artificial phallus was microscopically consistent with Henley's. Hair collected from the body box was consistent with that of Charles Cobble.

For the jury, Vance described the initiating incident when officers had arrived at Dean Corll's and brought in the three survivors. The detectives had taken statements before Henley had led them to the three mass grave sites. Vance brought Corll's body box, restraint board, and instruments of sexual torture into the room for display. The monstrous dildo had been lubricated in a way that Henley knew was contrived. Vance used diagrams of Corll's house to show where the items had been found, along with diagrams and photos of the exhumations at the three locations. Just seeing the images of decomposing remains had to have distressed the jury. When parents of the victims testified, Vance handed them clothing found with bodies to seal the identifications.

Detective David Mullican, the Pasadena detective who'd gone to Corll's home and spent three days with Henley, took the stand. He explained what he could about the torture board, with its holes cut out for better restraint. Henley gazed at it without expression. Mullican described Henley's admission about how Corll had used different types of torture tools on the boys. He said one boy, just fifteen, had been tied to the board for three terrible days, because Corll had "liked" him. He also talked about Henley tricking a friend, Frank Aguirre, into getting handcuffed so Corll could overpower him. Mullican offered the chilling statement that Henley had commented that strangling someone "was not as easy as you see it on TV." Corll had assisted him with several strangulations. "Once he made the first initial step," Mullican said, "he was caught. Also, Corll was an older person who showed him attention and approval. But as he got into it, he learned to like it. That's powerful stuff for someone who never had anything."

Vance led Mullican through Henley's statement, bringing out the fact that Corll had offered him "$200 at least for every boy that I could bring him and maybe more if they were real good-looking boys." This had all been framed within the notion of an organization in Dallas that trafficked in drugs, stolen goods, and boys-for-hire. Since little investigation had been undertaken on the latter point, it hung in the air as an unproven claim, maybe something the kid had made up.

Gray made multiple objections, especially about comments Henley had allegedly made. He claimed they should not be admitted. With only a few exceptions, Judge Dial repeatedly overruled him.

Assistant DA Don Lambright questioned the medical examiner and the various dentists. Dr. Joseph Jachimczyk had worked with families to make victim identifications and determine how each victim had been killed. Some still had ligatures around their necks and some had been too decomposed to determine a cause of death, but it was clear that most had been choked or shot, or both. Items of clothing and dental records assisted, but some identifications could not be made. A few remains had been misidentified. Jachimczyk described the evidence he'd found of sexual torture.

Henley steamed in silence. "I did not like Joseph Jachimczyk. He said things I thought were asinine, like that he had bodies buried for a length of time and he could tell that their sphincter muscles were distended. Granted, had they a fresh body, they might be able to see that, but you can't pull a body out of the ground that's been there for months or years and say that. Soft tissue is the first thing that goes."

Henley wanted to challenge statements he believed were false. "I'm sitting there with my stomach in a knot. People were lying and I wasn't supposed to react. Marty Jones's mother is screaming at me, and I can't react. That dildo that they got—they put axle grease on it. They had doctored it. Dean Corll was fastidious, so I knew that it didn't look like that [when they'd collected it], but what could I do about it? Then when Vance kept looking at me, asking me questions during his summation, I wasn't supposed to react. He'd turn and ask me a question and then say, 'See, he won't even answer.' "

For Henley, the trial was an ordeal. "I felt shame. A lot. I didn't like what they were making me. But I was totally dependent on those lawyers. I had started trying to study [the law], and Gray told me, 'I don't need you to know the law. I need you to sit there and be quiet.' All the lawyers, that's what they were supposed to do is handle me. You hear people lie and make you into something you weren't, but you can't *say* you weren't. It's your word against theirs. You can't say, for instance, 'To the best of my knowledge, any of those boys could have been released and there would not have been a mark on them up until the time they were killed.' They made it sound like they were beaten bloody, like they were cut and scraped. A lot was being said I couldn't argue about. When Marty Jones's mom testified, I was flat told, 'Do not look at her.' The things that she said were horrible, the fact that she was having to go through that. I understood it. But I'm being told not to react."

Whether Gray realized it or not, he'd compromised his ability to put on a solid defense. Henley had signed over to him the media rights to his story so he might earn something for the time he'd put into the case. This was the only means Henley had to pay his attorney. Such an arrangement wasn't unique, but it did raise the issue of a conflict of interests: Henley's story wouldn't sell for much, if at all, if he were found innocent. Gray, the defense attorney, had a vested interest in a conviction that would *enhance* Henley's notoriety. The result was that he hired no experts and called no character witnesses to the stand. He never even interviewed anyone Henley knew to see if there was any value in it.

"Will said he could get the case reversed," Henley explained. "I don't know of anyone who talked to him. None of my friends, none of my acquaintances, none of my teachers . . . so he did not do an investigation."

Henley's mother was kept out of the court during the entire trial. "My mother was not allowed to testify. She was supposed to, but they did that [put her on the witness list] to keep her out of the courtroom. My brothers and grandmother were there. I wasn't supposed to look at them.

But Mom had definite ideas. It was not going to appear that my family had turned away from me. That was important to her."

The prosecution team presented a summation, highlighting Henley's self-incriminating statements. Then the defense took the floor. Ed Pegelow pleaded for mercy. He hoped the jury would consider that Henley had helped to locate the victims and had brought the killing to an end.

"Gray didn't give the summation," Henley said. "He let Ed [Pegelow] do it. Ed wanted to help me, but he was not capable. I have a lot of problems with how it went down. Some of it I tuned out. I wanted to look these jurors in the eye. 'Hey, look at me. I'm the one you're trying.' It was very frustrating."

After presenting twenty-four witnesses and ninety-six pieces of evidence during five days of testimony, the prosecution rested. The defense followed suit. The case went to the jury. After just ninety-two minutes of deliberations, the jurors found Henley guilty of all six counts of murder with malice. He received six 99-year sentences. Judge Dial made them consecutive, for a total of 594 years.

"I don't know what we would have done without the cooperation of the two young defendants," Vance would later write. "As bad as they were, the older Corll had led both of them into this episode and was the driving force behind it, even offering them financial incentives." He even thought that Henley might have sensed that Corll would surely eliminate the two who knew best what he had done. Still, Vance did not think this mitigated their crimes. "Brooks and Henley had plenty of blood on their hands." He didn't consider that Henley might have remained silent, letting them discover the bodies on their own one day (or never).

Right after the conviction and before the sentencing, Gray had Henley speak to a writer, James Conaway, who stated that the interview was related to Gray's attempts to sell the story—a "literary audition." Henley said they met in the warden's office and Gray was not present, despite Conaway giving the impression he was. Supposedly, Gray had urged Henley to describe for Conaway "how you did it."

As he sat cross-legged and smoked a Marlboro, Henley gave his thoughts on killing his malignant mentor: "He'd have been proud of the way I did it." Conaway made it look as if Henley were bragging. "My only regret is that Dean isn't here now, so I could tell him what a good job I did killing him. . . . Dean had been training me to react fast and react greatly. And that's what I did."

Conaway described Henley with acne scars, oily curls, nastiness, and eyes too large, and he likened the convicted killer to "things best left under rocks." His distaste is palpable, but he appreciated the scoop that would enhance sales of his own book, *The Texans*. He acknowledged Henley's "reputed IQ of 126" but undermined any sense that Henley could think beyond his own sordid accomplishments. The kid came from a "seedy, lower-middle-class enclave" where kids sat around getting high, skipping school, playing pool, and wasting time.

Conaway viewed Brooks as emotionally dependent, but "Henley wanted money." He said that Henley delivered friends (vs. strangers) to Corll because this was "easier, less risky, more prestigious."

Henley talked freely about murder. "At first, I wondered what it was like to kill someone. Later, I became fascinated with how much stamina people have." On TV, strangling someone looked easy, but "sometimes it takes two people half an hour." He added, "Dean searched for a climax he never found."

Conaway explained Corll as "quite mad" but thought Henley represented "a larger problem because he seems to be quite sane." Henley admitted to Conaway that he'd enjoyed causing pain. "You either enjoy it or go crazy," he said. He just pushed it away afterward and didn't think about it. Henley admitted he'd felt no real remorse. "That's something I've tried to build in me. I don't really feel about it, you know?" Conaway interpreted his admission as a sign of callousness.

Looking back on these comments today, Henley said, "I understand now what remorse is. It's not the melodrama I'd see in church services. It is a deeply held belief that what you've done is wrong. In order to survive and move forward, you have to recognize not just your responsibility, but you have to take your remorse to heart and deal with it and move past it. If you spend every day feeling remorse-ridden and melodramatically guilty, I believe that's when you need a psychologist. I don't think we can survive like that."

To Conaway, Henley admitted he was glad he'd revealed everything he'd done and that he'd stopped Corll from "killing little kids." But for him, there was "no heartfelt emotion." An article like this left a negative impression. If people were on the fence about Henley, the published quotes made him look self-satisfied and utterly cruel.

"I'm not heartless about it," Henley said in retrospect. "When I [sometimes] think that I don't deserve to be locked up my entire life, I can't help but wonder, how can I ask to ever be let out when these victims never had anything past that? I don't have an answer for that. There's nothing you can do to fix it. If I survive, even in here, in order for their lives not to have been totally and senselessly lost, I have to strive to do the best things I can do. It may not mean anything to anybody else, but it means something to me."

Henley and Brooks communicated just once by letter, agreeing to keep in touch. Neither did. They'd shared a secret that Henley had revealed. He'd killed the person who'd kept them together. Other than that, they'd had no real bond. Henley heard from inmates who knew Brooks that he wanted Henley to stop giving interviews.

## Brooks in Court

In February 1975, ADA Lambright's team prosecuted David Brooks for the 1973 murder of Billy Lawrence. There was limited media fanfare. Although Brooks had not directly implicated himself in murder, he was tried as a principal. He'd stated he was present when Lawrence was killed. Henley did not testify as a witness, but the other murders were described as part of a pattern that Brooks had either known about or participated in. Brooks's statements were admitted, along with the photograph of Billy Lawrence that he'd identified. In one statement, he'd said he'd known about eight murders but had done nothing about it. His description of the time he'd spent while Corll still had Lawrence alive in the house was likely chilling to the jury, as was his description of going fishing before finally burying the body. His cold recitation of his experience in his confession, as well as his admission that it didn't bother him, endeared him to no one.

Billy's father, James, identified the image in the photograph as his son. Further evidence included statements about where the bodies of victims Brooks had named had been buried, and how they'd died. Ruben Watson Haney's mother testified that her son had called to say he was going to spend the night with Brooks. That was the last she'd heard from him. Stanley Blackburn's mother identified his driver's license, found in Corll's house. James Dreymala's father identified the bicycle found in Corll's boat stall, where his body was buried. Police officers described their search for victims with Brooks's assistance.

Ted Musick had left Brooks's case in November 1974 after a "squabble over sanity strategy" regarding his competency to stand trial. Musick thought Brooks was not competent. Brooks's new attorneys, Elaine Brady and Jim Skelton, attempted to show that his statement had been taken without first apprising him of his rights. However, Brooks had given his first statement voluntarily as an attempt to assist. At the time, he hadn't been under arrest or even suspected of any involvement. He could have completed his statement and left. Yet, once Henley had implicated Brooks upon hearing that he was at the Houston Police Department, Brooks had been warned and detained.

In addition, the defense attorneys presented Brooks as merely an accessory with little involvement in any murder. Assistant District Attorney Tommy Dunn told the jury, "This defendant was in on this killing, this murderous rampage from the very beginning. He attempts to inform you he was a cheerleader if nothing else. That's what he was telling you about his presence. You know he was in on it."

In just ninety minutes, the jury convicted Brooks of one count of murder with malice and gave him a life sentence. He remained mute. His wife, now the mother of their daughter, quietly wept.

Brady and Skelton lodged an appeal, contesting several points, including insufficient evidence, the erroneous application of certain legal arguments, and the erroneous admission of extraneous offenses. The prosecutor should not have introduced Brooks's homosexual activity with Corll, nor any of the murders in which he'd had no part. In addition, the trial court had misapplied the law of principal. At most, he'd been an accessory after the fact.

The court disagreed. At the very least, Brooks had known what Henley and Corll intended to do with Billy Lawrence and had remained at the house. He'd also assisted with the burial. Since Brooks had admitted being present to the murder while knowing Corll's intent, he wasn't merely an accessory. Brooks's appeal was dismissed.

### The Far Reach

Police in Los Angeles paid careful attention to the stories emerging from Houston. They had a series of eleven unsolved murders that bore many similarities to descriptions of the victims' remains in Houston. On September 20, 1976, HPD contacted Mullican to tell him that Detectives John St. John and Kent McDonald wanted to interview Brooks and Henley. They described their torture-murder cases to him, adding that they had a suspect who'd said he was a friend of Dean Corll and had been in Houston and Pasadena at Corll's residences. The detectives thought that associates of Corll's who could furnish a name of a California friend might corroborate the story. Mullican agreed to facilitate the interviews.

The Los Angeles detectives were talking about the so-called Trash Bag Murders. During the 1970s, multiple gay men had been murdered, mutilated, and dumped along highways around Los Angeles. Their main suspect was Patrick Wayne Kearney, an electronics engineer for Hughes Aircraft. He would eventually turn himself in and plead guilty to twenty-eight murders going back to 1968, eighteen of which were prosecuted. Kearney shot and mutilated his victims and sometimes beheaded them. He tied up many of them and put them in plastic garbage bags. He admitted he'd killed because it "excited" him and gave him "a feeling of dominance." It wasn't a stretch to imagine Corll among his acquaintances.

In the company of a team from HPD, the LA detectives traveled first to the Ramsey II Prison Unit to talk with Henley. Mullican went first, to explain their purpose. He found Henley to be "hostile," but Henley agreed to the interview.

"I talked to John St. John," he said. "I might have been hostile to Mullican because I thought he'd screwed me [at the trial], but I wasn't hostile to John St. John. He told me he was trying to connect Corll to the Trash Bag Murders. He suspected that Corll had been there when the murders began, and that Corll was an original member of the group and had splintered off and come home to Houston. The MOs were similar."

Henley couldn't help, so the detectives moved on to Clemens Prison Unit to ask Brooks the same questions. He was "most cooperative and talkative." Although he couldn't furnish names of Corll's California acquaintances, he told them Corll had been "super-secretive" about his post office mailbox. He'd read his mail there and then destroy it.

Mullican used the opportunity to ask Brooks about Henley's claim that four more bodies were buried around Freeport, Texas. (Only Mullican seemed to know about this claim, and he did not write it down anywhere in the records.) Brooks said he knew of none and thought Henley didn't either. As a burial spot, Freeport would have been "considerably less convenient."

Maybe Corll had told Henley something, Brooks said, but they hadn't transported any bodies out there during his association with Corll.

The LA detectives seemed to find nothing of interest for their case from Brooks or Henley. They never returned and never did make an official link to Dean Corll.

## New Proceedings

At the end of 1978, the Texas Court of Criminal Appeals reversed Henley's San Antonio conviction and awarded Will Gray a retrial, due to Judge Dial not allowing Gray to pursue a change of venue. Gray had shown that hundreds of stories had been published or broadcast prior to the trial, and the press had contacted eight of the jurors or their relatives. Gray had moved again and again to sequester the jury, but Judge Dial had always denied him. In addition, Dial had allowed newspeople into the bar, filling in extra seats across from the jury with media artists. Some had drawn the jurors and published their drawings in newspapers.

The new trial would take place in July 1979 before Judge Noah Kennedy in Corpus Christi in Nueces County. Although Kennedy imposed a limited gag order, rumors floated that Gray planned to use a "Hearst defense," i.e., that Henley had been brainwashed. Pegelow had read about F. Lee Bailey's strategy for defending Patty Hearst.

On February 4, 1974, the Symbionese Liberation Army (SLA), a terrorist group, kidnapped nineteen-year-old heiress Patricia Hearst from her apartment in Berkeley, California. The SLA hoped this high-profile act would help to bring down the capitalist state. They released recordings of their captive, who seemed to sympathize with their cause. Two months later, Hearst participated in an armed robbery. She was arrested that September. A debate ensued over whether she had been a willing "soldier" or the victim of brainwashing. In her 1976 trial, F. Lee Bailey used three mental health experts on thought reform to support the argument that the SLA had conditioned Hearst via "coercive persuasion." He presented it as a clear case of Stockholm syndrome. Only certain people were susceptible, the experts said, and the subject must first be destabilized. Psychologist Robert J. Lifton, famous for his analysis of the Nazi doctors, stated, "The mind is rather fragile. It can be broken down." The experts used examples from among prisoners of war who'd been "subjected to unusually intense and prolonged persuasion in a situation from which they could not escape." Hearst, a captive, fit this pattern. The brainwashing defense failed, and Hearst was convicted of bank robbery and felonious use of firearms.

Pegelow was not deterred. Aware that Corll had a stack of books on hypnosis (not listed in the police inventory), he believed Corll might have brainwashed his accomplices. Henley didn't buy it. He thought they should try a coercion defense. Gray said coercion wouldn't work because Henley had often been away from Corll's immediate control. At the time, no one considered coercion to be as much a psychological state as physical.

Judge Kennedy began pretrial hearings in April. Media interest had greatly diminished. Getting a trial reversed on technicalities changed no one's mind about Henley's guilt.

This time, Gray focused on Henley's youth at the time he'd met Corll to show that Corll had overwhelmed him. He suggested sentences of five to fifteen years. He requested that all jurors and alternates be sequestered, but Judge Kennedy said he'd sequester only the twelve actual jurors.

Assistant District Attorney Doug Shaver researched the Hearst trial in preparation. He told reporters this was like claiming that intoxication was a mitigating factor. "It would not be a legal defense." He said that if Henley's case were presented as an insanity defense, his legal team would have to give formal notice in a timely manner. He didn't expect this to happen.

Mary West, Corll's mother, offered her opinion to *Houston Chronicle* reporters. She reiterated that the two teens had done all the killings and framed her son. Press coverage had been biased and her son had been unfairly scapegoated. "When you know your son and when you know he would do anything to help anyone, especially young people—you know." She admitted she hadn't seen him in the five years before his death. She wanted to hire a lawyer to pressure Henley to describe what had really happened. "But I know he's not going to trial to clean his conscience. He's going to try to get free." She thought that if he succeeded, he'd be killed. "There's too many people bitter."

For the proceeding in Corpus Christi five years after the first trial, all the evidence and witnesses were still available. Once again, Gray put on no defense and called no witnesses. He made several motions about faulty procedure, all of which were denied. Although Vance offered to let him have five more juror strikes than the prosecution had, the judge allowed only two. Gray stated that there were at least three jurors who had prejudices and should be removed. One juror had even disclosed this. The judge ignored Gray's concerns. Due to these items, Gray believed Henley would get a third trial.

After deliberating just over two hours, the jury gave Henley six concurrent life terms (concurrent, because Henley's attorneys had agreed to trying the six cases together only if the potential sentencing would be concurrent). Kennedy added that Henley was incorrigible, which essentially deprived him of any real chance at parole. He'd get the requisite hearings, but he'd likely remain behind bars for the rest of his life.

Gray appealed again, but the Court of Criminal Appeals denied it. There would be no third trial. Henley was going to prison.

Will Gray never did get a book deal. Henley didn't hear from him again.

# CHAPTER 7

## The Right Hook

### Mind Probe

In prison, Henley began to suffer from post-traumatic stress disorder. He didn't know until later what it was, but he had frequent nightmares. He tried to lose himself in prison jobs.

"In the seventies and early eighties, I worked constantly. I kept busy from five thirty in the morning until ten or eleven at night every day. I didn't let myself sleep. I didn't want to dream. I had dreams that terrified me. [In a dream] I've gotten out and was home or I was never locked up, but it was always, 'We found more bodies' and I need to come with them. And I'd be hiding under houses because they're looking for me. I dreamed of how devastating it would be for them to come to my door and tell me that. The other variation was being chased. It was never someone in particular, but it was always someone I knew. Occasionally it was someone I knew from here [prison]. I had put it down to the idea that I was still under Dean Corll's control."

During the early days while appeals were pending, Gray had advised Henley not to correspond with anyone or do any interviews lest he say something that would hurt the case, so he tried to stay under the radar. He was allowed ten correspondents and he chose his family and a few friends. He hoped he could eventually redeem himself, but the message he heard from all sources was that he was as evil as Corll. He accepted this judgment. "They had me convinced that I was evil, and heartless, and homicidal. So many people said it. So many believed it. I seriously worried that I was all that and the best thing was to keep me locked up forever. But I couldn't reconcile that because I didn't have those thoughts and feelings."

Detectives visited several times over the years to see if Henley had remembered anything more. They still had a few unidentified victims. "Periodically, investigators would come and ask me some questions. I said 'Look, you keep coming. I've told you everything I know.' They said they believed me, but 'We keep coming back because something might have happened to jog your memory.' I said, 'Well, you have me doubting myself.' I asked if they believe in the efficacy of hypnosis. They said yes. I said I would undergo questioning, but I wanted immunity from being prosecuted anymore. I wanted to help but didn't want to risk going back to court. They said okay."

Texas had led the way in police training for investigative hypnosis. At the time, practitioners believed that memory was like a video recorder and that hypnosis was a tool that could refresh and restore memories that had degraded over time. The modern use of hypnosis is based on the notion that responses to hypnotic suggestion involve some capacity to access mental functions that are normally beyond the reach of conscious control. Hypnosis has been utilized as a tool to try to heal memory gaps, add details to accounts, facilitate or suppress certain behaviors, and enhance recall accuracy. In a typical scenario, the hypnotist induces a state of deep relaxation to exploit the subject's suggestibility and penetrate past their cognitive defenses.

However, during the 1980s, research began to show that memory was more of a reconstructed mix of experience, beliefs, biases, and other factors than a precise recording of life episodes. In addition, researchers discovered that hypnosis could facilitate the induction of false or confabulated memories. Many courts around the country banned its use in forensic cases.

In *State v. Hurd* (1981), a New Jersey case, the court set up guidelines for forensic procedures to safeguard reliability.

1. Witnesses must use a psychiatrist or psychologist trained and experienced in the use of hypnosis.
2. The hypnotist should be independent of, and not regularly employed by, the prosecution, police, or defense.
3. Information given by any party to the action to the hypnotist should be written or recorded and made available to all parties.
4. The hypnosis session(s) should be video- or audio-taped, including pre- and post-interviews.
5. Only the expert and the witness should be present during all phases of the hypnosis.
6. The subject's pre-hypnosis memories for the events in question should be carefully recorded and preserved.

Around 1986, the investigator for the Harris County District Attorney's Office, Gary F. Johnson, went to meet with Henley. He had a master's degree in psychology and had probably taken the basic course on hypnosis that was offered during those days for law enforcement and prison psychologists. With Henley, some of these *Hurd* guidelines were ignored, such as using an independent hypnotist, but the sessions were more an experiment than a search for something probative. Johnson videotaped them and Henley asked for the transcript. It never arrived. Requests in recent years suggest that all records have been lost. Nevertheless, the sessions were a turning point for Henley.

"I thought we spent about four hours," he recalled. "And since that session, no police officer has ever come back and asked me another question. He [Johnson] said, 'You will remember this as you're ready and capable of remembering.' Afterward, he told me, 'I will say this: you are not as bad a man as you think you are.' They said they'd give me a transcript, but it was never forthcoming. Since no cop from any county has come since then to ask me a question, they must have gotten everything they could ever get from me."

Nothing else turned up about more bodies, so the sessions seem to have provided no further enlightenment beyond what Henley had already said. When contacted for this book, Johnson declined to affirm or explain his comment to Henley or to provide more information about the sessions.

## Impression Management

Henley came up for parole several times but knew it was just a formality. "I did not actively campaign for parole because I wasn't sure I had any right to request to be released after what I had done." He was always turned down, but someone on a parole board said he should show more of himself to the public, to abate the 'monster' stigma. He wasn't sure about this. His attorneys had told him to remain silent. But they didn't represent him anymore, and many false stories had been published about various people who claimed to have had an encounter with him. He hoped to set the record straight. He had no knife wound inflicted by a boy who'd narrowly escaped him; he hadn't shooed anyone from a grave site; he had not fished at High Island every weekend with Corll or buried bodies at Freeport; he had not systematically picked off his friends to feed Corll's appetite. In fact, in prison, he'd been an exemplary inmate and many of the prison staff liked him. He thought media exposure might help.

In 1989, Henley did a brief interview with reporter Debbi Johnson for a local TV station. The following year, Henley agreed to an interview for the prime-time newsmagazine show *48 Hours*. Officials supported it and allowed the film crew to enter the prison. In the episode, "Man with a Past," Henley, thirty-four, is shown in prison whites, lighting up a cigarette. Correspondent Victoria Corderi sits cross-legged on a dining table next to him, leaning forward to ask, "How would you describe yourself?"

"Quiet," he says, "Friendly. I work hard. I'm not any different than anyone else." More in earnest, he states, "If a junkie can quit being a junkie, why can't I quit being what I was?"

Film footage from the body removal from the boat stall frames the story, as Corderi describes Henley's pending parole hearing and his hope to be considered reformed, with the potential for release. They cut to Mullican. On a page of a large tablet, Mullican, now the Pasadena Chief of Police, shows Corderi the extensive notes he took prior to Henley giving his written confession. He lists the victims Henley admitted to killing. It's clear he does not support any bid for parole.

The camera returns to Henley. "When I got involved with Dean Corll," he says, "it was like going through the looking glass. Nothing was real, nothing was right. I was living in a madman's world. . . . I was a *boy* in a madman's world." He says he feared Corll and "thought he was sick," but at the same time "I didn't want to displease him. . . . I wanted him to be proud of me."

Corderi asks if he thinks of himself as a victim. "Of Corll," he acknowledges. She counters with the fact that he's a serial killer. Henley denies this. The production continues with Mullican reading Henley's admissions to several murders.

"You say you're not a serial killer now," Corderi says, "but you've serially killed."

Henley shows discomfort. "That's semantics. . . . On my own there would have been no crime. It's not me." He shrugs. "I'm passive."

The crew films near his cell. He says he believes he can function in society again and even have a positive influence. "I just want to be decent people."

Corderi pushes him: maybe there's something out there that could trigger that dark part of him back into action.

"I'm a grown man now," he says. But the impression lingers, due to Mullican's gruesome delivery, that Henley was complicit in so many murders he can't remember them all. Audiences never saw the significance of Corderi being locked in his cell as the warden walks away, showing his confidence that she was safe with Henley. Due to the stark images from the victim exhumations, the show seemed to have had the opposite effect of what Henley had hoped. But he was willing to try again.

Other journalists and talk show hosts interviewed him as well, sometimes making him out to be a stone-cold psychopath. "Dean Corll ruined my life," Henley said in one interview. "I'm not an ugly person. I'm not a violent person. I'm not a hateful person, and I wasn't raised to be. Somehow or another, I got involved in that." But few listened.

Henley began to realize that media people could cut and paste and make him into anything they wanted, regardless of his intent. He withdrew. "You've seen a lot of the interviews I've done," he said to this author. "When they ask what I'd say to the families, I usually say, 'What can I say? Sorry's not enough.' I think that's probably all they air. They don't air the part where I say, 'Nothing I say to them is gonna help. Nothing I say to them will bring their child back, and nothing I say to them will convey how I really felt. So, what *would* I say?' "

His hope is to show that there's more to him than the time he spent with Corll. "I don't want people to only remember me as having killed people. That's just not who I want to be. I'm not proud of it and I don't talk about it. I'm ashamed of it."

Perhaps because of discussing the crimes, Henley began to experience panic attacks during the 1990s, where he believed he was about to die.

He sometimes wondered if it wouldn't have been better if Corll had killed him on the day Brooks had first brought him over. Two decades later, the man—the monster—still had power over him.

Late in the 1990s, the FBI's Behavioral Analysis Unit was conducting interviews with mass murderers and serial killers, an extension of an effort begun during the 1980s (which did not include Henley). Supervisory Special Agent James Beasley arrived to ask Henley to answer a few questions from a standardized questionnaire.

Henley recalled the encounter. "The FBI came here to do their serial killer survey. It was on my birthday. I asked him to come back the next day. He did." Henley answered those questions he could, but most were about such things as motivation, fantasy life, and feelings about murder. "After a while, he [the special agent] said, 'Nothing applies to you, so you're not a serial killer.' He said it would be a waste of time to ask me all those questions."

In essence, Henley had been an accomplice. He'd killed under the command of Dean Corll. He had no lust for blood, no fantasy-driven motivation, and no desire to have continued to kill, short of the need to please Corll. This was not the kind of material the FBI sought for its study of primary killers.

Around this time, Henley took up art. "Murderabilia" collector Rick Staton persuaded him to draw and paint some things that Staton thought he could sell. He'd had great success with serial killers like John Wayne Gacy. Staton had run some art shows and sold items to galleries. An acquaintance gave Henley a few art lessons and he discovered he enjoyed drawing and painting, along with making jewelry. He even made some money. In 2000, Henley was featured in a documentary, *The Collectors*, which covered an art show from 1997 at a gallery that displayed his work. In the production, Henley describes his sense of himself and his appreciation of nature. He comes across as thoughtful and quiet. However, advocates for the victims' families attend the art show and express outrage over the fact that Henley has creative outlets and a way to make money. They buy and burn one of his pieces.

Eventually, these advocates got the prison craft room shut down. After creating more than two hundred pieces, Henley's art career was over.

But it wasn't the last the public would hear of him. Other people came to interview him for documentaries, including Stéphane Bourgoin, a self-described expert on serial killers who would later be exposed as a fraud. He attempted to get Henley to describe the murders, which Henley refused to do. Henley repeated things he'd said before and talked about his father, but the interview produced no new insights.

For a documentary that was never screened, Teana Porras contrasted Henley with Richard Reyes, a child advocate, to ponder evil vs. salvation. Both had grown up in similar conditions in the Heights, but they went in quite different directions. Henley admits to Porras that he was a coward for not calling police right away. "That's the part I can't forgive myself." She says she believes him.

In 2008, Tim Kerley, a Corll survivor, told his story for the first time outside a courtroom, offering it to a Houston television station. He hoped it might bring peace to victims' families and encourage young people to be careful. At the time, he hadn't realized how close he'd come to being killed. In retrospect, the enormity of his close call had grown. "When someone ties you to a board, the odds are pretty good that you're not going to walk out of there." He said Corll had threatened to cut off his arm. He'd prayed to God for help. When Henley picked up the gun and told Corll to stop, Kerley recalled that "Dean stood up and I saw him change into a different person. There was somebody inside him and it wasn't him. It was a spirit from Hell."

He tried to be philosophical: "It was one day of my life. I have two choices—either accept it and move on or kill myself." He'd never contacted Henley. "I don't know if I would shake his hand and say thank you or beat the [expletive] out of him." Kerley described "a battle going on between good and evil in that room [at Corll's]. And good won. Maybe the victims' families can find some solace. We got him. You know, he's dead. He's dead and the other one is in the penitentiary forever."

Six months after this interview, at the age of fifty-five, Kerley died from a heart attack. (Some sources indicate he killed himself, but this was not confirmed.)

Rhonda Williams announced on social media her intention to write a book called *The Girl on the Torture Board*. Initially, she assisted film director Josh Vargas with details about her ordeal to help him make *In a Madman's World*, which focused on Henley's side of the story. Williams visited Henley several times at the prison to gain his cooperation. He agreed to help with the script and even asked his mother to let Vargas use his clothing from the 1970s. The movie was finished but not distributed. It shows the deteriorating Heights neighborhood and gives the sense of a kid with nothing much to do but walk around and hang out. Henley tried to correct some things, such as the fact that his mother did not swear and that he was working a lot, but Vargas appears to have ignored him. Vargas claimed one shirt bore a bloodstain, but Henley wasn't wearing a shirt when he shot Corll, and he told Vargas the stain on the shirt in question wasn't blood. "No bloodstained clothing would have come back to my house." They stopped communicating.

However, Vargas did add some notoriety to the case. When he sorted through Henley's items in storage, he claimed to have discovered a Polaroid photo of a boy who appeared to be bound, crouching near a toolbox—supposedly Corll's infamous toolbox. He told the press about this, which generated headlines announcing a possible twenty-ninth victim. In an exchange on social media, Rhonda Williams accused Vargas of photoshopping it. Henley's mother identified it as a photo of her son, Ronnie, out in the toolshed. Yet the news stories were not retracted or corrected.

In 2013, for the fortieth anniversary of the Houston Mass Murders, Williams reached out to the same Houston television ABC affiliate to which Kerley had provided an interview five years earlier. She said she'd been silent for long enough. She worried about death threats and talked about her difficult childhood. She'd been raped as a child, was sent to several foster homes, and had fallen into substance abuse. She said her father had physically abused her and she'd turned to Henley for help. She added that even when she was tied up at Corll's, she wasn't worried. "I couldn't see Wayne hurting me. I just trusted him."

Williams stated that Henley told her during a prison visit that he'd intended to shoot her that morning. "He was afraid that he wasn't going to be able to save me. So, he was going to sit down with me—you know, lay down with me like he'd been doing when we talked—and he was going to put the gun by my head while we were talking and then he was just going to shoot me." (Henley denied telling her this or making any such plan; he'd been too high that morning to think clearly.) Williams inflated her ordeal by saying she was tortured for hours. "I just kept looking to Wayne to get me out of there. He had always been my protector, so yes, I was like, 'When are you going to get me out of this?'" She described the fatal shooting. "Because I had all that faith, I gave him the courage to finally turn the gun on Dean."

Williams claimed she spent time in jail afterward, and in a hospital, and was told to never speak about that night again. "Physically and mentally," she said, "it's taken my life from me." Her father barred her from the house and her relatives believed she'd been part of the prior murders. Although Williams realized from Henley's statement that he'd taken her fiancé, Frank Aguirre, to Corll's house, which resulted in his death, she continued a relationship with Henley. "He's still my friend, but now I have a lot more questions to ask him and I'm learning more as I go."

The news reporter asked her, "Do you think he's told authorities everything he knows?"

"I think he's tried," she replied, adding that speaking with him was part of her own healing. "I would like to be known as a person who did do something. I am not the bad person who lured boys to a madman."

Williams never finished her book, but she did become a social worker with a focus on abused and neglected children. She died in 2019 at the age of sixty-one.

Another woman, who went by the name "Donna," also gave an interview to a blogger in 2012. She had visited Henley with Josh Vargas and claimed she knew a lot of things not previously reported. Most of what she said came from letters Henley had written to Vargas during his participation in the film. Supposedly, Henley had told her details about the murders that made her wonder how he could sleep. "He remembers thirteen faces." She said he'd told her that Corll had killed the Baulch brother (unclear which one) due to a vendetta. "After a while, as Wayne slipped closer to insanity, he did enjoy causing pain. . . . I was speechless to hear this . . . yet he comes across very gentle and kind." When Brooks had wanted to grab some girls for rape and murder, Corll had nixed the idea. "Wayne said that, towards the end, if Dean could have had a boy a day, [that] would have been his dream."

All during this time, efforts were still underway to identify Corll's victims. Mix-ups had occurred that required better forensic tools than were available during the 1970s.

## Mistakes Corrected

Reportedly, at least forty-two boys had vanished from the Houston Heights area during the time that Dean Corll was known to be operating. Some could have been runaways or victims of other predators, but based on several items discussed below, it's likely that Corll killed more boys and young men than the official count indicates. Most of his known victims were from the Heights area.

Work on their identifications had commenced as soon as the victim remains were exhumed. In some cases, this was simple. Dreymala's bike and fingerprints, some distinct items of clothing or an ID, and Henley's description of burying Cobble and Jones assisted. Henley and Brooks together knew most of the victims buried on the beach or at the lake. If they didn't know a name, they offered descriptors to compare with missing persons reports. Sometimes a unique wound was helpful, but Henley knew little about Corll's boat stall burials, and DNA analysis was long in the future. Some remains had decomposed to the point of needing a much more painstaking analysis. By August 16, the ME's office had identifications for a dozen victims and had a fair idea about several others, but dental records were still needed. In some cases, there were none. (A full list of where each victim was buried can be found in Appendix B.)

Errors occurred right away. Medical Examiner Joseph Jachimczyk recorded that, based on the identification of clothing from the father of the Waldrop boys, bodies #9 and #10 in a common grave in the center of the stall were identified as Donald and Jerry. The skeletal remains were consistent with their size. The remains were released and interred in Georgia, where the Waldrops then lived. Within a couple weeks, it was determined that the remains were instead those of David Hilligiest and Gregory Malley Winkle. The Waldrop boys were #13 and #14, buried along the east wall. The Waldrops were informed on September 7, 1973, and arrangements were made to correct the errors.

In 1983, the same year that the remains of Richard Kepner were finally identified, another body was found on Jefferson Beach, about four miles from where the Chambers County graves were located. The case had not been deemed "forensic," so a pathologist was not assigned at the time. It took twenty-six years to match these remains to seventeen-year-old Joseph Lyles, whom Brooks had known about. Lyles had lived near David Brooks and had been to Corll's home on Wirt Road. On some lists, he became victim #28, but since Jachimczyk had eliminated Sellars, Lyles was victim #27.

Mark Scott's distinct house key among Corll's collection of keys confirmed that he was a likely victim. Henley said Corll had collected these keys from the boys he killed so he could get into their families' homes to steal things. The keys had also served as trophies.

Jachimczyk's forensic team decided that the twelfth set of remains from the boat stall were those of Mark Scott. Henley was adamant that Scott had been buried "fetal position, head up" on High Island. But Jachimczyk ignored him. He even wrote in his report that Henley and Brooks had said that Scott's remains were in the boat stall. Neither one had. And the boat stall remains in question had a healed collarbone, which eliminated Scott. The Scott family refused the remains if the ME wasn't 100 percent certain. Their instinct was right. Victim #12 from Hole #7 eventually turned out to be Willard Karmon "Rusty" Branch Jr., the son of a cop who once set out to confront Corll. In a 1985 news report, Jachimczyk indicated that the remains matched Branch on fourteen comparison points that provided a "reasonable amount of probability." A BB was found embedded in a bone, and Branch had once been shot with a BB gun. He'd also sustained a skull fracture and a shoulder injury consistent with the remains. In addition, a braided leather bracelet on the victim's wrist matched one the sister had described.

In 1991, a bone sample from the fifteenth set of remains from the boat stall (ML73-3355) appeared to be consistent via rudimentary DNA analysis with Mark Scott. Oddly, Jachimczyk's report indicated that a hair analyst had found the dark brown hair on Unknown #15 to be consistent with Scott's blond hair. As forensic procedures improved, in 1994 the Harris County ME's office hired a forensic artist to create a drawing from a superimposed transparency of the skull believed to be Scott's. This artist thought the method was imprecise, but she agreed to do it. When she was finished, the ME was certain this skull was Mark Scott's, even though the skull showed tooth extractions that Scott never had. Except for one bone sliver, the remains were finally given to the Scott family, who cremated them. Then, in 2010, a more sophisticated DNA analysis on the withheld bone fragment contradicted the identification: The Scotts had cremated someone else's son. This victim turned out to be Steven Sickman. He'd lived a few blocks from Henley's father and was last seen leaving for a party he said was in the Heights.

Scott's remains might be lost for good, because after the High Island exhumations, a fresh layer of sand was spread across the beach, and in 2008 Hurricane Ike swamped High Island. Yet it's possible, although no one has proven this scientifically, that the extra bones found in the double grave containing Billy Baulch and Johnny Delome might have been scraped by the grader to this location from a grave that wasn't excavated. Mark Scott was reportedly buried near that grave. Possibly, those extra bones were from his remains. Investigative reporter Barbara Gibson claimed in a 2013 online post that she had discovered Mark Scott's remains, misidentified as someone else, but she provided no details. She said that a forensic dentist confirmed her discovery. There has been no confirming media report as of this writing, and she did not reveal her discovery in her 2023 book. Instead, she ended with #15 being identified as Mark Scott via Jachimczyk's 1992 PCR analysis of the DNA.

Henley said that on several anniversaries, Jachimczyk made statements to the press about his work. He'd suggest that if Henley would cooperate, they could finish the job. This bothered Henley. "I had done all I could to help from the beginning. Dr. Jachimczyk had never requested to talk to me. I thought the only way to get him to hush was by the two of us talking. Thing was, I was scared he'd misrepresent any conversation he and I had. The Texas Rangers had told me in the past that if I needed any help [that] they, as law enforcement, could provide, to write to them."

Henley sent off a letter explaining the situation. He just wanted a witness. The Rangers were willing, and they set up an interview. Assistant

Warden H. E. Kinker also wanted to attend. Henley warned him that the meeting might be adversarial. Kinker wanted to ensure that Henley was kept safe.

When Jachimczyk arrived, Henley had the impression that he wasn't keen about these witnesses. "He made it clear he was there to ask questions, not listen to me. Nor would he answer most of my own questions. Still, I gave him as honest answers as I was capable in hopes to get him to cease telling people I was not cooperative. In the end, Dr. J began to badger me and allude to the idea I was being less than frank. Finally, I told him I was sure I could not help him, that he did not seem to want my assistance, so we should stop. . . . He never would consider what I said about [Mark Scott] but stood on his identification. However, the interview did work in a way, as Dr. J quit telling people I would not cooperate."

Forensic anthropologist Sharon Derrick at the Harris County Institute of Forensic Sciences tested the DNA from each of three remaining unidentified victims and scoured through missing persons reports and police files from the 1970s. Two sets of remains had been removed from the boat stall and one set from Lake Sam Rayburn. Derrick interviewed Henley and Brooks, using an artist's renditions from the skulls of what the decomposed decedents might have looked like. Henley couldn't tell from the sketches, but Brooks recognized one. He said he didn't know the name. He drew a map to the house where the kid had lived and made a poignant statement: "I wish I'd told my mother what he [Corll] was doing to me. If I had told her, I wouldn't be here now."

In 2008, using Brooks's lead and confirming with some relatives, Derrick identified case ML73-3349 as Randell Lee Harvey, just fifteen when he disappeared in 1971 after riding his bicycle from his job at a gas station in Oak Forest. Items buried in the boat stall with these remains matched those that Randy had worn. Primitive DNA analysis in 1991 and 2004 had failed to identify him. He'd been shot in the eye with a .22-caliber firearm and had a nylon cord tied around his neck. A tipster had once fingered Brooks as a primary suspect since he'd made threats against Harvey.

Barbara Gibson, working with Derrick, found that numerous details in the autopsy reports for the remains identified as Michael "Tony" Baulch were inconsistent with Henley's statement about his death by strangulation and his burial spot at Lake Sam Rayburn. Baulch had disappeared on his way to get a haircut a year after his older brother, Billy, had been abducted. The Baulch boys' parents had identified a unique belt buckle for Michael, so Jachimczyk had given them remains from that hole in the boat stall to bury with Billy's. (This victim had been shot twice.) Other features seemed to confirm this identification, such as similar dental fractures, but better technology later put the identification into doubt.

Derrick analyzed the bones and found that the set from the woods (ML73-3378) was consistent with Michael Baulch, just as Henley had said (which suggests that the artist's sketch that he failed to recognize was not a good rendition). Thus, some other boy had been mistakenly buried as Baulch. Derrick found a report for Roy Bunton, a teenager missing since 1972 after leaving for work. The report on the remains identified as "Michael Baulch" described his unusually long legs. Baulch had not been that tall, but Bunton had. The shape of Bunton's teeth matched these remains as well. So Bunton had been buried as Michael Baulch, and Michael Baulch's remains had been placed with the unidentified sets. The errors were rectified and the Baulch brothers were finally buried together.

This left a lone unidentified victim from the boat stall. He likely went missing in 1971 or 1972. He was fifteen to seventeen, with brown hair, wearing or carrying a multicolored striped, belted swimsuit. With his remains were a pair of brown cowboy boots, a pair of cotton socks, a pair of dark blue corduroy trousers, some white jockey shorts, a leather ankle bracelet, and a long-sleeved tan shirt with a large peace symbol bearing tiny letters, LB4MF or L84MF. His case number is ML73-3356.

Derrick has tentatively linked him with a boy named Robert French, based on photos sent to her office. Many fragments of bone from this case were sent to the University of Northern Texas, where the Center for Human Identification has the technology to potentially identify this boy. Additionally, there now exist tools like forensic genealogical DNA, in which even a partial or degraded DNA profile can be traced to ancestors.

Brooks knew of several boys that Corll had grabbed, killed, and buried on his own: the unnamed Mexican, possibly the two boys at the Yorktown apartment, a nine-year-old son of a grocer, and an unnamed boy at the Columbia residence. Brooks also stated that Corll had said he'd buried at least one victim (maybe more) in California and had mentioned a potential killing while living at a Judiway Street address, before the murder of Jeffrey Konen. Henley had described picking up a hitchhiker, whom some sources identify as Willard Karmon Branch Jr. It is *not* Branch, so that's another boy without a name that Corll said he'd killed. The hitchhiker is unlikely to be ML73-3356, because the hitchhiker was thumbing in February, so he would probably not be wearing or carrying a swimsuit. In addition, there are bones from a grave on High Island that belonged to no as-yet identified remains. Brooks's and Henley's statements provide a framework for their collaborative crimes but might not reveal Corll's entire criminal career.

## Kids and Killers

Henley had used some clinical guidance about PTSD to try to get out from under the weight of his past, but he continued to wonder about his experience with Dean Corll. Nothing seemed consistent with his sense of who he'd been before Corll, and after. "The thing that I have problems with integrating into this line of thought is the positive and negative control.

I can't look back and see where I was experiencing reward or positivity. I don't understand why it would matter to me that Dean was proud of me or that he approved of what I did, or it was what he wanted. He hadn't done anything that I could point to and say, 'Oh, he was my hero. He was the person I wanted to grow up to be like.' Because there was never any of that. I didn't get paid. I received no material gain. He did not elevate me in his crew or his crowd. I was not treated very well. But Dean was there. If I called him, he was there."

It could be difficult for Henley as an adult to appreciate the way things would have looked to him as a teenager, since teen biology flushes the body with chemicals that make certain things much more significant than they will be later in life. And he wasn't alone.

## Other Accomplices

Adult offenders who sought to enlist accomplices were well aware of the endless pool of vulnerable teens that could be lured into crime. Sometimes the right hook was simply being a consistent presence in a kid's life and acting as if you know what you're doing—as Henley noted. Kids will do things they'd never have believed about themselves—even ghastly things—if they think the adult has life all figured out.

Like Dean Corll, Douglas Moore, thirty-six, was known among the teens in Mississauga, Ontario, in Canada, as the guy with the drugs. The provider. He sold dope at a spot across from an elementary school and offered his home as a hangout for teenage boys. He was also a serial pedophile.

At age eighteen, Moore was convicted of sexually assaulting four boys, twelve to sixteen. He was put on probation. He committed the same crime again with a twelve-year-old boy. This time, he got four years in prison. For good behavior, he received a one-day parole privilege. He used it to assault another boy. He got four more years. In the prison, he became a drug kingpin and entered a treatment program for sex offenders. He was considered cured, so he got an early release. That's when he moved near the elementary school. The Peel Regional Police would later say they were unaware that a serial pedophile lived in their jurisdiction, let alone near a school.

In the spring of 2004, Moore was arrested for molesting several disabled kids in foster care where he babysat. Alarmed about returning to prison, he committed suicide. His death deprived police of the ability to ask him what he knew about three missing persons, two young men and a boy.

In November 2003, close friends Robert Grewal, twenty-two, and Joseph Manchisi, twenty, had vanished. The father of one of them questioned people in the area and heard Moore's name repeatedly mentioned as an acquaintance of theirs. But when he told police about Moore, an officer allegedly said, "These types [sex offenders] are not usually violent." No one investigated. A month later, fifteen-year-old Rene Charlebois had disappeared from the same area, last seen leaving school. His mother would later say the police made little effort.

Early in 2004, two mutilated male torsos without heads and hands turned up in Montreal. They were identified as the remains of Grewal and Manchisi. Not long afterward, Charlebois's mutilated corpse was discovered in a landfill in Orangeville.

Moore's former common-law wife and a fourteen-year-old boy (unnamed in the Canadian press) were charged with accessory to murder after the fact for assisting Moore to dispose of evidence. The boy admitted he'd been present when Moore killed Grewal and Manchisi in the garage of his town house. Moore had tied one victim to a chair and strangled him with a skate lace and beat the other to death with a baseball bat. Moore believed they'd robbed him of thousands of dollars' worth of drugs, jewelry, and cash. (It turned out that the accomplice had robbed him and convinced him the other two had done it.) Why Moore killed Charlebois remains unknown. The fifteen-year-old victim had spent a lot of time in chat rooms, perhaps lured by Moore into a sexual situation. Whether he'd been sexually assaulted was not revealed.

The fourteen-year-old accomplice went to trial. Although his attorney argued that the boy had been under Moore's influence and was confused and afraid, the judges decided he'd exhibited "some initiative" related to the murders and thus was criminally responsible as an accessory. The teen had disposed of the knife that was used to dismember the bodies without Moore directing him to, and he'd held the victims' heads as Moore cleaned his car in a car wash before helping him to bury the dismembered parts in the woods. The boy was aware that Moore had intended to kill them over their alleged thievery and had done nothing to stop him or alert someone. The accomplice claimed he'd viewed Moore as a father figure, so he'd done what Moore wanted. Due to his youth, he received six months in prison.

No matter how much we educate kids about stranger danger (and even about questionable neighbors), as they grow up they want to explore. Sometimes they want to take risks or test themselves. Sometimes they just want to get close to someone like Moore with a bad reputation, or they want to try the drugs he offers. During this period, they're vulnerable to cults, misbehaving peers, and experimentation.

It is nearly impossible to prospectively determine who a sexual predator might be. Someone who looks "creepy" is not necessarily an offender, while someone who seems respectable cannot be eliminated as a child molester or a bad influence. Accurate prediction based on traits, appearance, or behavior remains outside our reach. We must be concerned with those who skillfully hide their predilections.

Pedophiles are often placed into one of four categories. *Mysopeds* molest and sexually abuse children to physically harm them; they're sadists. *Regressed child offenders* generally have relations with adults but offend against children when stressed; it helps them to feel in control. *Fixated child offenders* are stuck in an early stage of psychosexual development. They have little to no social contact with people their own age. They view their abuse as "affection." Finally, *naive pedophiles* have no sense of right and wrong, usually from mental instability or low intelligence. Corll seemed to be a cross between a mysoped and a fixated child offender.

Researchers Reuben Lang and Roy Frenzel interviewed fifty-two incest offenders and fifty pedophilic offenders and found that the average age of their study subjects for the period of offending was thirty-four (Corll was thirty to thirty-three). The typical modus operandi is to befriend the parents and offer to babysit targeted victims or keep them busy with things like pool, sports, trips to the beach, or computer games. They gradually ease into the victims' lives and make themselves indispensable. Corll had vehicles, a pool table, and a house, as well as access to liquor and drugs. He took boys to the beach or gave them rides elsewhere. Brooks and Henley both came to depend on him, giving them incentive to overlook his "thing."

Pedophiles often go undetected because they act as if they have nothing to hide, they do favors, and they're friendly. Friends and neighbors of the kindly fifty-four-year-old Anthony Barron were stunned when he was convicted of eighty-nine offenses against young girls. He was a volunteer treasurer for the Boy Scouts and was active in a parent-teacher organization. People trusted him. But for nine years, he'd been regularly molesting at least eleven girls, some as young as three. Barron had befriended the parents first. He came across as reasonable and caring, and he was a father and grandfather. Some parents allowed him to watch their children when they were away, and he used games, toys, and his charming manner to persuade the girls who came to his house to cooperate. He videotaped himself molesting them, using both still and video cameras to get images from various angles. He used candy as bribes to keep their secret.

Understanding the predatory sex offender is paramount to public safety, but it is equally important to know the types of children pedophiles target, including those they recruit for crime.

## How It Works

Some kids are wired for trouble. They might be anxious, passive, reactive, or in need of attention. Adverse life experiences reinforce their issues. Some negative behavior arises from family influence, the environment, social media exposure, and criminal role models. Some kids get into a situation and they're too scared to tell someone, or they don't want to be viewed as a narc. Even if they have appropriate moral upbringing, they can be confused. Their hesitancy plays into the predator's plan. The longer they wait to inform police or walk away, the easier it is for predators to convince them they're in too deep to leave.

After a tumultuous childhood, Lee Boyd Malvo clung to forty-one-year-old John Muhammad as the only stable force in his life. With no communication from his biological father, Malvo had been subjected to the whims of an unstable mother, who moved him around and often neglected or abandoned him. Muhammad took him in when he was a teen and treated him well. Malvo was the kind of kid Muhammad thought he could turn into one of his "soldiers." Little by little, Muhammad won Malvo's trust and leveraged him into blind obedience, until the boy finally agreed to kill for him. The synchrony described earlier was at work in this team.

"I trusted him completely," Malvo wrote. "Whatever he was or was not, he was consistent. . . . If he uttered it, it was as good as the next sun rising; not only have I accepted him, he became a pattern for me to follow, I absorbed his personality by way of osmosis. . . . He could depend on me because he understood me, what was my drive, how to motivate, chide, the

THE SERIAL KILLER'S APPRENTICE

intensity of my anger, and thus the outcomes of my action. Thought was a burden I left up to him. I was nothing without him."

For three weeks in 2002 as the "Beltway Snipers," Muhammad and Malvo shot thirteen people at random along the I-95 corridor in the eastern United States, killing ten. A subsequent investigation tied them to shootings in other states. Malvo, the primary shooter, was just seventeen. He was tried, convicted, and given ten life sentences without the possibility of parole, six in Maryland and four in Virginia.

Anthony Meoli, of Meoli Forensic Consulting, had extensive contact with Malvo, documented in *Interview with the DC Sniper*. He asked how Muhammad had been able to instill such a strong fatherly bond.

"He didn't really have to instill it," Malvo responded. "There was a hole there for the last fifteen years that I was trying to fill from my real parents, who really didn't give a f—. He just had to be there, show up and be consistent. He was bad, he was terrible, but he was consistent, he was there." When pressed to describe his struggle with things Muhammad required, Malvo said, "At the time, I did not have time to think. Twenty-four hours a day I was doing something. He [Muhammad] learned on two occasions if he left me and gave me time to think, I would start breaking down. So he just had to keep the ball rolling. If there was nothing to do, he had to create something. As long as I had something to do . . . then everything would be okay."

At his trial, Malvo put it more succinctly: "I was desperate to fill a void in my life, and I was ready to give my life for him."

According to forensic psychiatrist Neil Blumberg, Malvo had a dissociative disorder as a consequence of his preexisting vulnerability to Muhammad's indoctrination. Blumberg also diagnosed Malvo with depressive disorder and conduct disorder. He noted that the childhood of a perpetrator of violence provides red flags when there's abandonment, instability, abuse, neglect, and extreme inconsistency, especially for males.

The court ordered social worker Carmeta Albarus to find any information that might help mitigate a death sentence in the case. She worked with psychologist Jonathan H. Mack. Albarus met with Malvo numerous times and traveled to his Jamaican homeland to interview his relatives, teachers, and friends. She learned that he'd been a promising young man whose repeated abuse and abandonment had left him detached from his parents and desperate for guidance and support. John Muhammad, a veteran of the first Gulf War, had conditioned his protégé through brainwashing, sniper training, and race hatred to turn him into an angry, dissociated killer with no empathy for his victims. Yet just as Malvo's youth had made him susceptible, Albarus said, his malleable brain also made him salvageable. Under more favorable conditions, his former sense of purpose, dignity, and care for others could be restored. That is, he'd been psychopathic under a bad influence and controlled conditions rather than being a primary psychopath.

Malvo made progress and came to understand the enormity of his criminal acts. He asked the state of Maryland to reconsider his sentences. In *Miller v. Alabama* in 2012, the US Supreme Court had barred mandatory life sentences for juveniles, except for those rare few considered to be permanently incorrigible. The Court had decided that evaluating defendants for sentencing had to consider such factors as their development, their education, and their adverse circumstances. Adolescent immaturity, impulsiveness, vulnerability to negative influences, and tendency to take risks were recognized. Their actions as kids, in other words, were not necessarily "evidence of irrebuttable depravity." Although the US Supreme Court adjusted its criteria in 2021, stating that incorrigibility need not be the standard for decisions, the Maryland Court still determined that Malvo was entitled to a rehearing.

Malvo's public defender contended that he should benefit from Maryland's new law that enables those convicted as juveniles to seek release after serving twenty years. The Maryland Court of Appeals said it is unlikely that Malvo would be released from custody because he first must be granted parole in Virginia, where he has four life sentences, before beginning to serve his consecutive sentences in Maryland. On August 30, 2022, the

Virginia Parole Board denied Malvo's first application for parole after they considered him to be a "risk to the community." Yet, his shift in moral perspective once free from Muhammad has become his behavioral guide. Despite legal decisions, his story provides a positive model for mental health counselors and offender reentry teams.

## Henley's Perspective

Like Muhammad with Malvo, Corll made a series of moves that bypassed Henley's moral training, although Corll was not as intense or focused as Muhammad. Henley became Corll's apprentice, but he also suffered psychologically. Henley drank and took drugs to get high to distance and numb himself. Whenever he was away from Corll, he tried to pick up a normal life, hoping Corll would quit killing.

Henley understands how he has psychologically compensated. "I've had to compartmentalize. I was raised in a Christian household. I was raised to believe in family values. I was raised to be a good person, a Southern gentleman. And when I was with Dean, that was all put in abeyance. After Dean, I was able to get that person back and now it's a daily thing of being that person. It's hard for me to give myself the excuse that I was too young to deal with a serial killer. Objectively, I can say that no fourteen- or fifteen-year-old can be expected to adequately deal with a serial killer who is twice his age—a person that authorities today cannot adequately deal with. So why would they expect that fifteen-year-old to have been any better at it? But then the question comes up, how could I, Wayne Henley, who was raised this way, have allowed this to ever happen?"

After finding his way through panic attacks and persistent nightmares, Henley has a better grasp of the costs of his involvement with Corll. "I have to accept that any child—because that's what I was—any child could be manipulated, given that the right buttons were pushed. And Dean pushed all my buttons. He convinced me that there were higher powers of syndicates and hit men and amorphous bad guys in the background. So, I felt like they were a threat. There's no excuse in the eyes of the law. . . . But he made me aware that I had been involved in a murder that I did not know about. I thought, 'I'm going to the electric chair.'

"When I got arrested, I had no frame of reference to what had happened to me. I didn't understand it. And there for a long time, I just believed all the hype that I must be an evil person. But having been able to stand back from it, and with so many people concentrating studies on [grooming], I can see where Dean had walked me through a process. He would take me a few steps and get me there. And then take me a few more steps. He had brought me to a point where I participated in what I thought was a crime of white slavery, and then when I backed away from that, he forced the issue. He was able to look me in the eye and say, 'This is what I've done, and this is what you've been involved in. And this is what's going to happen to you. You don't have any choice. Deal with me or the police are going to kill you . . . or *I* will.'"

Henley is working his way through a narrative influenced by current research and awareness of malleable adolescence. He's identifying triggers that Corll used, such as his need to make his father proud of him, the need to stand up for himself, and Corll's use of positive and negative reinforcement. "It seems so silly, but one time he wanted me to do something to somebody, and when I got done, he was gonna go in and make blueberry muffins."

Henley has repeatedly said that Corll's approval mattered to him. "If I'm acting out of survival psychopathy, then Dean's approval means that I will survive."

Henley had mostly soft limits, something Corll could erode. Like others in his social groups, he was young, vulnerable, a bit rebellious, and willing to commit minor crimes. Corll saw how pliable he was. "Dean recognized someone he could manipulate," Henley states. "I've never allowed myself that. I've always said [to myself], no, you were a grown-up, you were responsible. You're an intelligent person. It should never have happened. But it happened because I was a child. . . . Dean Corll provided me with authority and approval, and a guilt-free purpose. Anything I did with him or for him was approved."

There's no formula for what any given predator seeks. Generally, they know it when they see it—the mur-dar. When they're looking for partners in crime among teens, they're vigilant for kids they think they can mold. Their narcissism makes them believe they can gain control; their sadism compels them, and their lack of remorse erases any sense of the harm they might do. Corll took a shy, insecure kid like Brooks and made him tolerant of sexual assault and murder by giving him things he wanted or needed. Corll viewed Henley as a social asset—a kid who could attract other kids—so he chipped away at Henley's beliefs and exploited his anger.

Becoming aware of the dynamics of such teams, especially those that manipulate child vulnerabilities, can help to form protective strategies. Nothing has changed about how vulnerable kids are to offenders who are intent on adopting one as a partner. However, the predator's playground and set of tools have expanded. Despite all the surveillance, education, warnings, and cautionary tales, there are still many ways for these criminals to victimize communities and their children.

# CHAPTER 8

## Closer Than They Appear

### How Predators See the World

C hristopher Wilder sensed trouble. Police were investigating the disappearance of several women associated with the thirty-nine-year-old Florida contractor. In 1984, he packed up and fled west. Along the way, he lured several young women into his clutches by exploiting typical teen aspirations. Sometimes he just stole their car, but others he tortured and sexually assaulted before killing them. However, he kept one girl alive to assist him. For nine days, she complied.

During his flight, Wilder followed young women in malls or parking lots to tell them he was a photographer in need of models. As bait, he used flattery about their beauty and the assurance of a glamorous career. He persuaded them to go with him to his car to see his portfolio, and he had one ready to show. As they looked at his photos and relaxed their guard, he forced them into his car.

On April 4, 1984, Wilder spotted sixteen-year-old Tina R. at a store in California. He presented his ruse. Tina, flattered, let him take pictures of her, but then he forced her at gunpoint to do as he said. He raped her but instead of killing her, he sensed he could use her and thereby minimize his risk of being seen with girls who disappeared. He drove Tina across the country to Indiana, where Wilder sent her to lure a girl who was filling out a job application. The bait would be the promise of a job interview. Tina introduced herself to this girl as Tina Wilder and learned that the jobseeker's name was Dawnette. Tina invited Dawnette to step outside to speak to the "store manager." Wilder abducted Dawnette and made Tina drive while he raped the girl. At a hotel, he tortured her. In New York, Wilder took Dawnette into the woods to suffocate her, but she fought him off. When he stabbed her, she pretended to be dead, so he left. She managed to find a road and get help.

Near Victor, New York, Wilder used Tina to help him steal another car. He shot the female driver. Then he took Tina to an airport and gave her enough money to fly home. Reportedly, he told her to kiss him on the cheek and urged her to write a book.

When she arrived in Los Angeles, she directed a cab driver to a lingerie store so she could purchase clothes. "My mind was just so blank," she would later say. Then she reported her ordeal to police. By this time, a New Hampshire state trooper who'd recognized Wilder had approached him but failed to stop him from shooting himself.

Wilder was dubbed the "Beauty Queen Killer" because he sought young women at beauty pageants and had a portfolio to support his ruse. He apparently saw a quality in Tina that let him trust her when she was out from under his immediate control. She did what he said for more than a week. Identified later in the press, she credited a turbulent childhood raised among outlaw motorcycle gangs for helping her to handle Wilder and survive. "There's something inside of me that I knew how to play along," she admitted. Although Wilder focused on victims he expected to kill, with

Tina he'd shifted his modus operandi from murder to manager because he sensed something in her he could use to his advantage.

Predators evaluate everyone they meet as potential obstacles, targets, partners, or enablers. Often, they use a contrived persona to falsely engender trust.

Dr. Jon Conte, associate professor in social sciences at the University of Chicago, conducted a study, published in 1989, that invited twenty male sex offenders in a community treatment program to describe how they had targeted, recruited, and maintained a sexual abuse situation with a child. Most believed they had a special ability to spot a vulnerable kid. Most also used systematic desensitization to prepare the child for abuse. Many were attracted to a friendly child, but some of these men looked specifically "for some kind of deficiency." The offenders also evaluated children who seemed likely to keep a secret, usually because they were socially isolated or seemed desperate for guidance from an adult. They didn't have friends and would be willing to do something that gained them one: "Use love as a bait," one offender said, and "Show the kid extra attention." Gifts, flattery, attention, and sympathy assisted with their approach and with maintaining the abuse. The opening strategy for several offenders was introducing sexual jokes (like Corll) and verbal seduction. "Get on their level, ask how their day was going, what did they like."

In addition, they worked on the people around the child: "Get as many people who are close to the victim to trust you" and "separate them from adults who might protect them." The goal was to get the child to believe they have given tacit consent. This would make them less likely to tell someone.

Although this offender group focused on abuse victims, the strategies for recruiting youthful accomplices are similar. For predators, it's a matter of studying human nature through a lens of exploitation, then manipulating common human tendencies and expectations.

In a pivotal study about persuasion, social psychologist Robert Cialdini crystallized the core principles of influencing others based on hundreds of research studies about compliance and conformity. He identified six key aspects of human nature that will "move someone in your direction." Good persuaders, he explained, "strum strings that are inside all of us." Their goal is to create a state of mind that is ready to respond. Predators can strum these strings to bait accomplices and victims alike.

One strategy is posing as an authority, a person with knowledge or power. Successful predators offer false personas, spiked with a strong dose of confidence, or they acquire actual positions of authority to gain the aura of privilege and trust. If they're verbally fluid, they have another advantage because those who speak faster than normal are viewed as confident in their claims. Predators watch for uncertainty in people, then step in with clear instructions; people who feel safe are more likely to cooperate, especially with the person who clarified things.

Similarly, says Cialdini, successful persuaders are aware that people tend to do things for those they like. Predators use compliments, common interests or problems, or similar gestures, clothing, and posture to increase rapport. They also give gifts because people tend to feel a need to reciprocate. They also try to elicit commitments, because most people want to honor what they state they will do.

Dean Corll used some of these ploys to secure his accomplices or to acquire victims when he worked alone: gifts, resources, a pleasant facade, a place to hang out, a sense of confidence, a car or a ride, and the promise of alcohol or drugs. To get Henley's compliance in his first kidnapping, Corll used humor, pressure, money, and lies. After killing that young man, Corll sprang the trap: Henley was now complicit in murder. "He led me on to that point where I was willing to accept as a fact that he had killed, and I had participated."

Corll framed this collusion with the intimidating authority of a sex trafficking organization in Dallas. Henley believed he'd been caught up in organized crime. It was beyond Henley's ability to navigate such perilous circumstances, given his youth and inexperience.

## Spotting the Markers

Despite the notion that most people have a solid sixth sense about conning and duplicity, predators know how to deflect this. No one whom police interviewed about Corll said they'd sensed something sinister in him. Even when he commented to coworkers about the ease of killing someone, they attributed his knowledge about such things to his military experience.

Humans are hardwired to focus. They need to see *important* things rather than *everything*, so they're selective. In addition, their perceptual system takes shortcuts by imposing a context based on their limited knowledge and experience. They typically see what they expect to see, and they behave accordingly.

In 2015, YouTube prankster Joseph Saladino performed a social experiment. With permission from three parents, he videotaped encounters with their young children on a New York City playground. Each child had been warned not to talk with strangers. Then Saladino used a puppy to lure them to a place where they'd be vulnerable. All were quickly hooked. They even put their hands in his. The parents were shocked at how easy it had been for Saladino's ploy to undo their training. The idea of seeing a cute dog had silenced alarm bells.

Saladino's work was criticized. Some said the kids had seen him talking with their parents, so he wasn't a stranger. Therefore, they felt safe. However, being familiar to the kids doesn't necessarily diminish his potential to be dangerous.

In one terrible case, Alfred Dyer, a thirty-two-year-old elementary school crossing guard, approached three girls he knew, ages seven to nine, and asked if they wanted to hunt bunnies. They recognized him from school and they wanted to see the bunnies, so they followed him. It was the middle of the day in a city park. He made sure to walk well in front so he wouldn't seem to be escorting them away. Once he got the girls behind some bushes, he sexually assaulted and strangled them. He said later that he'd been surprised how easy it had been to persuade them. Given the right bait, even kids who've been warned can still be lured if the predator can make the situation seem safe.

In another experiment conducted in Florida in 2014, adolescents were offered an opportunity to be cast in a reality show that could make them famous. Some subjects willingly entered a windowless van and surrendered their phones. "In less than one hour, we approached nineteen students, everyone from freshmen to grad students. Six of them got into our minivan and handed over their cell phones—their only lifeline to get help." One had even participated recently on a Safe Walk program. "He admitted he didn't think twice about sitting in the van and said the safety test was a good reminder." Kids can easily make poor decisions without being aware of possible consequences.

Still, predators often do exhibit red-flag behaviors. You *can* read them, but you must be informed, alert, and willing to recognize the signs. During a conversation, there might be subtle self-stimulation with hands and fingers ("preemptive tactile contact"), as well as physical contact with the child. Touching, squeezing the shoulders, giving back rubs, standing too close, or any form of intimacy done without permission is reason for concern. If an older adult acts like a child's peer, parents should be watchful, especially if the adult enters the child's bedroom (as Corll did at the Henley home).

Voice tones are a powerful part of the arsenal. They can be dominating, intimate, and inviting all at once, gradually entrancing the target. An accent can have this effect, as can a deep voice. A quiet voice tone draws someone closer, especially when matched with calculated body language.

Strategically, many predators these days have moved from the streets to the anonymity of the internet. Kids are generally savvier about online socializing than their parents but still fail to realize that freely offering their personal information is what predators notice. These kids are the equivalent of the "friendly" kids the twenty offenders-in-treatment had described as their preferred targets.

With smartphones, kids now hold in their hands the thing that makes them most vulnerable. It offers predators a portal. It also contributes to the kids' anxiety and insecurity, based on "likes" or negative comments, especially when they lack healthy role models. They can see where their friends are, whether they've been excluded, how they're falling short of "influencers" their age (or younger), and how to harm themselves should those thoughts arise. This makes kids susceptible to strangers—especially adults—who seem to have answers. But on the internet, predators can also pose more easily as someone younger. Austin Lee Edwards, twenty-eight, catfished a fifteen-year-old girl online in November 2022 by posing as a teenage boy. In a failed attempt to abduct her, he murdered her mother and grandparents. Edwards was no ordinary predator; he was a sheriff's deputy.

Most kids fail to realize how much data they're exposing. Between 2019 and 2020, the National Center for Missing and Exploited Children (NCMEC) reported a shocking increase in reports about online sexual enticement, from nineteen thousand reports to nearly thirty-eight thousand. "We've noticed a clear and disturbing uptick in our CyberTipline reports of online enticement. In the year 2020 alone, we've seen the rate of these types of incidents increase 97.5% compared to the year prior." With photo filters, predators can make themselves resemble other teens, even of the opposite sex. They study their specialized jargon, learn their cultural touchstones, and exploit opportunities to converse. AI tools might enhance their ability to falsely pose.

Sexual predators seeking children, says the NCMEC, are generally male, and between the ages of thirteen and sixty-five. They're generally collectors of images or videos involving child pornography, chatters who just like to engage kids to talk about sex, or "travelers," who encourage offline face-to-face contact. Whether online or in the street, most sexual predators look for a few key behaviors that signal vulnerable kids:

- Being unpopular or the subject of teasing
- Being isolated
- Expressing feelings of being neglected or unloved
- Looking for attention
- Have low self-esteem and a lack of confidence
- Lacking in resources
- Lacking parental supervision
- Having significant family problems such as divorce, substance abuse, or crime
- Feeling uncertain about their sexuality
- Wishing for money, drugs, or adventure
- Having a pliable morality (soft limits)
- Having parents who easily trust others with their child

Corll noticed that Brooks had no family ties. His parents were divorced and neither paid him much attention. He was an easy target. Corll saw that Henley was angry about his father's abuse—the thing that had disintegrated Corll's own family and soiled his sense of himself. Corll played on this affinity. He knew how to meet Brooks's needs for respectful attention and to manipulate Henley's simmering coals. Some predators will offer a "mentoring" relationship, as Corll did; others act as if they're the same age as their target. Corll did this too, as he posed as the cool adult with a youthful attitude. Thus, predators appear to offer a bridge between the doubts of adolescence and the stability of adulthood. Henley described this aspect of Corll as a particular appeal. Multiple people said that Corll knew how to make them feel special, as if they really mattered. That's captivating.

Kids also like to experiment. Some specific behaviors turn up in those who've reported an encounter with a sexual predator. One study showed that youths who engaged in at least four of the following behaviors were most likely to become victims:

1.  Making contact with people in a wide variety of online venues
2.  Talking freely about sex with strangers
3.  Allowing strangers to be part of their personal buddy list or social network
4.  Making rude or vulgar comments online
5.  Visiting sexually explicit sites

Once engaged with a target, predators will emphasize secrecy, with rewards attached for loyalty. They might make kids believe they'll be in trouble should they tell, or believe that their families will shun them, or that they'll spoil the "special" relationship they have with the predator. They might even threaten to hurt someone in the child's family.

When predators contact kids, there can be telltale signs. There might be gifts or phone calls from strangers, or more secretive behavior with phones or on computers. When children start to behave differently, especially more aggressively, more withdrawn, or with increased substance abuse, parents should investigate who might be influencing this. Any behaviors that indicate increased stress, such as trouble sleeping or eating, anxiety, irritableness, or aggression should be viewed as potentially more than a developmental stage. Henley exhibited all these behaviors, causing his friends and relatives to worry and his mother to make an appointment with a psychiatrist. She'd seen the signs but by the time she acted, it was tragically far too late.

Like the Dallas-based trafficking organization that Corll described to threaten his teen procurers, the internet has created a trade in child pornography and sex trafficking that stays steps ahead of law enforcement and legislative regulation. The digital industry of child pornography that thrives today came from previously established networks, according to Melanie Weaver's 2019 doctoral research at Arizona State University. She showed how the caches of child pornography today trace back to master lists like those that John David Norman had generated. The internet, especially the dark web, has only encouraged networks among child molesters who might otherwise have remained solitary wolves. They pass around productive strategies, describe new opportunities, and support one another's criminal activity. Lucrative child porn networks have grown enormously, expanding internationally, using trade in victims or their images to indemnify one another.

To ensure a child's safety, parents and guardians are the front line of defense. They must set up clear rules about internet use and remain firm, engage in regular monitoring, keep open communication, and discuss the reality of online and cell phone lures that predators use. Some kids will still follow the enticements, but others, when educated, might be deterred.

There are self-help guides about "reading people" and some provide lists of red alert behaviors. Among good resources are Robert Hare's *Without Conscience*, David Givens's *Crime Signals*, and Gavin de Becker's *The Gift of Fear* and *Protecting the Gift*.

## Guidelines

There's a lot to consider. Based on what's known about the experiences of accomplices, including who they were before and after their involvement on a criminal team, it's possible to formalize a set of tips:

1. Beware of adults who spend most of their time with kids, especially if they never invite a parent to join an outing or gathering.
2. Teach kids about grooming behavior and the importance of telling someone if it happens. Then *listen* to those who say they're in trouble. They might not know quite how to

reveal it, or they might describe something that's difficult to believe, but it's important to take them seriously.

3.  Talk with kids about not keeping harmful secrets and explain that responsible adults would not ask children to do this. Make sure children know they can confide in their parents or guardians if someone—even a trusted friend—asks them to do something they're uncomfortable with.

4.  Discuss the concepts of respect, consent, and gut feeling, so children clearly understand when someone has crossed a line. Parents might use situations in movies or novels to open lines of communication. Kids should also be taught the meaning of consent and be told they can withdraw consent at any time.

5.  Be present in the child's life. Give them a clear sense of where it's safe to go. Pay attention to how they're feeling, especially if they're acting in an uncharacteristic manner. Be careful not to dismiss such behavioral shifts as "just a teenage phase." They might really be in trouble. Be supportive without being controlling or judgmental. Shame should not be a reason they stay silent.

6.  Know who the child interacts with. Be aware of "friends of friends." No matter how trusting an older adult might seem, take care to know in what manner your child is interacting with them. Talk with neighbors about what they know too. (It's likely that greater communication in the Heights might have helped the parents of missing kids to piece together the connections to Brooks and Corll.) These days, it's easier to run a check on someone using internet sources, and this should be done.

7. In settings outside the home, such as a camp, an organized trip, or a community center, check on the creden-
   tials of adults who work there. More than one predator
   has used such organizations to get close to kids, since
   they're free of direct parental supervision. In fact, having
   status as an authority figure often aids these offenders, as
   parents prefer to believe that predators would not acquire
   such positions.

8. As daunting as this might be, take time to understand
   the online world in which your children are interacting.
   Predators anticipate that parents will be too busy or
   clueless to do much more than check in now and then.
   (They're not wrong.)

9. Be careful about how information about family is displayed on social media, on cars, or with other types of
   signs. First, it presents a model to kids. Also, predators
   use any and all information for their own purposes.
   They're skilled data-miners.

10. Verify claims made by people who will be supervising or
    caring for your children. Call their references. The most
    prolific abusers have come from communities deemed
    safe.

11. Realize that grooming often starts in the presence of
    adults to normalize it for the targeted child. Psychologists
    Carmit Katz and Zion Barnetz investigated grooming
    in a sample of ninety-five children, five to thirteen years
    old. They found that 68.4 percent of victims reported that
    their abuser had also manipulated their family members.

12. Don't believe you can spot a predator by appearance or
    from a gut reaction. The most benign facade can conceal
    the most malignant intent. You must watch for patterns,

inconsistencies, and evidence of deception. Document it
so you have a record and a reminder.

13. Recognize that sexual predators can be female. It's a myth
to believe that sexually molested boys are not victims. Of
those who were manipulated by female teachers, many
described the difficulty they had in later years with trust
in relationships and with personal emotional issues.

14. Never assume that a child can fend off a skilled predator.
Children make decisions differently from adults because
they value things differently. Even if they're smart and
believe they know what to do, under certain types of
pressure, they might make poor choices.

15. If a local law enforcement agency offers a program about
predators, attend it, if only to become acquainted with
police personnel and resources.

Henley views point #2 as the most important piece of advice.

"Please listen to anyone who comes with a problem or seeking advice.
Even if it's beyond your ken to try to correct things, *listen*. Hear them.
Take it to heart and take time to investigate. We have to realize that young
people have very real problems that require a mature adult's action. They
may well be inarticulate and ashamed or embarrassed. If they try to broach
the subject and are rebuffed, they may never approach it again. It may have
taken them months to be able to tell their mom or dad, or whoever their
authority figure is, that this man sexually molested me. Many of them
feel like they're at fault. If they finally decide to tell and someone does
not immediately let them know, 'I hear you and I believe you,' they're not
gonna come back."

Had any of the adults checked on the things Henley tried to tell them,
they might have been able to stop Corll. They could have checked on the
names Henley knew to see if boys were missing; they could have gone

with him to one of the graves; they could have helped him set up a sting operation. Instead, they decided he was crazy or drunk.

## Application

These cases are like puzzles with missing pieces. We can put together enough to see what the finished picture will look like, but the holes—the missing information—prevent a complete image. Many criminal cases are made from a totality of the circumstances, which consists of everything available. Often, that's not everything there is, but the evidence can still have sufficient suggestive power to confirm the connections between offenders and their crimes.

The point of this book was to show the considerable reach of predatory networks and to explore how one boy's vulnerability applies more broadly to kids today. Corll tested Henley's soft limits with innocuous petty crimes. Then he proposed a far more lucrative activity. Once he succeeded at getting Henley to act, he had sufficient leverage to erode Henley's moral code—his hard limits. Little by little, Henley took the bait, and then complied.

Yet he still refused to do certain acts, such as use a sword on someone or have sex with a bound victim. Another hard limit that he didn't realize until Corll tested it was his duty to females. Seeing a girl about to be killed drew on his upbringing, his sense of himself as a protector, and his respect for his mother and grandmother. His naive idealism, mixed with the hard reality of an abusive father, had made him easy to hook with the right bait. So did his yearning for an authority figure. Corll, twice his age, with a job, a car, and a place to hang out, modeled manhood for Henley.

Corll shredded the teen's ideas about God before he stepped in as a substitute. He also exploited an addicting rotation of cruelty and kindness to keep Henley coming back for more. But once Corll's influence was subtracted, Henley gradually recovered his former sense of himself. During the period when Corll dominated Henley, the boy had been as psychopathic as Corll. He'd thought it was cool to be part of the Syndicate. But as he assisted with locating bodies for the cops, the influence wore off. Henley wondered how he could have been part of something so vile.

Today, Henley hopes to help prevent others from becoming unwitting accomplices. He understands better now how trauma can manifest in someone's life and make them vulnerable. Although parents might believe they've trained their kids to be aware and to protect themselves, research shows that predators have evolved too. Kids are still shockingly vulnerable.

"Before I met Dean Corll," says Henley, "I had no idea that such evil existed in the world. He dragged me into his world; it was a crazy world, it was a scary world, and I handled it badly. Today, after fifty years in the penitentiary, I can't help but see myself as Dean's last victim. I understand that people are going to say I'm not a victim, I'm a perpetrator. But on my own, I worked, I went to church, I went to the movies with my kid brothers. I hold myself responsible and have guilt—and I've done my best to assume that—but at the same time, I was targeted by Dean. I wake up every day, and I'm still under Dean's thumb, I'm still living Dean's life. I understand why people are mad at me. But be mad at me for what *I've* done. Be mad at me because I was weak. Be mad at me because I was young and made poor choices. Don't be mad at me for Dean's crimes."

# Acknowledgments

## Katherine Ramsland

The first person I want to acknowledge is my coauthor, Tracy Ullman. She had already established a relationship with Wayne Henley and was willing to make an introduction. His trust in her transferred to me. She is the most diligent researcher I've ever worked with, and she quickly acquired the items we needed. It was terrific to work through ideas with her and get immediate feedback. We spent many mornings on the phone, grappling with tough topics. Next, I thank Wayne Henley. Despite the emotional difficulty for him of reliving the horrific events from 1972–73, he willingly described and explored the experience of being an accomplice in murder. The value of his contribution cannot be overstated. Also, I thank Mary Henley and Brittany Burns for their perspectives on Wayne's experiences. In addition, I appreciate the support from my colleagues at DeSales University, especially Brother Dan Wisniewski and Amy Jenkins.

Our editor, Tom Wickersham, gave us invaluable tips and guidelines for improving the story. I thank him for his enthusiasm for this project and his astute sense of direction. And I was fortunate to have good readers for early drafts: Susan Lysek, Sally Keglovits, Dana DeVito, and Brittany Burns. They helped to improve this manuscript by brainstorming with me and by catching errors. Sally Keglovits, in particular, provided significant guidance about Truman Capote.

My friend and literary agent, John Silbersack, has long been my strongest support in the publishing world. He was my first commercial editor more than three decades ago and has stuck with me as my agent. He saw the value of this book and found the right home for it.


## Tracy Ullman


In addition to Dr. Ramsland's acknowledgments—for whom I am also grateful—and her incredible work as a criminologist that truly brought this book's message home, I'd like to thank Dr. Sharon Derrick and Dr. Jennifer Love, formerly of the Harris County Institute of Forensic Sciences, for conversations that informed my larger journey of discovery; Michele Arnold from the Harris County Institute of Forensic Sciences for information that furthered my knowledge; Claudia German from the Houston Police Department for so diligently filling my FOIA requests; Randy White for sharing his immense archive about John David Norman; Ken Wooden, who described his first-person interactions with the devastation brought by child sex trafficking; Meredith Mann for helping me access Truman Capote's files at the New York Public Library; and Sergio Montemayor at the Nueces County District Clerk who accessed and digitized all of the original court files. I'd also like to thank Alison True and Steve Becker, who locked arms with me as we discovered the trafficking ring and its current relevance. Lastly, thank you Dan Glomski for being there.

# Bibliography

Abrams, Zara. "What Neuroscience Tells Us About the Teenage Brain." *Monitor on Psychology* 53 (5), July 2022. https://www.apa.org/monitor/2022/07/feature-neuroscience-teen-brain.

Albarus, Carmeta and Jonathan Mack. *The Making of Lee Boyd Malvo: The D.C. Sniper.* New York: Columbia University Press, 2012.

Apter, Michael. *The Dangerous Edge: The Psychology of Excitement.* New York: The Free Press, 1992.

Barlow, Jim. "Henley Case Began in 1973 with Teen's Report of Killing." *Houston Chronicle.* December 21, 1979.

Becker, Steven W. "Human Trafficking, Homicide, and Current Prevention Efforts in the United States of America." *Hrvatski Ljetopis za Kaznene Znanosti I Praksu* November 29, 2022, 565–580. https://doi.org/10.54070/hljk.29.2.11.

"Behavior: The Mind of the Mass Murderer," *Time*, August 27, 1973.

Berliner, L. "The Concept of Grooming and How It Can Help Victims." *Journal of Interpersonal Violence* 33 (1), January 2018, 24–27. https://doi.org/10.1177/0886260517742057.

Blakemore, Sarah-Jayne. *Inventing Ourselves: The Secret Life of the Teenage Brain.* New York: Doubleday, 2018.

Bliss, George, and Michael Sneed. "Probe Destruction of Mail-Order Sex List," *Chicago Tribune*, May 30, 1977, 1.

Brandt, John Randall, Wallace A. Kennedy, Christopher J. Patrick, and John J. Curtin. "Assessment of Psychopathy in a Population of Incarcerated Adolescent Offenders." *Psychological Assessment* 9 (4), 1997, 429–435. https://doi.org/10.1037/1040-3590.9.4.429.

Caldwell, Michael, Jennifer Skeem, Randy Salekin, and Gregory van Rybroek. "Treatment Response of Adolescent Offenders with Psychopathy Features: A Two-year Follow-up." *Criminal Justice and Behavior* 33 (5), 2006, 571–596. https://doi.org/10.1177/0093854806288176.

Capote File on Houston, Brooke Russell Astor Reading Room for Rare Books and Manuscripts, The New York Public Library.

"Capote Starts Work on Houston Murders," *Milwaukee Journal*, January 7, 1974.

Capote, Truman. *In Cold Blood*. New York: Random House, 1966.

Carlisle, A. C. "The Dark Side of the Serial-Killer Personality." In *Serial Killers*, edited by Louis Gerdes. San Diego, CA: Greenhaven Press, 2000, 106–118.

Casey, B. J., Rebecca M. Jones, and Todd A. Hare. "The Adolescent Brain." *Annals of the New York Academy of Sciences* 1124, March 2008, 111–126. https://doi.org/10.1196/annals.1440.010.

Chriss, Nicholas C., and Robert Rawitch. "Corll's Portrait: Polite, Quiet, Neat, 'Always with Young Boys.' " *Los Angeles Times*, August 19, 1973.

Cialdini, Robert. *Influence: The Psychology of Persuasion*. New York: Harper, 2006.

Cole, Sharline, and Susan R. Anderson. "Family Interaction and the Development of Aggression in Adolescents: The Experiences of Students and Administrators." *American International Journal of Contemporary Research* 6 (4), August 2016. https://api.semanticscholar.org /CorpusID:168164675.

Collin-Vézina, D., M. De La Sablonnière-Griffin, A. M. Palmer, and L. Milne. "A Preliminary Mapping of Individual, Relational, and Social Factors that Impede Disclosure of Childhood Sexual Abuse." *Child Abuse and Neglect* 43, 2015, 123–134. https://doi.org/10.1016/j.chiabu.2015.03.010.

Conaway, James. "The Last Kid on the Block." *Texas Monthly*, April 1976. Excerpted from *The Texans*, New York: Alfred A. Knopf, 1976.

Conte, Jon R., Steven Wolf, and Tim Smith. "What Sexual Offenders Tell Us About Prevention Strategies." *Child Abuse and Neglect* 13 (2), 1989, 293–301. https://doi.org/10.1016/0145-2134(89)90016-1.

Costa, Silvia and Peter Shaw. " 'Open Minded' Cells: How Cells Can Change Fate." *Trends in Cell Biology* 17 (3), 2006, 101–106. https://doi.org/10.1016/j .tcb.2006.12.005.

Dallas Police Prosecution Report on John David Norman apartment search, ID # 121699, August 15, 1973.

Da Silva, Diana R., Daniel Rijo, and Randall T. Salekin. "Child and Adolescent Psychopathy: A State-of-the-Art Reflection on the Construct and Etiological Theories." *Journal of Criminal Justice* 40 (4), 2012, 269–277. https://doi.org/10.1016/j.jcrimjus.2012.05.005.

Davis, David Martin. "Forensic Hypnosis is Big in Texas. Here's How It Got Its Start." Texas Public Radio, December 14, 2021. https://www.tpr.org /news/2021-12-14/forensic-hypnosis-is-big-in-texas-heres-how-it-got -its-start.

Dean, Andy C., Lily L. Altstein, Mitchell E. Berman, Joseph I. Constans, Catherine A. Sugar, and Michael S. McCloskey. "Secondary Psychopathy, But Not Primary Psychopathy, is Associated with Risky Decision-Making in Noninstitutionalized Young Adults." *Personality and Individual Differences* 54 (2), 2013, 272–277. https://doi.org/10.1016/j.paid.2012.09.009.

De Becker, Gavin. *The Gift of Fear: Survival Signals that Protect Us from Violence.* New York: Little, Brown & Co., 1997.

———. *Protecting the Gift: Keeping Children and Teenagers Safe (and Parents Sane).* New York: Dial Press, 1999.

Declercq, Frederic, Joachim Willemsen, Kurt Audenaert, and Paul Verhaeghe. "Psychopathy and Predatory Violence in Homicide, Violent, and Sexual Offences: Factor and Facet Relations." *Legal and Criminological Psychology* 17 (1), 2012, 59–74.

Dietz, Park, Robert R. Hazelwood, and Janet Warren. "The Sexually Sadistic Criminal and his Offenses." *Bulletin of the American Academy of Psychiatry and Law* 18 (2), 1990, 163–178. https://api.semanticscholar.org /CorpusID:19298269.

Dunne, Dominick. "Greenwich Murder Time." *Vanity Fair*, June 2006.

Easton, Scott D., Lela Saltzman, and Danny Willis. "Would You Tell Under Circumstances Like That? Barriers to Disclosure for Men Who Were Sexually Abused During Childhood." *Psychology of Men and Masculinity* 15 (4), 2014, 460–469. https://doi.org/10.1037/a0034223.

"Five Ways Parents Can Deter Predators." *The Mama Bear Effect.* May 16, 2019. https://themamabeareffect.org/five-ways-parents-can-deter-predators/.

Flynn, George. "3 Sunny Days in August Cast a Cloud Over Houston." *The Houston Post*, February 14, 1974.

Forth, Adelle, Sune Bo, and Mickey Kongerslev. "Assessment of Psychopathy: The Hare Psychopathy Checklist Measures." In *Handbook on Psychopathy and Law*, edited by K. Kiehl and W. Sinnott-Armstrong. New York: Oxford University Press, 2013, 5–33.

Frick, Paul J. "Extending the Construct of Psychopathy to Youth: Implications for Understanding, Diagnosing, and Treating Antisocial Children and Adolescents." *Canadian Journal of Psychiatry* 54 (12), 2009, 803–812. https://doi.org/10.1177/070674370905401203.

Gao, Y., Adian Raine, F. Chan, P. H. Venables, and S. A. Mednick. "Early Maternal and Paternal Bonding, Childhood Physical Abuse and Adult Psychopathic Personality." *Psychological Medicine* 40 (6), 2010, 1007–1016. https://doi.org/10.1017/S0033291709991279.

Garbarino, James. *Miller's Children: Why Giving Teenage Killers a Second Chance Matters for All of Us.* Oakland, CA: University of California Press, 2018.

Gibney, Bruce. *The Beauty Queen Killer.* New York: Pinnacle, 1984.

Gibson, Barbara. *Houston Mass Murders—1973: A True Crime Narrative.* Self-published, 2023.

———. "The Forty Year Search for Houston Mass Murder Victim May be Over." 2015. https://www.houstonmassmurders.com/finding-mark-scott, accessed December 2022.

Givens, David. *Crime Signals: How to Spot a Criminal Before You Become a Victim.* New York: St. Martin's Press, 2008.

Gnerre, Sam. "Christopher Wilder's Savage Crime Rampage Included Stop Off in the South Bay." *Daily Breeze*, July 19, 2021.

Gurwell, John. *Mass Murder in Houston.* Houston: Cordovan Press, 1974.

Hanna, David. *Harvest of Horror: Mass Murder in Houston.* New York: Belmont Tower, 1975.

Harbers, Scott, and Ed Jackson. "Dean and His Boys: A Tale of Sex and Death." *The Advocate*, September 12, 1973.

Hare, Robert D. *The Psychopathy Checklist-Revised, 2nd Edition.* Toronto, Ontario, Canada: Multi-Health Systems, 2003.

———. *Without Conscience: The Disturbing World of the Psychopaths among Us.* New York: Simon and Schuster, 1993.

Hare, Robert D., David J. Cooke, and Stephen D. Hart. "Psychopathy and Sadistic Personality Disorder." In *Oxford Textbook of Psychopathology*, edited by T. Millon, P. H. Blanney, and R. D. Davies. New York: Oxford University, 1999, 555–584.

Hazelwood, Robert R., and Janet Warren. "Sexual Sadists: Their Wives and Girlfriends." In *Practical Aspects of Rape Investigation*, 3rd edition, edited by Robert R. Hazelwood and Ann Burgess. Boca Raton, Florida: CRC Press, 2001.

"Henley: Corll 'Like Two Different People.'" *Abilene Reporter-News*, August 11, 1973.

Hernandez, Katelyn A., Sara Ferguson, and Thomas Kennedy. *A Closer Look at Juvenile Homicide*. Cham, Switzerland: Springer Nature, 2020.

Hewitt, Don, executive producer. "Kiddie Porn," *60 Minutes*, May 15, 1977. Bentley Historical Library, University of Michigan.

Hickey, Eric. *Sex Crimes and Paraphilia*. Upper Saddle River, NJ: Pearson, 2006.

———. *Serial Murderers and their Victims, 6th edition*. Belmont, CA: Wadsworth, 2013.

Hilberry, Conrad. *Luke Karamazov*. Detroit, MI: Wayne State University Press, 1987.

Hollandsworth, Skip. "The Lost Boys." *Texas Monthly*, April 2011.

"John David Norman—A Case Study." *Illinois State Police, Criminal Intelligence Bulletin* 39, December 1986.

Johnson, Sarah. "Investigative Hypnosis: What Is It and Does it Have a Place in Our Courts?" Bill Track 50, November 17, 2021. https://www.billtrack 50.com/blog/investigative-hypnosis/.

Junge, Justin A., Brian J. Scholl, and Marvin M. Chun. "How is Spatial Context Learning Integrated over Signal Versus Noise? A Primacy Effect in Contextual Cueing." *Visual Cognition* 15 (1), 2007, 1–11. https://doi.org/10.1080/13506280600859706.

Katz, Carmit. "'What Do You Mean the Perpetrator? You Mean My Friend?' Spotlighting the Narratives of Young Children who are Victims of Sexual Abuse by Their Peers." *Psychology of Violence* 10 (1), 2020, 30–37. https://doi.org/10.1037/vio0000238.

Katz, Carmit, and Z. Barnetz. "Children's Narratives of Alleged Child Sexual Abuse Offender Behaviors and the Manipulation Process." *Psychology of Violence* 6 (2), 2016, 223–232, https://doi.org/10.1037/a0039023.

Kennedy, T. "No Link Found to Homosexual Ring." *Houston Post*, n.d.

Kiehl, Kent. *The Psychopath Whisperer*. New York: Broadway Books, 2014.

Konnikova, Maria. *The Confidence Game: Why We Fall For It . . . Every Time*. New York: Penguin, 2016.

Labella, Madelyn H., and Ann S. Masten. "Family Influences on the Development of Aggression and Violence," *Current Opinion in Psychology* 19, February 2018, 11–16. https://doi.org/10.1016/j.copsyc.2017.03.028.

Lang, Rueben, and Roy Frenzel. "How Sex Offenders Lure Children." *Annals of Sex Research* 1 (2), 1988. https://doi.org/10.1177/107906328800100207.

Lebeau, Jean-Charles, Sicong Liu, Camilo Sáenz-Moncaleano, Susana Sanduvete-Chaves, Salvador Chacón-Moscoso, Betsy J. Becker, and Gershon Tenenbaum. "Quiet Eye and Performance in Sport: A Meta-Analysis." *Journal of Sport and Exercise Psychology* 38 (5), 2015, 441–457. https://doi.org/10.1123/jsep.2015-0123.

LeMaigre, Charlotte, Emily P. Taylor, and Claire Gittoes. "Barriers and Facilitators to Disclosing Sexual Abuse in Childhood and Adolescence: A Systematic Review." *Child Abuse and Neglect* 70, 2017, 39–52. https://doi.org/10.1016/j.chiabu.2017.05.009.

Lewis, Dorothy Otnow, Ernest Moy, Lori D. Jackson, Robert Aaronson, Nicholas Restifo, Susan Serra, and Alexander Simos. "Biopsychosocial Characteristics of Children Who Later Murder: A Prospective Study." *The American Journal of Psychiatry* 142 (10), 1985, 1161–1167. https://doi.org/10.1176/ajp.142.10.1161.

Lifton, Robert J. *The Nazi Doctors: Medical Killing and the Psychology of Genocide.* New York: Basic Books, 2nd edition. 2017.

Linedecker, Clifford. *Children in Chains.* New York: Everett House, 1981.

Lopez-Villatoro, J. M., N. Palomares, M. Díaz-Marsá, and J. L. Carrasco. "Borderline Personality Disorder with Psychopathic Traits: A Critical Review." *Clinical Medical Review and Case Reports* 5 (8), 2018, 227–35. https://doi.org/10.23937/2378-3656/1410227.

Lloyd, Robin, and Birch Bayh. *For Money or Love, Boy Prostitution in America.* New York: Vanguard Press, 1976.

Lynam, Donald. "Pursuing the Psychopath: Capturing the Fledgling Psychopath in a Nomological Net." *Journal of Abnormal Psychology* 106 (3), 1997, 425–438. https://doi.org/10.1037/0021-843X.106.3.425.

Lynam, Donald R., Avshalom Caspi, Terrie Moffitt, Adrian Raine, Rolf Loeber, and Magda Stouthamer-Loeber. "Adolescent Psychopathy and the Big Five Results from Two Samples." *Journal of Abnormal Child Psychology* 33 (4), August 2005, 431–443. https://doi.org/10.1007/s10648-005-5724-0.

McVicker, Steve. "Killer Art." *Houston Press*, January 30, 1997.

Macknik, Stephen, Susana Martinez-Conde, and Sandra Blakeslee. *Sleights of Mind: What the Neuroscience of Magic Reveals about our Everyday Deceptions.* New York: Henry Holt and Co., 2010.

Marchocki, Kathryn. "Spader Won't Contest Life Sentence." *New Hampshire Union Leader*, April 22, 2013.

Meckel, Rob. "Body Identified After 12 Years in Local Morgue." *The Houston Post*, July 4, 1985.

Mellor, Lee. "Sexually Sadistic Homicide Offenders." In *Homicide*, edited by Joan Swart and Lee Mellor. Boca Raton, FL: CRC Press, 2016.

Montgomery, Paul L. "A Body Ruled Out as Victim of Ring." *The New York Times*, July 12, 1974.

Moore, Thomas. *Dark Eros: The Imagination of Sadism*. Dallas, TX: Spring, 1990.

Moreira, Diana, Susana Oliveira, Filipe Nunes Ribeiro, Fernando Barbosa, Marisalva Fávero, and Valeria Gomes. "Relationship Between Adverse Childhood Experiences and Psychopathy: A Systematic Review." *Aggression and Violent Behavior* 53, 2020, https://doi.org/10.1016/j.avb.2020.101452.

Myers, Wade C., David S. Husted, Mark Safarik, and Mary Ellen O'Toole. "The Motivation Behind Serial Sexual Homicide: Is it Sex, Power, and Control, or Anger?" *Journal of Forensic Sciences* 51 (4), 2006, 900–907. https://doi.org/10.1111/j.1556-4029.2006.00168.x.

Myers, Wade C., Heng Choon Chan, Eleanor J. Vo, and Emily Lazarou. "Sexual Sadism, Psychopathy, and Recidivism in Juvenile Sexual Murderers." *Journal of Investigative Psychology and Offender Profiling* 7 (1), 2010, 49–58. https://doi.org/10.1002/jip.113.

Niehoff, Debra. *The Biology of Violence*. New York: The Free Press, 1999.

Nightbyrd, Jeff. "Runaway Murder in Texas." *Crawdaddy*, 1973, 38–45.

Oberg, Ted. "Bodies Exhumed of Victims of Serial Killer." ABC 13, February 8, 2011.

———. "DNA Test Confirms Serial Killer Victim's Body Misidentified." ABC 13, November 30, 2011.

———. "Man Recalls Encounter with Serial Killer's Accomplice." ABC 13, February 8, 2012.

———. "Surviving a Serial Killer." ABC 13, August 8, 2008.

———. "The Texas Following: Under a Serial Killer's Spell." ABC 13, February 4, 2013.

Ogilvie, Claire, Emily Newman, Lynda Todd, and David Peck. "Attachment and Violent Offending: A Meta-Analysis." *Aggression and Violent Behavior* 19 (4), 2014, 322–339.

Olafson, Steve. "DNA Test Puts Face on '70s Murder." *The Houston Post*, January 6, 1994.

Olsen, Jack. *The Man with the Candy: The Story of the Houston Mass Murders*. New York: Simon and Schuster, 1974.

Olsen, L., J. Daggs, B. Ellevold, and T. Rogers. "The Communication of Deviance: Toward a Theory of Child Sexual Predators' Luring Communications." *Communication Theory* 17, 2007, 231–251.

Olsen, Lise. "After Decades, Another Serial Killer Victim Identified." *Houston Chronicle*, December 1, 2011.

Ortiz, Adam. "Adolescent Brain Development and Legal Culpability." Office of Justice Programs, #204311, 2003.

Pisano, Simone, Pietro Muratori, Chiara Gorga, Valentina Levantini, Raffaella Iuliano, Genaro Catone, Giangenaro Coppola, Annarita Milone, and Gabriele Masi. "Conduct Disorders and Psychopathy in Children and Adolescents: Aetiology, Clinical Presentation and Treatment Strategies of Callous-Unemotional Traits." *Italian Journal of Pediatrics* 43 (1), 2017, 84–104. https://doi.org/10.1186/s13052-017-0404-6.

Porter, Stephen, Michael Woodworth, Jeff Earle, Jeff Drugge, and Douglas P. Boer. "Characteristics of Sexual Homicide Committed by Psychopathic and Nonpsychopathic Offenders." *Law and Human Behavior* 27 (5), 2003, 459–470. https://doi.org/10.1023/a:1025461421791.

Raine, Adrian. *The Anatomy of Violence: The Biological Roots of Crime.* New York: Vintage, 2013.

Ramsland, Katherine. "The Care and Feeding of Serial Killers." In *A History of Evil in Popular Culture*, edited by Sharon Packer and Jody Pennington. Santa Barbara, CA: Praeger, 2014.

———. *Confession of a Serial Killer: The Untold Story of Dennis Rader, the BTK Serial Killer.* Lebanon, NH: ForeEdge, 2016.

———. "The Moors Murderers." *Serial Killer Quarterly* 3, 2014.

Ramsland, Katherine, and Patrick McGrain. *Inside the Minds of Sexual Predators*, Santa Barbara, CA, ABC/CLIO, 2010.

Reilly, Jill. "Could There Be Even More? 29th Victim of Candy Man 'Revealed' after Photo of a Terrified Handcuffed Young Boy Discovered." *Daily Mail*, February 9, 2012.

Rhor, Monica. "Coroner Still Seeks Names of Houston Mass Murder Victims After 35 Years." *The Canadian Press*, June 6, 2008.

Rignall, Jeff, and Ron Wilder. *29 Below.* Chicago: Wellington Press, 1979.

Ringenberg, Tatiana R., Kathryn C. Seigfried-Spellar, Julia M. Rayz, and Marcus K. Rogers. "A Scoping Review of Grooming Strategies: Pre- and Post-Internet." *Child Abuse and Neglect* 123, 2022. https://www.sciencedirect.com/science/article/abs/pii/S0145213421004610.

Rosella, Louie. "Notorious Meadowvale Serial Killer Left a Suicide Note." Mississauga News, 2015. https://www.mississauga.com/news-story/5733577 -50th-anniversary-notorious-meadowvale-serial-killer-left-suicide-note/.

Rouner, Jef. "Real Horror: Local Filmmaker Brings the Horrific Crimes of Dean Corll to the Screen." *Houston Press*, December 4, 2013.

Salekin, Randall T., and John E. Lochman. "Child and Adolescent Psychopathy: The Search for Protective Factors." *Criminal Justice and Behavior* 35 (2), 2008, 159–172. https://doi.org/10.1177/0093854807311330.

Sapolsky, Robert. "Dude, Where's my Frontal Cortex?" *Nautilus*, June 25, 2014. https://nautil.us/dude-wheres-my-frontal-cortex-234980/.

Schaffer, Lisa, and Julie Penn. "A Comprehensive Classification System." In *Sex Crimes and Paraphilia*, edited by Eric Hickey. Upper Saddle River, NJ: Pearson, 2006, 69–94.

*Sexual Exploitation of Children—Hearings Before the Subcommittee on Crime*, 95th Congress, 1st Session, May 23, 25, June 10, and September 20, 1977.

Shivers, Rob. "Raid on 'Call-boy' Service Nets up to 100,000 Names." *The Advocate*, September 12, 1973.

Smallbone, Stephen W., and Richard K. Wortley. "Child Sexual Abuse: Offender Characteristics and Modus Operandi." *Trends and Issues in Crime and Criminal Justice* 193, 2001. https://www.researchgate.net/publication /29458465_Child_Sexual_Abuse_Offender_Characteristics_and_Modus _Operandi.

Spanos, Staci. "College Kids Easily Lured into Stranger's Van." News4Jax, November 14, 2014. https://www.news4jax.com/news/2014/11/14/ college-kids-easily-lured-into-strangers-van/.

Spivey, Michael J. *Who You Are: The Science of Connectedness*. Cambridge, MA: MIT Press, 2020.

Stevenson, Robert Louis. *The Strange Case of Doctor Jekyll and Mr. Hyde*. New York: Scribner's, 1886.

Stone, Michael H. "Sadistic Personality in Murderers." In *The Psychopath: Antisocial, Criminal, and Violent Behavior*, edited by Theodore Millon, Erik Simonsen, Roger D. Davis, and Morten Birket-Smith. New York: Guilford Press, 1998, 346–355.

Stone, Michael H., and Gary Brucato. *The New Evil: Understanding the Emergence of Modern Violent Crime*. New York: Prometheus, 2019.

True, Alison. "Vito Marzullo's Grandson and Gacy: The Biggest Open Secret in Chicago History" *John Wayne Gacy's Other Victims* (blog). February 24, 2013. www.johnwaynegacynews.com.

Van Dam, Carla. *Identifying Child Molesters: Preventing Child Sexual Abuse by Recognizing the Patterns of the Offenders*. New York and London: Routledge, 2001.

Vance, Carol S. *Boomtown DA*. Houston, TX: Whitecaps Media, 2010.

Vronsky, Peter. *American Serial Killers: The Epidemic Years 1950–2000*. New York: Berkley, 2020.

Warren, Janet I., and Robert R. Hazelwood. "Relational Patterns Associated with Sexual Sadism: A Study of Twenty Wives and Girlfriends." *Journal of Family Violence* 17, 2002, 75–89.

Weaver, Melanie. "Long-Term Survivors of Commercial Sexual Exploitation: Survivor Voice and Survivency in the Decades after Exiting." A Dissertation Presented in Partial Fulfillment of the Requirements for the Degree Doctor of Philosophy, Arizona State University, October 2019.

Wilk, Miss. "Reporter's Notebook: Is There Another Victim of the Houston Serial Killers?" April 10, 2012. https://crimeculture.wordpress.com /2012/08/10/reporters-notebook-is-there-another-victim-of/.

Wittenberg, Pete. "Henley Says Fear Prompted Slaying." *The Houston Post*. January 25, 1974.

**Media clips:**

Corderi, Victoria, "Man with a Past." *48 Hours*: 1990. Accessed on Youtube January 2022, https://www.youtube.com/watch?v=wAm6Oil9sG4

Hobbes, J. P., "Interview with Elmer Wayne Henley, Jr.," *Collectors*. 2000. KRPC-TV footage, August 8, 1974.

Vargas, Josh. *In a Madman's World*. 121 minutes, YouTube video, accessed January 2022, https://www.youtube.com/watch?v=Mf64WRQ6-e4

**Legal documents and cases:**

David Brooks affidavit

David Brooks witness statement

Elmer Wayne Henley Jr. affidavits

Timothy Kerley affidavit

Rhonda Williams affidavit

*David Owen Brooks v. State of Texas*, 580 S.W.2d 825 (1979)

*Elmer Wayne Henley v. State of Texas*, 644 S.W.2d 950 (1978)

*State [of New Jersey] v. Hurd*, 432 A.2d 86 (NJ 1981)

Houston Police Department reports

Pasadena Police Department reports

**Personal interviews:**

Steven Becker—Tracy Ullman, 2011–2012

Dr. Al Carlisle—Katherine Ramsland, 2013

Dr. Robert Hare—Katherine Ramsland, 2003, 2014, 2019

Robert R. Hazelwood—Katherine Ramsland, 2000

Elmer Wayne Henley Jr.—Tracy Ullman, 2020–present; Katherine Ramsland, 2021–present

Mary Henley—Tracy Ullman, 2018–present

Dr. Eric Hickey—Katherine Ramsland, 2014

Sally Keglovits—Katherine Ramsland, 2022

Dr. Kent Kiehl—Katherine Ramsland, 2014

Don Lambright—Tracy Ullman, July 2022

Gregg McCrary—Katherine Ramsland, 2014

Freddie Majors—Tracy Ullman, July 2022

Anthony Meoli—Katherine Ramsland, 2014

# APPENDIX A

# Photos

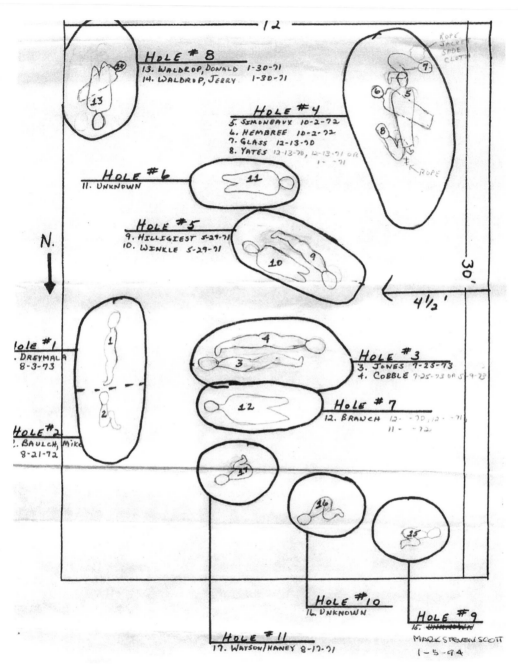

A police drawing that details where victims' bodies were buried at the boat stall on Silver Bell Street in Houston, with an erroneous correction for the victim in Hole #9.

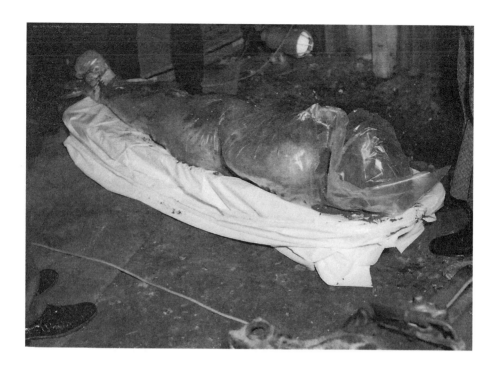

ABOVE: Evidence photo of a body exhumed by Houston Police at Corll's boat stall. BELOW: The 1973 mugshot of David Owen Brooks.

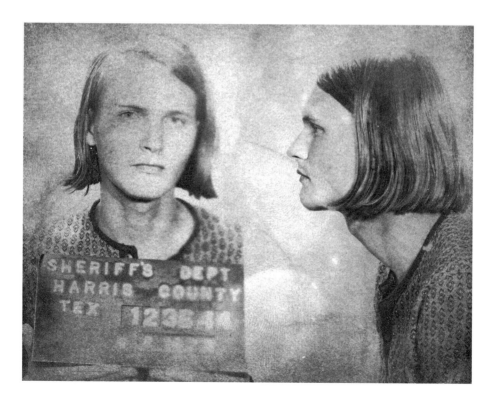

ABOVE: One of the few known photos of Dean Corll. BELOW: Evidence photo of Dean Corll shooting in his home in Pasadena, Texas, on August 8, 1973.

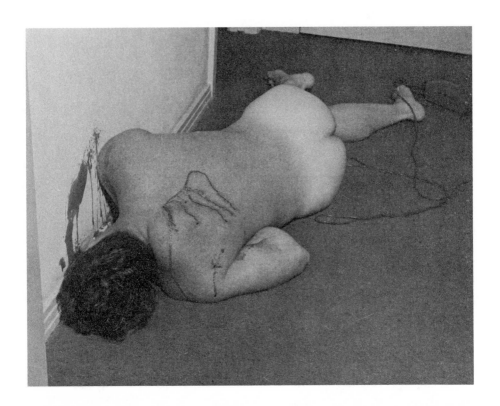

ABOVE: Police officers digging up bodies in area of Lake Sam Rayburn. BELOW: The 1973 mugshot of Elmer Wayne Henley Jr.

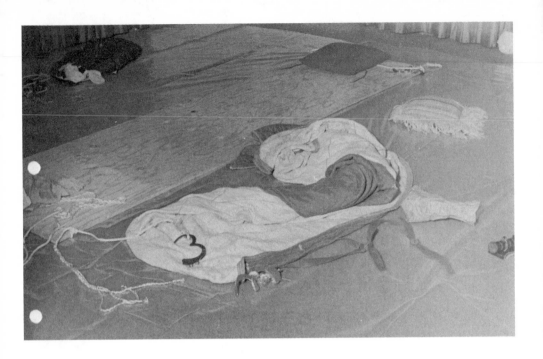

ABOVE: The torture board attributed to Dean Corll. Note the handcuffs nearby and the plastic sheeting underneath for easy disposal. BELOW: Evidence photo of a double-sided dildo and lubrication used during Corll's sexual torture sessions.

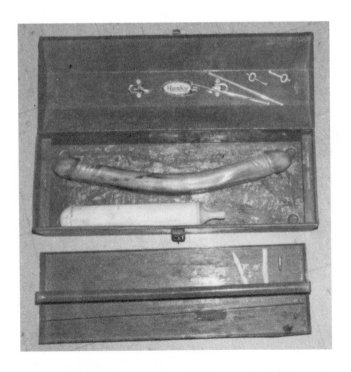

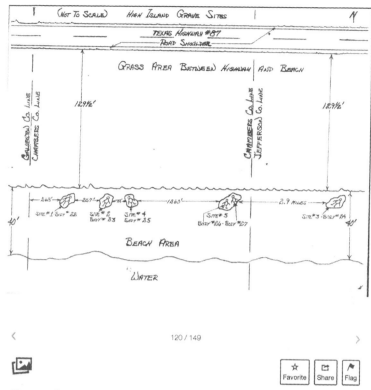

< 120 / 149 >

☆ Favorite    ⬏ Share    ⚑ Flag

## Dean Corll records from Pasadena PD

ABOVE: Henley and Brooks showed police the locations of victims' remains at High Island Beach in Texas. BELOW: After Henley received art lessons in prison, he created paintings like this for sale until he was prohibited from continuing. *By permission of Elmer Wayne Henley Jr.*

Missing persons poster for fifteen-year-old James Eugene Glass, with identifying characteristics.

The 1973 mugshot of John David Norman after he fled Dallas once he posted bail for numerous charges.

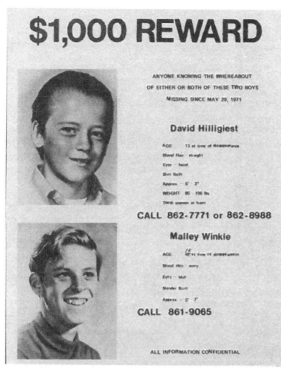

Some of the first victims to go missing in the Houston Heights were Mally Winkle and David Hilligiest. David was a friend of Wayne Henley's, and Henley helped with the search.

An early 1970s snapshot of Mary Henley and her four sons, Ronnie, Elmer Wayne, Paul, and Vernon. *By permission of Mary Henley.*

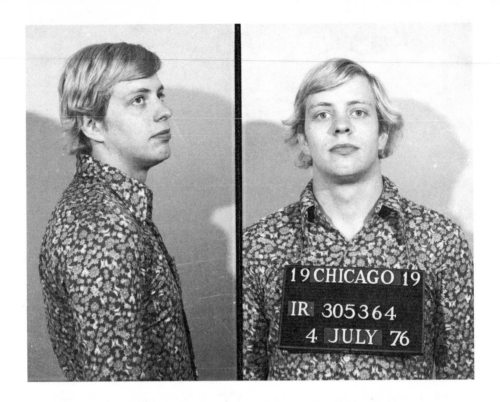

ABOVE: The 1976 mugshot of Phillip Paske, a close associate of John David Norman. BELOW: The 1977 mugshot of Roy Clifton Ames, whose warehouse police raided for child pornography.

TOP: Police removing bagged victim remains from a hole near Lake Sam Rayburn. CENTER: While police searched the beach at High Island for victim remains, Henley and Brooks directed them. BOTTOM: As the rising victim count painted Houston as the US mass murder capital, the roles that Henley and Brooks played came under intense police scrutiny.

# APPENDIX B

# The Victim Locations and Identifications

Known victims, locations, assigned numbers, ages, and year they went missing:

| Boat Stall | High Island Area | Lake Sam Rayburn |
|---|---|---|
| #1 James Dreymala (13) 1973 | #18 Jeffrey Konen (18) 1970 | #20 Raymond Blackburn (20) 1973 |
| #2 Roy Bunton (19) 1972 | #19 Richard Kepner (19) 1972 | #21 Homer Garcia (15) 1973 |
| #3 Marty Ray Jones (18) 1973 | #23 John Sellars (17) 1972 (probably excluded) | #22 Michael "Tony" Baulch (15) 1973 |
| #4 Charles Cobble (17) 1973 | #24 Frank Aguirre (19) 1972 | #27 Billy Lawrence (15) 1973 |
| #5 Wally Simoneaux (15) 1972 | #25 Johnny Delome (16) 1972 | |
| #6 Richard Hembree (13) 1972 | #26 Billy Baulch (17) 1972 | |
| #7 James Glass (14) 1970 | #28 Joseph Lyles (17) 1973 (remains found 1983 on Jefferson County Beach) | |
| #8 Danny Yates (14) 1970 | | |
| #9 David Hilligiest (13) 1971 | Mark Scott (17) 1972 (no number assigned; not identified) | |
| #10 Gregory Malley Winkle (16) 1971 | | |
| #11 Randell Harvey (15) 1971 | | |
| #12 Willard Branch Jr. (17) 1972 | | |
| #13 Donald Waldrop (15) 1971 | | |
| #14 Jerry Waldrop (13) 1971 | | |
| #15 Steve Sickman (17) 1972 | | |
| #16 Unknown | | |
| #17 Ruben Watson Haney (17) 1971 | | |

# APPENDIX C

# David Brooks Statements

Before me, the undersigned authority, this date appeared David
Brooks, who is a credible person and who, after being duly sworn
did depose and say:

My name is David Brooks. I am a White Male 18 years old, having been born
2-12-55. I live at 1445 Pech #6 with my wife, Bridget. I now work for the
Alton Brooks Paving Company, which is owned by my father.

I first met Dean Corll when I was in the 6th grade at Helms Elementary
school. He was working at the Candy Kitchen on W.22nd street, which was
owned by his mother. This was approx 6 years ago.  The reason that I knew
him was that he would give candy to the kids leaving school, which was
located across the street from the store. Also he owned a motorcycle and
would give the kids rides and take some of the kids to the movie.

I moved to Beaumont shortly after I met him and lived in Beaumont for about
3 years, during which time I had contact with Dean only on Holidays and
during the summer when I would visit Houston.

My first Homosexual contact with Dean was during the time I was living in
Beaumont. I was visiting Houston and I had called Dean and told him that
I was in town and he came and picked me up at my Grandmothers house and took
me to his house on 22nd street in about the 900 or 1000 block. He gave me
a 4 foot black light at that time.  At that time he sucked my dick. After
that I just sat around and watched TV for a little while and then he
took me back to my grandmothers. This has been approx 4 years ago.

During the next four years I visited Deans house on many occasions. Sometime
I went overthere just to visit and sometimes he would suck me when I went
over. He started out by giving me $5 when he sucked me off and then later
he raised that to $10 a time. Also during this time I knew of several
other people who were involved with him both sexually and as just friends.
It appeared that not all of his friends were involved with him sexually.

Approx. 3 years ago, I went to Dean's apartment, when he was living in the
Yorktown Townhouses. I just walked into the apartment without knocking and
when I got inside I saw that he had two boys strapped down on his bed.
Their hands were tied to the bed stead. Both of the boys were nude. When
Dean had heard me open the door he came out of the bedroom and he was nude
and I just walked into the bedroom to see what was going on and that is when
I saw the boys. Dean asked, " WHAT ARE YOU DOING HERE,?" I just told him
I had just come by  and I wanted to know what was going on and he told me
that he was just having some fun. We sat and talked for a little while and
during that talk he promised me a car if I wouldn't say anything about what
I had seen and so I left and hitch hiked back home, and didn't mention what
I had seen. I did not know either of the boys involved at this time.

Shortly after this incident Dean moved to the Place one Apartments on
Magnum I also visited that location. It was just before he moved over to
this location that Dean first told me that he had killed some boys. I just can't
remember what the entire conversation was but I do remember him telling
me about Killing someone.

Next Dean moved to a house at 915 Columbia and it was while he was living
here that I introduced Wayne Hennley to Dean. This was about 2 or 2½ years
ago. I don't know how involved with Dean Henlly immediatly became but
eventually they became close friends and Hennly became involved with Dean
sexually to some extent, but I don't know how much. Also during the time
Dean was living on Columbia he gave me a car, it was a Corvette, 1969, which
he had bought for me! He reminded me that the car was for keeping my mouth
shut about what I had seen at the Yorktown apartments. D.A.B.

page #2 of statement of David Brooks.

There were several time that Dean told me about killing people.
One time he told me about a Mexican boy who he had killed while he was
living on Belfontain. He told me that this mexican boy had been coming at
him and he shot the boy one time in the head and it didn't seem to do
anything so he shot him again and that killed the boy. He didn't mention
what he had done with the body.

Another time he told me about killing a boy in a bath tub and mentioned that
broken a piece of tile offof the tub.

Sometime when we were talking he would say how hard it was strangle someone
and that the way that they did it on TVwasn't realistic,because it took
quite a while to do it.

All during the period of time that Dean talked to me about the
killings I got the impression that he had killed perhaps as many as 25 or
30 people,over about a three year period. I can't remember exactally how
many he said were buried at the boat house but it seems like it was 19 that
had buried at that one location. Also at one time he mentioned burying some
on a beach somewhere but he never showed me that location.

I am not sure when the first time Dean took me to the boat house was,but it
has been over a year ago. At that time he told me that he had buried bodies
in the boat house,at the time he was telling me this Wayne Henley was also
with us.He told me that there were rows of bodies buried and pointed out the
ruffled ground. The reason we had gone to the boat house was to pick up
something but  don't remember exactally  what it was. I went out to the
boathouse several times and one time I noticed what appeared to be a fresh
grave but I didn't even mention this to Dean.

During one of our conversations Dean mentioned that there was a group of
people in Dallas which had similar activities to his. He mentioned a man
by the name of Art who he said had also killed some boys in Dallas. One
day while  was at his house I picked up a piece of paper with the name
Art on it and all of a phone number but the last number and the area code
was 214. Dean also mentioned that Art has a wife. Lately Dean has been
wanting to go to Dallas and I believe was supose to go at the end of this
month.

About a year and a half ago I was living with Dean and I came home one
night and Henly came with me, we had been over to some girls house. When
we went in the house, at about 11:30PM,we walked back to Deans  bedroom
and when we walked through the door Henley hit me in the head with a hydroli
jack handle and I fell across the bed, and then Dean jumped on me. They
handcuffed me to a board with Eye rings in it. Dean made me suck him then
and suck his ass hole and then he wanted me to kiss him and he fucked me
in the ass and this went on all night long. Henley did not participate
in this but  he was in the other room. When he first took me down he told me
that he was going to kill me but that it had to be a joint dicision
between him and wayne Henley and that he would try to talk Wayne out of
killing me. I begged and pleaded with him all night and the next day and
about 5PM he let me go. I got up and took a bath and cleaned up. I
continued to live with Dean for about 4 or 5 months after that. This inciden
happened when he was living on Schuler and then we moved to the Westcott
apartments and we changed apartments at Westcott and moved into a two bedroo
apartment  and shortly after that is when I left. Wayne had told me that
Dean was talking about getting me again and so I just packed up and left.
When I moved out Dean got all excited because he didn't know what I was goin
to do so I moved back in with him and stayed for about a month and  a half
and this was the last time that I lived with at Westcott. Shortly after I
left this time he moved to the Francessa Apartments on Wirt Rd. and I lived
with there for about 2 months and then I moved in with my Grandmother.

Dean moved to the house in Pasadena about 6 months ago and he lived with his folks in the house for a while and I didn't visit him while they were living there. After they moved out I visited Dean several times.

One time ,when we were living on Schuler, Wayne and Dean planned to get a boy that I know by the name of Billy Bux Ridinger. I was there when he came over to the house with Dean and when they got there we sat and watched TV for a while and then they were pretending to show him a handcuff trick and that is when they got him down. I told him to just be quite or I though they would kill him. Then Dean fucked him in the ass and I don't know what all else that he did. Wayne said that he wanted to kill Billy but Dean talk him in to letting Billy go. Billy works for INTERNATIONAL HARVESTER on Washington and lives on either Auburnforrest or Spruce Forrest.

I knowof two boys that were involved with Dean who are now missing one is a Ruben Haney who was about 18 years old, and I know that the last time he was seen was at 6363 San Felipe where Dean was living. I was at the house when he came in and then I left. That was the last time that I know that anyone saw him.

I also know a Mark Scott who is 17 or 18 years old and he came to the hous on Schuler with Wayne. I was there when Mark got there and I stayed for a short time. Then it looked like they were going to take Mark down I left the house and that is the last time that I know of anyone seeing him.

I can remember something about a boy by the name of Glass. I don't remember waich one of them xxmaxbxxxxx mentioned his name but I remember the name.

I can read and write the English Language and I have read this statement and it is true and correct. I have made this statement of my own free will and was not threatened or mistreated in any way in order to make me give this statement.

SIGNED: _David Owen Brooks_

SWORT AND SUBSCRIBED TO BEFORE ME THIS THE 9th DAY OF AUGUST, 1973

J.L.TUCKER 8-9-73 1:20PM

SIGNED: _Edwin Duschinsky_
Notary Public in and for Harris Co.Texas

These are the statements given to police on August 8, 9 and 10. The errors are retained.


# DAVID BROOKS
## WITNESS STATEMENT, AUGUST 9, 1973


My name is David Brooks. I am a white male 18 years old, having been born 2-12-55. I live at 1445 Pech #6 with my wife, Bridget. I now work for the Alton Brooks Paving Company, which is owned by my father.

I first met Dean Corll when I was in the 6th grade at elms elementary school. He was working at the Candy Kitchen on W. 22nd street, which was owned by his mother. This was approx 6 years ago. The reason that I knew him was that he would give candy to the kids leaving school, which was located across the street from the store. Also he owned a motorcycle and would give the kids rides and take some of the kids to the movie.

I moved in Beaumont shortly after I met him and lived in Beaumont for about 3 years, during which time I had contact with Dean only on holidays and during the summer when I would visit Houston.

My first homosexual contact with Dean was during the time I was living in Beaumont. I was visiting Houston and I had called Dean and told Him that I was in town and he came and picked me up at my Grandmothers house and took me to his house on 22nd street in about the 900 or 1000 block. He gave me a 4 foot black light at that time. At that time he sucked my dick. After that I just sat around and watched TV for a little while and then he took me back to my grandmothers. This has been approx 4 years ago.

During the next four years I visited Deans house on many occasions. Sometimes I went over there just to visit and some-times he would suck me when I went over. He started out by giving me $5 when he sucked me off and then later he raised that to $10 a time. Also during this time I knew of several other people who were involved with him both sexually and as just friends. It appeared that not all of his friends were involved with him sexually.

Approx. 3 years ago, I went to Dean's apartment, when he was living in the Yorktown townhouses. I just walked into the apartment without knocking and when I got inside I saw that he had two boys strapped down on his bed. Their hands were tied to the bed stead. Both of the boys were nude. When Dean had heard me open the door he came out of the bedroom and he was nude and I just walked into the bedroom to see what was going on and that is when I saw the boys. Dean asked, "WHAT ARE YOU DOING HERE?" I just told him I had just come by and I wanted to know what was going on and he told me that he was just having some fun. We sat and talked for a little while and during that talk he promised me a car if I wouldn't say anything about what I had seen and so I left and hitch hiked back home, and didn't mention what I had seen. I did not know either of the boys involved at this time.

Shortly after this incident Dean moved to the Place one Apartments on Magnum. I also visited that location. It was just before he moved over to this location that Dean first told me that he had killed some boys. I just can't remember what the entire conversation was but I do remember him telling me about killing someone.

Next Dean moved to a house at 915 Columbia and it was while he was living here that I introduced Wayne Henley to Dean. This was about 2 or 2 1/2 years ago. I don't know how involved with Dean Henley immediately became but eventually they became close friends and Henley became involved with Dean sexually to some extent, but I don't know how much. Also during the time Dean was living on Columbia he gave me a car, it was a Corvette 1969, which he had bought for me. He reminded me that the car was for keeping my mouth shut about what I had seen at the Yorktown apartments.

*Brooks, witness statement, page 2:*

There were several times that Dean told me about killing people. One time he told me about a Mexican boy who he had killed while he was living on Belfontain. He told me that this Mexican boy had been coming at him and he shot the boy one time in the head and it didn't seem to do anything so he shot him again and that killed the boy. He didn't mention what he had done with the body.

Another time he told me about killing a boy in a bath tub and mentioned that broken a piece of [crossed out] off of the tub.

Sometime when we were talking he would say how hard it was strangle someone and that the way that they did it on TV wasn't realistic, because it took quite a while to do it.

All during the period of time that Dean talked to me about the killings, I got the impression that he had killed perhaps as many as 25 or 30 people, over about a three year period. I can't remember exactly how many he said were buried at the boat house but it seems like it was 19 that had buried at that one location. Also at one time he mentioned burying some on a beach somewhere but he never showed me that location.

I am not sure when the first time Dean took me to the boat house was, but it has been over a year ago. At that time he told me that he had buried bodies in the boat house, at the time he was telling me this Wayne Henley was also with us. He told me that there were rows of bodies buried and pointed out the ruffled ground. The reason we had gone to the boat house was to pick up something but don't remember exactly what it was. I went out to the boathouse several times and one time I noticed what appeared to be a fresh grave but I didn't even mention this to Dean.

During one of our conversations Dean mentioned that there was a group of people in Dallas which had similar activities to his. He mentioned a man by the name of Art who he said had also killed some boys in Dallas. One day while - was at his house I picked up a piece of paper with the name Art on it and all of a phone number but the last number and the area code was 214. Dean also mentioned that Art has a wife. Lately Dean has been wanting to go to Dallas and I believe was suppose [sic] to go at the end of this month.

About a year and a half ago I was living with Dean and I came home one night and Henl[e]y came with me, we had been over to some girls house. When we went in the house, at about 11:30PM, we walked back to Deans bedroom and when we walked through the door Henley hit me in the head with a hydrolic jack handle and I fell across the bed, and then Dean jumped on me. They handcuffed me to a board with Eye rings in It. Dean made me suck him then and suck his ass hole and then he wanted me to kiss him and he fucked me in the ass and this went on all night long. Henley did not participate in this but he was in the other room. When he first took me down he told me that he was going to kill you me but that it had to be a joint dicision [sic] between him and Wayne Henley and that he would try to talk Wayne out of killing me. I begged and pleaded with him all night and the next day and about 5PM he let me go. I got up and took a bath and cleaned up. I continued to live with Dean for about 4 or 5 months after that. This incident happened when he was living on Schuler and then we moved to the Westcott apartments and we changed apartments at Westcott und moved into a two bedroom apartment and shortly after that is when I left. Wayne had told me that Dean was talking about getting me again and so I just packed up and left. When I moved out Dean got all excited because he didn't know what I was going to do so I moved back in with him and stayed for about a month and a half and this was the last time that I lived with at Westcott. Shortly after I left this time he moved to the Francessa Apartments on Wirt Rd. and I lived there for about 2 months and then I moved in with my Grandmother.

*Brooks, witness statement, page 3:*

Dean moved to the house in Pasadena about 6 months ago and he lived with his folks in the house for a while and I didn't visit him while they were living there. After they moved out I visited Dean several times.

One time, when we were living on Schuler, Wayne and Dean planned to get a boy that I know by the name of Billy Ridinger. I was there when he came over to the house with Dean and when they got there we sat and watched TV for a while and then they were pretending the show him a handcuff trick and that is when they got him down. I told him to just be quiet or I thought they would kill him. Then Dean fucked him in the ass and I don't know what all else that he did. Wayne said that he wanted to Kill Billy but Dean talked him in to letting Billy go. Billy works for INTERNATIONAL HARVESTER on Washington and lives on either Autumforrest or Spruce Forrest.

I know of two boys that were involved with Dean who are now missing one is a Ruben Haney who was about 18 years old, and I know that the last time he was seen was at 6363 San Felipe where Dean was living. I was at the house when he came in and then I left. That was the last time that I know that anyone saw him.

I also know a Mark Scott who is 17 or 18 years old and he came to the house on Schuler with Wayne. I was there when Mark got there and I stayed for a short time. When it looked like they were going to take Mark down I left the house and that is the last time that I know of anyone seeing him.

I can remember something about a boy by the name of Glass. I don't remember which one of them mentioned his name but I remember the name.

I can read and write the English Language and I have read this statement and it is true and correct. I have made this statement of my own free will and was not threatened or mistreated in any way in order to make me give this statement.

#2

## CONFESSION WITH MAGISTRATE'S WARNING

Date __August 1),1973__
Time __9AM__

Statement of __David Owen Brooks__ taken at

__#61-Biesner Police Administration Building__ Harris County, Texas,

On the __9th__ Day of __August__, 19__73__, at __5:28__ o'clock p M.

I, __David Owen Brooks__ was taken before __Michael Gordon__

a Magistrate at his office in __Houston__ Harris County, Texas,

who informed me:

(1) Of the accusations made against me and of any affidavit filed;
(2) That I have the right to retain counsel; (3) That I have the right
to have an attorney present during my interview with peace officers or
attorneys representing the State; (4) That I have the right to terminate
the interview at any time; (5) That I have the right to request appointment of counsel if I cannot afford counsel; (6) That I have the right to
an examining trial; (7) That I have the right to remain silent and that
I am not required to make any statement, and any statement I make may be
and probably will be used against me.

I fully understand all of these rights; and, desiring to waive all
of them, I hereby make the following voluntary statement to _____
__JIM D. TUCKER__.

My name is David Owen Brooks. I am a white male 18 years old. I was
born February 12,1955. I live at 1445 Pech #6 with my wife Bridget.
I went to the 10th grade inschool and I read and write the English
language.

I came to the police station on August 9th in order to made a witness
statement about what I know about Dean Corll. I came down of my own free
will and I gave that statement to Set. Tucker. In the statement what
I said was partially the truth but I left out the fact that I was pres
when most of the killings happened. I never actually killed anyone but
I was in the room when they happened and was supose to help if somethi.
went wrong.

The first killing that I remember happened when Dean was living at the
Yorktown Town houses. There were two boys there and I left before they
were killed but Dean told me that he had killed them afterwards. I don
know where they were buried or what their names were. The first few
that Dean killed were supose to have been sent off somewhere in califor:

The first killing that I remember being present at was on 6363 San Fel:
That boy was Ruben Haney. Dean and I were the only people involved in t
one but Dean did the killing and I just was present when it happened.

I also remember two boys who were killed at the Place One Apartments on
Mangum. They were brothers and their father worked next door where they
were building some more apartments. I was present when Dean killed them
by strangling them but again I didn't participate. I believe that I was
present when they were buried but I don't remember where they were bur:
The youngest of these two boys is the youngest that was killed I think.

I remember one boy who was killed on Columbia at Deans house. This was
just before Wayne Henley came into...

most of the killings that occured after Wayne came into the picture involved all three of us. I still did not take part in the actual kill but nearly always all three of us were there.

I was present when Mark Scott was killed at the schuler street address I had told yesterday in my witness statement about Mark Scott being at the Schuler house but I did not say that I was present, which I was. Mark had a knife and he tried to get Dean. He swung at him with a knife and caught deans shirt, and barely broke the skin. He still had one han tied and Dean grabbed the hand with the knife. Wayne ran out of the ro and got a pistol and Mark just gave up. Wayne killed Mark Scott and I think that he strangled him. Mark was either buried at the beach or th boat house.

There was another boy killed at the Schuller house, actually there wer two at this time. A boy named Billy Balsch and one named Johnny and I think that his last name was "alone. Wayne strangled Billy and he said "HEY JOHNNY" and when johnny looked up Wayne shot him in the forehead with a .25 automatic. The bullet came out of his ear and he raised up and about three minues later he said," AYNE PLEASE DON'T". Then Wayn  strangled him, and Dean helped.

It was while we were living on Schuler that Wayne and Dean got me down and started to kill me. I begged them Dean not to kill me and he fina  let me go. I told about this in my witness statement and that part of my statement was absolutly true. It was also at this address that the  got Billy Ridinger and what  said in my witness statement was true abo  him. I took care of aim while he was there and I believe the only reas  he is alive now is because I begged them not to kill him.

Wayne and Dean got one boy by themselves while we were on schuler. It  a tall skinny, guy. I just happened to walk in the house and there he w  I left before they killed this one.

In the first apartment we lived in at Westcott Towers t think that the  were two boys killed. These were both young boys from the heights are  but I don't know there names. Wayne accidentally shot one of them. Th  was about 7AM. I was in the other room asleep when this happened. Dea  told me that Wayne had just come in waving the .22 and accidently sh  one of the boys in the jaw. The bullet just went in a little and then  it was just under the skin. The didn't kill the boy right then. They  killed these two boys later on that day.

Dean moved to the Prencesa Apartments on Dirt and I remember him gett  one boy there by himself. He wanted me to help him but I wouldn't do  I didn't want to mess with this one because I had someplace I wanted  go so I tried to get him mad so he would leave but he wanted to stay.  Dean Grabbed the boy and within 3 minutes of when he grabbed him I wa  gone. At that time I was using Deans car so I was in and out all of  time.

After the Prencesa apartments Dean moved to Pasadena. I know of two  that were killed there. One was from Baton Rouge and one was a small  blond boy from South Houston. I saw the boy from South Houston for ab  45 minutes. I took him a Piazza and then I left and he wanted me to  come back. I wasn't there when either of these boys were killed. I d  come in just after Dean had killed the boy from Baton Rouge, that was  on a different day from the blond boy.

In all I guess there were between 25 and thirty boys killed and they  were burried in three different places. I was present and helped bury  many of them but not all of them. Most of them were burried at the bodys at the beach of in a row down the beach for perhaps a half a mile or so. I am willing to showoffieers where this location is and will try to locate as many of the graves as possible.

I regret that this happened and I'm sorry for the kids familys.

I am making this statementof my own free will and I have not been mistreated or abus ed in any way. I understand my rights and I have waived them to make this statement. I have not been promised anything to get me to make this statement.

I have read this statement and it is true and correct.

SIGNED: *David O. Brooks*

WITNESSES: *Alton Brooks*

WITNESSES: *Caryl Stout*

taken by JD tucker 8-10-73 10:30AM

# DAVID BROOKS
## SECOND STATEMENT, AUGUST 10, 1973:

My name is David Owen Brooks. I am a white male 18 years old.
I was born February 12,1955. I live at 1445 Pech #6 with my
wife, Bridget. I went to the 10th grade in school and I read
and write the English language.

I came to the police station on August 9th in order to make
a witness statement about what I know about Dean Corll. I came
down of my own free will and I gave that statement to Detective Tucker. In the statement what I said was partially the
truth but I left out the fact that I was present when most of
the killings happened. I was in the room when they happened
and was supposed to help if something went wrong.

The first killing that I remember happened when Dean was
living in Yorktown Townhouses. There were two boys there and
I left before they were killed but Dean told me that he had
killed them afterwards. I don't know where they were buried
or what their names were. The first few that Dean killed were
supposed to have been sent off somewhere in California.

The first killing that I remember being present at was on
6363 San Felipe. That boy was Ruben Haney. Dean and I were the
only people involved in that one but Dean did the killing and
I was just present when it happened.

I also remember two boys who were killed at the Place One
Apartments on Magnum. They were brothers and their father worked
next door where they were building some more apartments. I was
present when Dean killed them by strangling them, but again
I didn't participate. I believe I was present when they were
buried, but I don't remember where they were buried. The youngest
of these two boys is the youngest that was killed I think.

I remember one boy who was killed on Columbia at Dean's house.
This was just before Wayne Henley came into the picture. Dean kept
this boy around the house for about four days before he killed
him. I don't remember his name but we picked him up on Eleventh

and Rutland; I think I helped bury this boy also, but I don't remember where it was. This was about two years ago. It really upset Dean to have to kill this boy because he really liked him.

A boy by the name of Glass was also killed at the Columbia address. I had taken him home one time, but he wouldn't get out because he wanted to go back to Dean's. I took him back and Dean ended up killing him. Now that I think about it I'm not sure whether it was Glass that I took home or another boy, but I believe that it was Glass.

It was during that time that we were living on Columbia that Wayne Henley got involved. Wayne took part in getting the boys at first and then later he took an active part in the killings. Wayne seemed to enjoy causing pain and he was especially sadistic at the Schuler address.

### Brooks, second statement, page 2:

Most of the killings that occurred after Wayne came into the picture involved all three of us. I still did not take part in the actual killing, but nearly always all three of us were there.

I was present when Mark Scott was killed at the Schuler address. I had told yesterday in my witness statement about Mark Scott being at the Schuler house, but I did not say I was present, which I was. Mark had a knife and he tried to get Dean: he swung at him with a knife and caught Dean's shirt and barely broke the skin. He still had one hand tied: Dean grabbed the hand with the knife. Wayne ran out of the room and got a pistol, and Mark just gave up. Wayne killed Mark Scott and I think that he strangled him. Mark was either buried at the beach or at the boathouse.

There was another boy killed at the Schuller house, actually there were two at this time. A boy named Billy Baulch and one named Johnny and I think that his last name was Malone. Wayne strangled Billy and he said "HEY JOHNNY" and when Johnny looked up, Wayne shot him in the forehead with a .25 automatic. The bullet came out of his ear and he raised up and about three minutes later he said, "WAYNE PLEASE DON'T." Then Wayne strangled him, and Dean helped.

It was while we were living on Schuler that Wayne and Dean got me down and started to kill me. I begged Dean not to kill me and he finally let me go. I had told about this in my witness statement yesterday and that part of my statement was absolutely true. It was also at this address that they got Billy Ridinger and what I said in my witness statement was true about him. I took care of him while he was there and I believe the only reason he is alive now is because I begged them not to kill him.

Wayne and Dean got one boy by themselves while we were on Schuler. It was a tall, skinny guy. I just happened to walk in the house and there he was. I left before they killed this one.

In the first apartment we lived in at Westcott Towers I think that there were two boys killed. These were both young boys from the Heights area, but I don't know their names. Wayne accidentally shot one of them. This was about 7AM. I was in the other room asleep when this happened. Dean told me that Wayne had just come in waving the .22 and accidentally shot one of the boys in the jaw. The bullet just went in a little and then it was just under the skin. The[y] didn't kill the boy right then: they killed these two boys later on that day.

Dean moved to the Frencesa Apartments on Wirt and I remember him getting one boy there by himself. He wanted me to help him but I wouldn't do it. I didn't want to mess with this one because I had someplace I wanted to go, so I tried to get him mad so he would leave, but he wanted to stay. Dean grabbed the boy and within three minutes of when he grabbed him I was gone. At that time I was using Dean's car so I was in and out all the time.

After the Frencesa Apartments, Dean moved to Pasadena. I know of two that were killed there: One was from Baton Rouge and one was a small blond boy from South Houston. I saw the boy from South Houston for about forty-five minutes. I took him a pizza and then I left and he wanted me to come back. I wasn't there when either of these two boys were killed. I did come in just after Dean had killed the boy from Baton Rouge, that one was on a different day from the blond boy.

In all I guess there were between 25 and 30 boys killed and they were buried in three different places. I was present and helped bury many of them but not all of them. Most of them were buried at the boat stall. There are three or four buried at Sam Rayburn, I think. I am sure that there are two up there. On the first one at Sam Rayburn I helped them bury him, then the next one we took to Sam Rayburn when we got there Dean and Wayne found that the first one had come to the surface and either a foot or a hand was above ground. When they buried this one the second time, they put some type of plastic sheet on top of him to keep him down.

The third place that they were buried was on the beach at High Island. This was right off the Winnie Exit where that road goes to the beach. You turn east on the beach road and go till the pavement changes, which is about a quarter or half a mile and the bodies are on the right hand side of the highway about 15 or 20 yards off of the road. I never actually buried one here but I always drove the car. I know that one of the graves had a large rock on top of it. I think that there five or more bodies buried at this location.


### Brooks, second statement, page 3:

The bodies at the beach are in a row down the beach for perhaps a half mile or so. I am willing to show officers where this location is and will try to locate as many of the graves as possible.

I regret that this happened and I'm sorry for the kids familys.

CONFESSION WITH MAGISTRATE'S WARNING

Date ___ August 10, 1973
Time 10:07PM

Statement of ___DAVID OWEN BROOKS___ taken at

#61 _____ POLICE ADMINISTRATION BUILDING _____ Harris County, Texas,

On the _9th_ Day of _August_____, 19_73_, at _5:20PM_o'clock _P_ M.

I,___DAVID OWEN BROOKS_____ was taken before ___MICHAEL GORDON___

a Magistrate at his office in ____HOUSTON____Harris County, Texas,

who informed me:

(1) Of the accusations made against me and of any affidavit filed;
(2) That I have the right to retain counsel; (3) That I have the right
to have an attorney present during my interview with peace officers or
attorneys representing the State; (4) That I have the right to terminate
the interview at any time; (5) That I have the right to request appointment of counsel if I cannot afford counsel; (6) That I have the right to
an examining trial; (7) That I have the right to remain silent and that
I am not required to make any statement, and any statement I make may be
and probably will be used against me.

I fully understand all of these rights; and, desiring to waive all
of them, I hereby make the following voluntary statement to
___JIM D. TUCKER___ I was also warned by Mike Hinton of the District.
Attorneys Office, and I understand this and I want to give this statement
about Billy Ray Lawrence.

About July 10th, 1973 I tried to call Dean's house, Dean Croll, and it
was a long time before I could get him or anyone to answer. Finally,
Wayne answered and I asked him if they had anyone there and he said
yes. I asked him "It's not a friend, is it?" and he said "sort of".
He wouldn't tell me who it was so I went over there just to see who
it was. He was still alive when I got there but he was tied to the
bed. I recognized him only as a friend of Wayne's.

The boy wasn't doing anything but lying there when I got there. He
didn't have any clothes on. I don't remember them calling him by name
but I have just now been shown a picture of him which I will initial
with this date and time and it is the same boy I have been talking
about. In fact, I have seen this same piture before at Dean's house.

I was tired so I went to bed in the opposite bedroom. Before I did
go to bed I then took Wayne home. Then I went back to Dean's house
and went to bed. The boy was still alive but Dean was awake because I remember he let me in. The next morning I went back to get
Wayne and Dean was supposed to pay me $10.00 for doing this but he
never did. That is, the 10.00 was for taking Wayne home th night
before.

I'm not sure about the time but I think it was the next evening when
Wayne's mother called. She was drunk and insisting Wayne come home
but he told her no, that he was going to the lake for a couple of
days. The boy was still alive. We left about 6:00 p.m. to go to
the lake and I know he was dead and in a box when we left so I must
have been there when he was killed because I didn't leave to go
anywhere before we left for the lake. However, I do not remember

When Wayne and I got back from fishing, we ate and I went to
sleep. I slept until about 5:00 p.m. and then Dean and I dug the
grave. Wayne was keeping lookout in the van. The spot was by a
trench near a dirt road. It was probably a few miles from Lake
Sam Rayburn itself.

We took the body out of the box, that is, Dean did, and I held the
boy's feet about half way to the grave. The body was already
wrapped in plastic. I went back to the van to get the carpet and
a flashlight. The carpet is to shovel extra dirt on and take it
some place else so there wouldn't be a mound showing.

I almost took too much dirt off and Dean griped at me for it.

This is the second page of a two page statement, I have read it
completely and understand it. It is true and correct and it is
completely voluntary on my part. It took a pretty long time but
it is because I wanted to be sure of everything I am saying.

_David Owen Brooks_
David Owen Brooks

Witnessed by:

_Larry E. Cooper (HOUSTON CHRONICLE)_          August 10,1973, 11:30 P.M.
                                                            D.O.B.

_Dan O M Mullen_

# DAVID BROOKS
## THIRD STATEMENT, AUGUST 10, 1973:

I want to give a statement about Billy Ray Lawrence.

About July 10th, 1973, I tried to call Dean's house, Dean Corll, and it was a long time before I could get him or anyone to answer. Finally, Wayne answered and I asked him if they had anyone there and he said yes. I asked him "It's not a friend, is it?" and he said "sort of". He wouldn't tell me who it was so I went over there just to see who it was. He was still alive when I got there but he was tied to the bed. I recognized him only as a friend of Wayne's.

The boy wasn't doing anything but lying there when I got there. He didn't have any clothes on. I don't remember them calling him by name but I have just now been shown a picture of him which I will initial with this date and time and it is the same boy I have been talking about. In fact, I have seen this same picture before at Dean's house.

I was tired so I went to bed in the opposite bedroom. Before I did go to bed I took Wayne home. Then I went back to Dean's house and went to bed. The boy was still alive but Dean was awake because I remember he let me in. The next morning I went back to get Wayne and Dean was supposed to pay me $10.00 for doing this but he never did. That is, the $10.00 was for taking Wayne home the night before.

I'm not sure about the time but I think it was the next evening when Wayne's mother called. She was drunk and insisting Wayne come home but he told her no, that he was going to the lake for a couple of days. The boy was still alive. We left about 6:00 p. m. to go to the lake and I know he was dead and in a box when we left so I must have been there when he was killed because I didn't leave to go anywhere before we left for the lake. However, I do not remember how he was killed. I don't know if I saw it or not. It didn't bother me to see it.

I saw it done many times. I just wouldn't do it myself. And I never did do it myself.

We left for the lake about 6:00 p. m. and got there about 9:30 or quarter to ten. We then went fishing. Wayne and me. This was after we slept. We fished from about 6:30 A.M. to 10:00 A.M. Dean told us he had already picked a spot and started digging, but he actually hadn't done very much.

### Brooks, third statement, page 2:

When Wayne and I got back from fishing, we ate and I went to sleep. I slept until about 5:00 p.m. and then Dean and I dug the grave. Wayne was keeping lookout in the van. The spot was by a trench near a dirt road. It was probably a few miles from Lake Sam Rayburn itself.

We took the body out of the box, that is, Dean did, and I held the boy's feet about half way to the grave. The body was already wrapped in plastic. I went back to the van to get the carpet and a flashlight. The carpet is to shovel extra dirt on and take it some place else so there wouldn't be a mound showing.

I almost took too much dirt off and Dean griped at me for it.

This is the second page of a two-page statement. I have read it completely and understand it. It is true and correct and it is completely voluntary on my part. It took a pretty long time but it is because I wanted to be sure of everything I am saying.

# Elmer Wayne Henley Jr. Statements

# AFFIDAVIT

THE STATE OF TEXAS

COUNTY OF HARRIS

BEFORE ME, the undersigned authority, a Notary Public in and for the County of
Harris, State of Texas, on this day personally appeared **Elmer Wayne Henley**

_____**White male 17 years old**_____, to me well known, and who, after being by

me duly sworn, deposes and says:

My name is Elmer Wayne Henley Jr, I am a white male 17 years old and was born
on 5-9-56 in Houston Texas. I have completed the 8th grade in school and can read and
write the English language. I am unemployed at the time and presently reside at 325
West 27th Street in Houston. I live there with my Mother and my Grandmother.

I have been knowing Dean Corll for about 2 or maybe three years. I have known him real well
for about 2 years. I met Dean through a friend of mine by the name of David Brooks. After I
met him, Dean would come by my house and pick me up and we would go riding and he would
buy beer for us and stuff like that. After I knew him for awhile, I began to figure that
he was queer, homosexual. Then after awhile, I just came out and asked him if he was queer
and he said yes, that he liked to have sex with boys by going down on them, and then he
asked me if he could do it to me and offered me ten dollars to let him do it. I told him
no. Then he asked me several more times after that, but I never would let him. At the
time, he was living in some apts on Yorktown street and since then has lived in several
different Apts. About three months ago , he moved into a house on Lamar Street in Pasadena.
I have another friend by the name of Tim Karley that I introduced to Dean several months
ago and right after Dean met Tim, he started talking about he would like to have sex with
him and asked me to get Tim to come over to his [Dean's) place so that he could do
unnatural sex acts with him. Also during this time, Dean told me about a Warehouse that
he had over on Hiram Clarke where he had killed some boys and buried them after he had
had sex with them. His reason for killing them was that he couldn't afford to let them
know that (that is everybody else) that he was a queer and what he had done to the boys.
I thought that he was just kidding me about that part of it, but he took me over to the
warehouse several times and the only thing that I ever saw in there was a car that he
said was stolen. It was all stripped out, and I don't remember what color it was. We
went on just being friends and fooling around for quite a while while and then about
2 months ago, we started talking about him quiting his job and we would go traveling.
We decided to do this about the first of September. I knew a girl by the name
who was having a big hassle with her parents and wanted to leave home so we
were going to take her with us. Then yesterday, when Dean got off work, he picked me
up at the corner of 15th and Shepherd Drive, and we rode around for awhile and drank a
couple of beers, then he wanted me to get Tim to come over to his house so that he could
have sex with him. I told him I didn't want to, but we went by Tim's house anyway. Dean
said he was going to fill his van up with gas, and I stayed there at Tim's house. I guess
I stayed there until after midnight, then me and TIM went over to Dean's house in Tim's
car. We stayed there for about an hour bagging, then me and Tim went over and met
at a washateria down the street from her house. brought her overnight bag and
some stuff because she wasn't planning on going back home. Then we all three went over
to Dean's house. I don't remember if he got up and let us in or if I just used my key,
but when we got there, we all sat around and bagged for awhile..End of page one.

I am aware of Article 310 of the Penal Code of Texas, which that any person who
shall, deliberately or willfully, under oath or affirmation legally administered,
make a false statement by a voluntary declaration or affidavit, which is not
required by law or made in the course of a judicial proceeding, is guilty of
false swearing, and shall be punished, if found guilty, by confinement in the
penitentiary for not less than two

THE STATE OF TEXAS

COUNTY OF HARRIS

BEFORE ME, the undersigned authority, a Notary Public in and for the County of Harris, State of Texas, on this day personally appeared _____

_____, to me well known, and who, after being by

me duly sworn, deposes and says:

" Page two of Affidavit:
The three of us, me ████████, and Tim sat around in the living room bagging on some acrylic, and we got pretty high, and then it must have been just before daylight, I woke up and Dean was in the process of putting a pair of hand-cuffs on me, with my hands behind my back, and I said hey, what are you doing, and Dean said you just pissed me off by bringing ████████ over here this early. I guess he was mad because I wasn't supposed to bring her over for several more days so she could go on the trip with us. Then I noticed that both ████████ and Tim were both on their stomachs, with their hands cuffed and their feet tied. Also, they had tape over their mouths. Then Dean brought a transistor radio in and turned it up real loud by ████████ and Tim. Then he picked me up and took me in the kitchen and told me again that he didn't appreciate me bringing ████████ over there because it interfered with his plans. I started talking to him and begging him to take the hand cuffs off of me because I was afraid that he was going to kill me. I told him that I would do anything he wanted me to if he would just take the cuffs off of me. Then he said I ought to just keep you tied down like the rest of them, but I'm going to let you loose, but I'll keep the gun and knife. Then he let me loose, and went back in the living room and chained and tied them to a long board that he had there in the bed room. (He picked both of them up and carried them into the room where the board was). Then he took Tim's clothes off, and told me to take ████████ clothes off. I cut ████████ pants and panties off with a knife. At first he wanted Tim to have sex with ████████, and Tim said he couldn't, then he told me to have sex with her, and he (Dean) would have sex with Tim. Dean had stripped himself completely naked. Then I got up and went to the bathroom, and came back and was just sort of walking around. I don't remember then whether Dean left the room or not, but he was down on top of Tim rubbing his penis on Tim's rear and I reached over on a little table on one side of the room and got the pistol that Dean had laid there. This was the pistol that he had had for quite a while and he had been pointing it at us earlier. I told Dean to stop what he was doing that I wasn't going to let him do anymore to Tim and ████████, and to get away from them. I was pointing the pistol at him and told him I would kill him if he didn't stop. Then he said, you wont kill me, and started towards me. That is when I started shooting him. I don't remember exactly how it happened, but I just kept pulling the trigger and Dean fell through the door into the hall. Then I let ████████ and Tim loose and they got dressed, and we talked about what we should do, and we decided to call the Police Dept, so I called them, and the Police came out to the house.
I am aware of Article 310 of the Penal Code of Texas, which that any person who shall, deliberately or willfully, under oath or affirmation legally administered, make a false statement by a voluntary declaration or affidavit, which is not required by law or made in the course of a judicial proceeding, is guilty of false swearing, and shall be punished, if found guilty, by confinement in the penitentiary for not less than two, nor more than five years."

# ELMER WAYNE HENLEY JR.
## AFFIDAVIT (UPON ARREST), AUGUST 8, 1973

My name is Elmer Wayne Henley Jr, I am a white male 17 years old and was born on 5-9-56 in Houston Texas. I have completed the 8th grade in school and can read and write the English language. I am unemployed at the time and presently reside at 325 West 27th Street in Houston. I live there with my Mother and my Grandmother.

I have been knowing Dean Corll for about 2 or maybe three years. I have known him real well for about 2 years. I met Dean through a friend of mine by the name of David Brooks. After I met him, Dean would come by my house and pick me up and we would go riding and he would buy beer for us and stuff like that. After I knew him for awhile, I began to figure that he was queer, homosexual. Then after awhile, I just came out and asked him if he was queer and he said yes, that he liked to have sex with boys by going down on them, and then asked me if he could do it to me and offered me ten dollars to let him do it. I told him no. Then he asked me several more times after that, but I never would let him. At the time, he was living in some apts on Yorktown Street and since then has lived in several different apts. About three months ago, he moved into a house on Lamar Street in Pasadena. I have another friend by the name of Tim Kerley that I introduced to Dean several months ago and right after Dean met Tim, he started talking about he would like to have sex with him and asked me to get Tim to come over to his (Dean's) place so that he could do unnatural sex acts with him. Also during this time, Déan told me about a Warehouse that he had over on Hiram Clarke where he had killed some boys and buried them after he had had sex with them. His reason for killing them was that he couldn't afford to let them know that (that is everybody else) that he was a queer and what he had done to the boys.

I thought that he was just kidding me about that part of it, but he took me over to the warehouse several times and the only thing that I ever saw in there was a car that he said was stolen. It was all stripped out, and I don't remember what color it was. We went on just being friends and fooling around for quite a while and then about 2 months ago, we started talking about him quiting [sic] his job and we would go traveling. We decided to do this about the first of September. I knew a girl by the name [redacted] who was having a big hassle with her parents and wanted to leave home so we were going to take her with us. Then yesterday, when Dean got off work, he picked me up at the corner of 15th and Shepherd Drive, and we rode around for awhile and drank a couple of beers, then he wanted me to get Tim to come over to his house so that he could have sex with him. I told him I didn't want to, but we went by Tim's house anyway. Dean said he was going to fill his van up with gas, and I stayed there at Tim's house. I guess I stayed there until after midnight, then me and TIM went over to Dean's house in Tim's car. We stayed there for about an hour bagging, then me and Tim went over and met [redacted] at a washateria down the street from her house. [Redacted] brought her overnight bag and some stuff because she wasn't planning on going back home. Then we all three went over to Dean's house. I don't remember if he got up and let us in or if I just used my key, but when we got there, we all sat around and bagged for awhile. End of page one.

## Henley, affidavit, page 2:

The three of us, me [redacted], and Tim sat around in the living room bagging on sone acrylic, and we got pretty high, and then it must have been just before daylight, I woke up and Dean was in the process of putting a pair of hand-cuffs on me, with my hands behind my back, and I said hey, what are you doing, and Dean said you just pissed me off by bringing [redacted] over here this early. I guess he was mad because I wasn't supposed to bring her over for several more days so she could go on the trip with us. Then I noticed that both [redacted] and Tim were both on their stomachs, with their hands cuffed and their feet tied. Also, they had tape over their mouths. Then Dean brought a transistor radio in and turned it up real loud by [redacted] and Tim. Then he picked me up and took me in the kitchen and told me again that he didn't appreciate me bringing [redacted] over there because it interfered with his plans. I started talking to him and begging him to take the hand cuffs off of me because I was afraid that he was going to kill me. I told him that I would do anything he wanted me to if he would just take the cuffs off of me. Then he said I ought to just keep you tied down like the rest of them, but I'm going to let you loose, but I'll keep the gun and knife. Then he let me loose, and went back in the living room and chained and tied them to a long board that he had there in the bed room. (He picked both of them up and carried them into the room where the board was). Then he took Tim's clothes off, and told me to take [redacted] clothes off. I cut [redacted] pants and panties off with a knife. At first he wanted Tim to have sex with [redacted], and Tim said he couldn't, then he told me to have sex with her, and he (Dean) would have sex with Tim. Dean had stripped himself completely naked. Then I got up and went to the bathroom, and came back and was just sort of walking around. I don't remember then whether Dean left the room or not, but he was down on top of Tim rubbing his penis on Tim's rear and I reached over on a little table on one side of the room and got the pistol that Dean had laid there. This was the pistol that he had had for quite a while and he had been pointing it at us earlier. I told Dean to stop what he was doing that I wasn't going to let him do anymore [sic] to Tim and [redacted] and to get away from them. I was pointing the pistol at him and told him I would kill him if he didn't stop. Then he said, you wont [sic] kill me, and started towards me. That is when I started shooting him. I don't remember exactly how it happened, but I just kept pulling the trigger and Dean fell through the door into the hall. Then I let [redacted] and Tim loose and they got dressed, and we talked about what we should do, and we decided to call the Police Dept, so I called them, and the Police came out to the house.

DATE: August 9th, 1973

TIME: 11:55 AM

Statement of __Elmer Wayne Henley_____, Taken at

__1114 Davis, Pasadena Police Dept_____Harris County, Texas.
   (Building)

On the __8th__ day of __August_____, 19_73_, at

__10:55__ o'clock _A_. M, I __Elmer Wayne Henley_____,

was taken before ____Judge Russell Drake_____, a Magistrate at

his office __Pasadena, Harris County,_____, Harris County, Texas,
who informed me:

Of the accusations made against me;
That I had a right to retain counsel;
That I had a right to remain silent;
That I had a right to have an attorney present during
my interview with peace officer or attorneys representing the state;
That I have a right to terminate an interview at any time;
That I have a right to request appointment of counsel if I cannot afford counsel;
That I have a right to an examining trial;
That I am not required to make any statement, and any statement I make may be used
against me.

I have now been warned by __Detective D.M.Mullican_____, the person to whom
I am making this statement, and was so warned by __Detective D.M.Mullican_____
prior to any questioning of me by police while I was under arrest:

(1) that I have the right to have a lawyer present to advise me either prior to any questioning or during any questioning; (2) that if I am unable to employ a lawyer I have the
right to have a lawyer appointed to counsel with me prior to or during any questioning,
and (3) I have the right to remain silent and not make any statement at all and that
any statement I make may and probably will be used in evidence against me at my trial,
and (4) I have the right to terminate the interview at any time.

I do not want to consult with a lawyer before I make this statement, and I do not
want to remain silent, and I now freely and voluntarily waive my right to a lawyer and
to remain silent and make the following voluntary statement.
XXX My name is Elmer Wayne Henley, I am a white male 17 years old and was born on
5-9-56 in Houston, Texas. I have completed the 8th grade in school and can read and
write the English Language. I presently live with my Mother at 325 West 27th Street
in Houston, Texas.

About 3 years ago, I met a guy by the name of Dean Corll. Dean was a lot older than
me and a school friend by the name of David Brooks introduced me to him. David was
always riding around in Dean's car and everything. I was only about 14 at the time
and I thought this was great. David Brooks told me that he could get me in on a
deal where I could make some money, and he took me to Dean Corll. Dean told me
that he belonged to an organization out of Dallas that bought and sold boys, ran
whores and dope and stuff like that. Dean told me that he would pay me $200.00 at
least for every boy that I could bring him and maybe more if they were real good
looking boys. I didn't try to find any for him until about a year later, and I
decided that I could use the money to get better things for my people so one day
I went over to Dean's Apt on Schuler street and told him that I would find a boy
for him. Dean had a GTX at the time, and we got in it, Dean and me and started
driving around. We picked up a boy at 11th and Studewood, and I talked to him
since I had long hair and all and it was easier for me to talk to him. I talked
him into going to Dean's Apt to smoke some marijuana, so we went over to Dean's
Apt. Dean left some handcuffs laying out where they could be seen, and we had this
little deal set up where I would put the handcuffs on and then could get out of
them. Then we talked this boy(I don't remember his name) into trying to get out
of them. The only thing was we put them on where the locks were turned in where he
couldn;t get the key into them. Then Dean took the boy down and tied his feet and
put tape over his mouth. I thought Dean was going to sell him to this organization
that he belonged to, so I left. Then the next day, Dean paid me $200.00. Then a day
or so later I found out that dean had killed the boy. Then I found out that Dean
screwed him in the ass before killing him. This was the start of the whole thing,
and since then, I have helped Dean get 8 or 10 other boys, I don't remember exactly
how many. Dean would screw all of them and sometimes kill them and make them suck
him. Then he would kill them. I killed several of them myself with Dean's gun
and helped him choke some others. Then we would take them and bury them in different
places. David Brooks was with us on most of them.

Witness _____

Witness _____         Person Giving Statement Wayne Henley

I think the only three that David Brooks wasn't with us on was the last ones at
the house on Lamar Street in Pasadena. The ones that I can remember by name
are: David Hildegeist who Dean told me he had killed and buried in his boat stall
a boy by the name of Malley Winkle, who David and Dean told they had killed and
put in the boat stall, Charles Cobble who I killed and we buried in the boat
Stall. I shot Charles in the head with Dean's pistol, over on Lamar Street in
Pasadena, then we buried him in the boat stall. Then Manty Jones, me and Dean
choked him and buried him in the boat stall. We killed a boy by the name of Billy
Lawrence, I dont remember how we killed him, but we buried him up at Dean's place
on Sam Rayburn Lake. We killed him at the house on Lamar Street too. Dean told me
about one named Rueben Haney that he killed and buried on the beach at High Island.
I shot and killed Johnny Delone, and we buried him at High Island. Then me and
Dean and David Brooks killed two brothers, I think we choked them, anyway, we
buried Billy Balch at High Island, and Mike Balch at Rayburn. We choked Mark
Scott and Frank Aguirre and buried them at High Island. The last one that I cna
remember their name is Homer Garcia, and I shot him in the head and we buried him
at Rayburn. I don't remember the dates on all these, because there has been too
many of them. Some of them were hitch-hikers and I can't remember their names.
Dean told me that there was 24 in all, but I wasn't with him on all of them.
I tried to tell me mother two or three times about this stuff and she just
wouldn't believe me. I even wrote a confession one time and hid it, hoping
that Dean would kill me because the thing was bothering me so bad. I gave the
confession to my Mother and told her if I was gone for a certain length of time
to turn it in. Me and David talked about killing Dean so that we could get away
from this whole thing and several times, I have come within an inch of killing
him but I just never got up enough nerve to do it until yesterday, because Dean
had told me that his organization would get me if I ever did anything to him.
This statement covers all that I can remember about all this killings and all
that I know about where they are buried.

While making this statement, I have not asked for nor wanted the presence or advise
of a lawyer. At no time during the making of this statement did I ask to stop or
want to stop making this statement.

I have read the __2__ page(s) of this statement, each page of which bears my signature, and the facts contained there in are true and correct.
This statement was finished at 12:40 PM. on the __9th__ day of __August__ ,19 __73__ .

WITNESS: _____

WITNESS: _____

_____
Signature of person giving
voluntary statement.

# ELMER WAYNE HENLEY JR
## FULL CONFESSION, AUGUST 9, 1973:

My name is Elmer Wayne Henley. I am a white male 17 years old
and was born on 5-9-56 in Houston, Texas. I have completed the
8th grade in school and can read and write the English Language. I presently live with my Mother at 325 West 27th Street
in Houston, Texas.

About three years ago I met a guy by the name of Dean Corll.
Dean was a lot older than me and a school friend of mine named
David Brooks introduced me to him. David was always riding
around in Dean's car and everything. I was only 14 back then
and I thought this was great. David Brooks told me he could
get me in on a deal where I could make some money, and he took
me to Dean Corll. Dean told me that he belonged to an organization out of Dallas that bought and sold boys, ran whores
and stuff like that. Dean told me that he would pay me $200.00
for every boy I could get for him and maybe more if they were
real good looking boys. I didn't try to find any for him until
about a year later, and I decided that I could use the money
to get better things for my people so one day I went over to
Dean's apartment on Schuler Street and told him I would find
a boy for him. Dean had a GTX at the time and we got in it.
Dean and me started driving around. We picked up a boy at
11th and Studewood and I talked to him since I had long hair
and all and it was easier for me to talk to him. I talked him
into going to Dean's Apartment to smoke some marijuana, so we
went over to Dean's Apt. Dean left some handcuffs laying out
where they could be seen, and we had this little deal set up
where I would put the handcuffs on and then could get out of
them. Then we talked this boy (I don't remember his name) into
trying to get out of them. The only thing was we put them on
where the locks were turned in where he couldn't get the key
into them. Dean then took the boy down and tied his feet and
put tape over his mouth. I thought Dean was going to sell him

to the organization that he belonged to, so I left. Then the next day, Dean paid me $200.00. A day or so later, I found out that Dean had killed the boy; then I found out that Dean had screwed him in the ass before killing him. This was the start of the whole thing and since then, I have helped Dean get 8 or 10 other boys, I don't remember exactly how many. Dean would screw all of them and sometimes suck them and make them suck him. Then he would kill them. I killed several of them myself with Dean's gun and helped him choke some others. Then we would take them and bury them in different places, David Brooks was with us on most of them.

### Henley, confession, page 2:

I think the only three that David Brooks wasn't with us on were the last ones at the house on Lamar Street in Pasadena The ones that I can remember by name are: David Hildegeist [Hilligiest] who Dean told me that he had killed and buried in his boat stall[,] a boy by the name of Malley Winkle who David and Dean told me they had killed and put in the boat stall, Charles Cobble who I killed and we buried in the boat stall. I shot Charles in the head with Dean's pistol over on Lamar Street in Pasadena, then we buried him in the boat stall. Then Marty Jones, me and Dean choked him and buried him in the boat stall. We killed a boy by the name of Billy Lawrence, I dont [sic] remember how we killed him, but we buried him up at Dean's place on Sam Rayburn Lake. We killed him at the house on Lamar Street, too. Dean told me about one named Reuben Haney that he killed and buried on the beach at High Island. I shot and killed Johnny Delone, and we buried him at High Island. Then me and Dean and David Brooks killed two brothers, I think we choked them, anyway, we buried Billy Baulch at High Island and Mike Baulch at Rayburn. We choked Mark Scott and Frank Aguirre and buried them at High Island. The last one I can remember the name of is Homer Garcia, and I shot him in the head and we buried him at Rayburn. I don't remember the dates on all of these, because there has been too many of them. Some of them were hitch-hikers and I can't remember their names. Dean told me that there was 24 in all, but I wasn't with him on all of them. I tried to tell me [sic] mother two or three times about this stuff and she just wouldn't believe me. I even wrote a confession one time and hid it, hoping that Dean would kill me because the thing was bothering me so bad. I gave the confession to my mother and told her if I was gone for a certain length of time to turn it in. Me and David talked about killing Dean so that we could get away from this whole thing and several times, I have come to within an inch of killing him but I just never got enough nerve to do it until yesterday, because Dean told me that his organization would get me if I ever did anything to him.

This statement covers all that I can remember about all this [sic] killings and all that I know about where they are buried.

# Index